Our Fatal Sincerity

Our Fatal Sincerity

How I Loved God Out of Existence

Alexandra

Mullinghouse Press

Mullinghouse Press

The events and conversations in this book have been set down to the best of the author's ability, although some names and details have been omitted to protect the privacy of individuals.

Our Fatal Sincerity: How I Loved God Out of Existence
Copyright © Alexandra, 2022. All rights reserved. For more information email alexandraofquestions@gmail.com. Book design by Alexandra.

First paperback edition 2022

ISBN 979-8-9856368-0-2

Published by Mullinghouse Press
nihilistshavemorefun.com

I've written this little book in case it might help someone like me out there to get some peace.

Contents

Preface i

A Note on My Approach v

A Note on Tolerance in the Church xv

1. My Testimony 1

2. Love & Personhood vs. Fear & Abstraction 99

    #1 The doctrines of hell and salvation only make sense if access to and understanding of information is more important than love. 102

    (#1.1 Does predestination solve the problem?) 125

    #2 Pascal's Wager doesn't work. 129

    #3 There is no Christian consensus on foundational spiritual questions. 142

    #4 You're not supposed to act as if God were actually real. 160

        (1) You're not supposed to actually follow God's commands unless your culture says it's okay. 160

        (2) You're not supposed to actually depend on God to provide for you. 170

        (3) You're not supposed to actually expect God to be present in your life. 175

        (4) You're not supposed to actually think about life in the way the Bible and church traditions suggest you should. 182

3. Truth vs. Manipulation 189

    A: "Everyone has an innate knowledge of God, but some people deny it." 194

B: "Your logic has to be based on faith in something. Put your faith in God's word first and then develop your logic from there. Any logic that contradicts something God has said is faulty." 206

C: "Truth is a person." 213

D: "Everything in the world has been damaged by sin, including your conscience." 219

E: "God is paradoxical." 225

F: "You know that God is speaking to you when you have a thought you definitely wouldn't have come up with on your own." 228

G: "Can't you see God working through all the good things that have come together in your life?" 233

H: "You need to manage your expectations and guard your heart against bitterness." 236

I: "Don't be so legalistic." 239

4. Brave Old World 243

    Eternity 247

    Meaning or Purpose 263

    An Objective Moral Standard 270

Additional Resources 287

Preface

There are two primary reasons I wrote this book.

One, because I thought the people whose presence in my life I have valued over the years deserved a real, comprehensible explanation of why at 27 years old I would leave the faith that had been everything to me until that point.

Two, because once I had come to the unavoidable conclusion I finally reached about theology, I was astounded at how much time and energy I had wasted trying to avoid it all my life, and soon I began to think back on all the frustration I had heard expressed from the mouths of high-schoolers sitting in circles on the floors of church camp cabins and pastors preaching on stages and middle-aged parents phoning their friends asking for prayer—I had listened to the distress of so many of those around me fighting to believe in an all-loving, all-powerful God despite so many circumstances that suggested no one was really running this universe. I had listened to them blaming themselves again and again for overlooking God's goodness. And once I had come to terms with my realizations about religion and discovered that the loss I had thought would mean the end of everything good had actually made me freer and happier than I had ever been before, I felt that I needed to tell all these people that they could be free too.

What I do not want to do is destroy the beliefs of people who would be devastated to lose them. That's why I recommend that you not read this book if you hold Christian beliefs and feel that the quality of your life would be lessened if you lost certainty in them.[1] My story might have no effect on you, but then again it might, and I didn't write it down in order to make anyone miserable. Some people have told me not to worry because anyone with such a strong need to believe in God will find a reason to keep believing no matter how good the contradictory evidence is, but I seriously doubt that that's the rule. There are times when people come across information that they cannot deny and yet never fully learn to live with and perpetually regret learning.

You might criticize me as you read that. You might be thinking now that if what I say is true I should say it without caring who hears and write it without caring who reads. You might be thinking that the truth is the best thing for people whether they feel like it or not. And in all probability you're right. I just don't have the heart to spring hard realities on people who have invested their lives in beautiful dreams.

What I very much want to do is talk to anyone whose Christian experience has been marked by depression, loneliness, doubt, or failure that you feel must be your fault because you know God only wants to give his people victory—anyone who feels a need to seek relief in the words of those musicians and authors on the edge of accepted Christian media who don't hold back from talking about despair and anger—anyone who loves to know what is true but has always been too afraid to research some subjects thoroughly because you've noticed that the world too frequently doesn't work the way your beliefs predict that it should—anyone who is ashamed of the moral beliefs they hold because they can't explain *why* they are moral but also

---

[1] See the "Additional Resources" page after Chapter 4, where a couple starting points for those wondering how to adjust to a loss of beliefs are listed.

can't give them up or deny holding them because this would go against God's laws—anyone who feels that as a Christian they can't be themself because as themself they would never choose to do some things that it seems necessary for a Christian to do—anyone who feels that everything is always wrong and there's no way out.

If this is you, I would love for you to have the experience of life finally making sense that I had. I would love for you to find yourself in the midst of simply feeling happy one day and realize that you had felt happy the day before and the day before that too. If something I say helps just one other person to shake themself free from the compulsion to keep saying they are evil so that they can keep saying God is good, I'm elated.

I have no idea who you are, so even if your situation matches what I've described I can't promise that its causes are the same as what I experienced or that changing your mind in the way I did will deliver the same results. I can't promise you happiness. Still, I ask you to read if you can in any way picture yourself surviving the loss of God, and if you have so much as a small seed of faith that all the good you've known in this world will still exist even if your understanding of its origin changes.

A Note on My Approach

I come from the Evangelical tradition. As I write this, the portion of my life I've spent outside of it makes up less than one tenth of the time I lived within it. In the Evangelical tradition, there is great respect for pastors and teachers who have no formal theological training and who craft moving messages built on their personal testimony and the words of the Bible alone. In keeping with this style of communication, I've chosen not to write a book heavy on data but to focus on these same types of sources. There are many works in existence that provide scientific and historical data related to religious questions, so no one in search of this information should have trouble finding it. Where opportunities to digress on details of such frequently discussed topics arise, I've tried to avoid digression. It was not those types of details that convinced me to change my mind about God anyway; it was my own personal experiences and my lifelong familiarity with the teachings of the Bible that brought me to finally realize all I had been wrong about.

There is also a methodological reason for focusing on personal experience and theological ideas, which is that the method of using disciplines such as science or history to prove a supernatural claim is a flawed one. These disciplines are ways of studying the natural world. They depend on our ability to reliably observe phenomena, measure them, quantify them, define them, understand them, test them, and finally begin to predict them. These disciplines cannot work if the objects of their study do not follow natural laws. And that is why they are only used to study and arrive at theories about the natural world. The supernatural is by definition other than and beyond the natural. The God that my community worshipped is said to be a supernatural being, a being who cannot be quantified, tested, or subjected to experiment. The works of God are miracles, and God also works imperceptibly through the natural, being the unseen cause behind events that also have full natural explanations. Using science or history to make decisions about supernatural claims would be like using a yardstick to measure the breadth of a galaxy—or, more accurately, like holding a yardstick up to your eye trying to see a distant galaxy. Just like a yardstick and a telescope have completely different functions and abilities, science and theology are utterly different tools designed to deal with utterly different experiences.

As long as God is supernatural, as long as we maintain that his ways are not confined within natural laws that make them understandable and predictable, we cannot use science, history, or any other empirical study of the natural world to prove or disprove claims about him. Picture with me a simple example of this:

Imagine that a woman discovers a tumor on her arm and understandably becomes quite worried. That night, she has a vivid dream of Jesus reaching out his hands to her, and when she wakes up the next morning, the tumor is gone. Can a scientist prove that the Christian God of the Bible appeared to her and healed her?

A scientist could not perform any sort of medical test on the site of the tumor to find a mark or residue left by God. There is no form of brain scan or psychological principle that could reveal whether the dream originated from a supernatural source rather than from the woman's own thoughts and her familiarity with Jesus as a comforting figure. There is no predictable pattern or rule that miracles have to follow, and so there is no way to hold an event up to a pattern or rule and say that it is a miracle if it fits and is not a miracle if it does not fit. The claim that the dream and the healing were supernatural cannot be proven or disproven.

Now, let's add more information to the story. The woman goes to a doctor, who examines her arm and finds that the lump she noticed wasn't a tumor but only a harmless cyst that has now all but disappeared—she might have broken it simply by rolling over on it while sleeping. Can a scientist now prove that God did not heal her or appear to her? No, there is still no way to prove or disprove whether a supernatural element was involved in the events. God could have turned a dangerous tumor into a harmless cyst miraculously, and there's no particular reason he wouldn't have performed the healing in this way instead of making the tumor completely disappear or guiding the woman to a doctor who would remove the tumor or bringing about any other resolution. Again, since the supernatural does not have to work within the rules of the natural, a scientist can't devise an experiment that would have one result if the supernatural was involved and another result if the supernatural was not involved.

Finally, there's one more important piece to the story. The woman feels convinced that Jesus healed her, but this woman isn't Christian. She's Hindu and believes that Jesus is one wonderful, powerful incarnation of divinity, just like many of the other great gods worshipped around the world, although he is one of her favorites. Her Christian friend insists that God or the divine as she pictures it isn't real at all. Her friend says that either the exclusively Christian triune God healed her, or nothing supernatural happened: Her arm was fine the whole time and she dreamed up an image of Jesus because she likes (her idea of) Jesus and thinks of him often. Either way, a Jesus who is synonymous with all the other divine figures of the world certainly was not responsible for the healing because no such Jesus exists. Now, can a scientist come up with any experiment to prove which supernatural cause was involved? No. There is no scientific test to identify the difference between a miracle worked by a God who only accepts Christians as true worshippers as opposed to a miracle worked by a divine power worshipped around the world under different names.

If we change the story a bit so that it describes a claim of a miracle experienced by someone 100 years ago, we could ask these same questions about a historian. Could a historian use recorded accounts or forensic evidence of the supposed healing and appearance to prove whether the events were supernatural? No. They could only study the natural side of the events. If the story once again involves the sudden disappearance of a lump on someone's arm, a historian could attempt to identify the most likely answer to a question such as, "Did the person have a tumor to begin with?" They could then point to details in the historical data they are studying that appear to support or oppose the idea that the person had a tumor and arrive at the answer they think is most likely to be true. This is because natural things such as human bodies do operate predictably by natural laws, even if they are very complex, and so the historian at least has a hope of comparing a description of a disease to the symptoms of a disease we know today and determining whether it is highly likely, somewhat likely, or unlikely that a historical person experienced that disease. A historian could not answer the question of whether a miracle took place for the same reason a scientist could not answer it. Miracles don't need to be confined to natural laws, so there is no pattern or rule to reliably distinguish an account of an event that was truly miraculous from an account of an event that someone mistakenly thought was miraculous, and no reliable mark of the miraculous left behind to find forensically. Neither is there a rule for identifying *which* supernatural entity worked a miracle.

This is all a lengthy way to say that I didn't write this book to make a scientific case against the existence of God. I think it's important to realize that over the years science and history have provided natural explanations for things that people once claimed had no natural explanation, but to go on from there to say that as long as something doesn't have a known natural explanation, God did it, or as long as something does have a known natural explanation, God wasn't involved in it, does not make sense. To do that is to claim that the supernatural operates by the same rules as the natural.

Paradoxically, the community I came from, while viewing God as supernatural and beyond human understanding, also thought that they could use certain types of historical and scientific data to prove his existence. In my account of my own experiences, I mention points at which I encountered information that conflicted with what my community said was true about science or history. Some of this information disproved specific historical or scientific claims that were common in this community, although I maintain it can't technically be used to disprove God's existence, for all the reasons I've just gone over.

Again, I am not making a scientific case against God's existence. What I am doing is making a theological case that it doesn't matter whether a person believes in the Christian God or not. Chapter 2, Section #1 is the heart of this book; the rest is all here more or less to give that discussion context. While I list many reasons throughout the text why I think it is most logical to conclude that God and the supernatural are not real, my goal isn't necessarily to get everyone to agree with me on that point.

It's more to show why I myself can't honestly accept any other conclusion as true.

The thesis of this book is that because studies of the natural world cannot be used to demonstrate the existence or identity of a particular supernatural being, any supernatural being that wants me to know about its existence and identity would have to reveal itself to me in a personal way I would understand, and if the Christian God has not done this and I therefore have no reason to think he is real, the theological contradictions one has to embrace in order to conclude I am condemned to hell for this are too severe to be allowed.

By way of this thesis and the related discussions it leads to, I am also trying to make the practical point that Christians should not feel any pressure or put pressure on anyone else to conform their life to the dictates of any theological idea. To give an example of what I mean, people in the community I grew up in believed that anyone who did not confess Jesus as God would go to hell. They also believed that the Bible placed many moral restraints on human behavior, some of which, as I discuss in the text, do not make sense from an ethical perspective.[2] These

---

[2] While the words "moral" and "ethical" are often used interchangeably, for convenience I use them to label contrasting concepts at several places throughout this book. When contrasted with each other in this book, the terms will be used to make the following distinction: "Morals" will refer to rules intended to define good and bad that a person feels bound to for any reason, including but not limited to reasons of tradition, familiarity, or instinct. "Ethics" will refer more specifically to the process of deliberately, carefully trying to identify what is beneficial to people as objectively as possible. In talking about my own experiences, this gives me a way to label the difference between the ideas about right and wrong I held

beliefs dictated how the people around me interacted with their neighbors and how they voted. Instead of basing these decisions, which affect people's lives in the natural world, on the findings of natural disciplines, they based them on theological ideas. Even if the decision made someone's life worse in this natural world, it could be justified if it promised to push the person towards heaven instead of hell. While I think that all the problems I discuss throughout this book invalidate the very idea that there is a God or a hell, I don't so much care that people come to that exact conclusion as that they come to understand why they shouldn't be making other people's lives worse on the basis of "facts" they only know by personal revelation and that cannot be demonstrated via principles that apply to everyone.

Thus, I have chosen to attack several Christian theological claims harshly, not because my goal is to make people abandon Christianity necessarily, but because my goal is to make people see how indefensible and self-contradictory the sorts of theological ideas that compel them to devalue other people's present, natural-world priorities really are. I don't want to destroy people's faith in something that brings them joy or gives them comfort, but I certainly want to make them scrutinize to the core anything that asks them to look down on or mistreat another person. I'm fine with Christians continuing to believe that there is a God who loves everyone out there; I just want the ones who think this loving God is going to let the majority of humanity end up in hell to seriously consider that perhaps their own beliefs about theology aren't as airtight as they assume.

---

mainly because someone told me to and those that I could articulate a satisfying, non-arbitrary reason for holding.

Do I want everyone to become atheist though? Well, yes, but mainly for the same reasons I want everyone to stop saying that juices and herbs can "detox" your body. I don't like the idea of people believing something is true when it isn't, just for the sheer nitpicking technicality of the thing, but I'm also uneasy about the negative results that could come from misplaced faith. For some people, the latest unfounded health crazes are nothing more than a harmless distraction, in which case I suppose I can control my urge to pester them about not falling for ridiculous claims. And when it comes to some people, belief in God doesn't stop them from living well and making choices that benefit everyone in the long run, in which case I suppose I can admit that there are more important things to focus on than the technical details of one's position on the supernatural. It is hard to rest easy just assuming that a person's acceptance of an inaccurate claim won't eventually lead to problems, but I don't see the good in becoming a nuisance to people who do manage to avoid the negatives of a belief I disagree with.

While it would be nice if people walked away from what I've written agreeing with me on theological points, it's much more important that they walk away from this book with a new or renewed commitment to stop and think about how their actions influence those whose views differ from their own. If it is up to God to convince people of various supernatural ideas and he hasn't convinced some people, is it really right for Christians to try to force faith into existence through shunning, condescension, pestering, or threats of damnation? If some moral taboos are not ethically wrong (and are thus matters of ritual purity more than anything else) is it truly right for Christians to try to force adherence to their religious purity rules on people who do not share their religious beliefs? If some supposedly undesirable behavior cannot be proven harmful by scientific principles shared among people of all theological positions, then why should Christians be trying to enforce their taboo against it on atheists and don't-really-care-ists any more than Orthodox Jews (or Muslims or Wiccans etc., etc.) should be trying to enforce adherence to their rituals and taboos on Christians? I certainly hope I can encourage some reflection on these sorts of questions!

In the end, it is most important that people choose to live by love and truth. If they want to continue to personify these values as God, I suppose that's fine with me. With my background, I can't help but fear the ease with which the personification can end up coming into conflict with those greater concepts and overthrowing them, but I'm willing to believe that there are communities in which this is not the case. The experiences I discuss throughout this text provide an abundance of guidelines on what *not* to do if you want your community to put love and truth first, regardless of your theological position.

A Note on Tolerance in the Church

Throughout the text, I bring up the topic of Christian views on same-sex romances several times and mention how the ethically indefensible negativity of my home church towards them, and towards other things that are not ethically wrong, was one factor in making me realize the shortcomings of Christianity. I'm aware that some readers might say I'm making it seem like people have to choose between Christianity and tolerance for various groups of people when in fact there are many churches who accept all these groups. That is definitely not what I'm trying to do, so let me explain my thinking here.

I'm not trying to discourage churches from accepting everyone. If people are going to practice Christianity, I'd far rather they practice it in a form that is accepting of everyone, but I have to be honest about how the Bible was taught to me, and that was in a form that said many behaviors that actually do no harm to anyone were sins, sins that could possibly lead to hell if the sinner made no effort to change their ways. I had heard a little about possible alternate interpretations of some of these things, but they seemed to be reaching and straining to make the Bible more palatable to modern readers. I find it far easier to believe in most of these cases that the authors who wrote the Bible many centuries ago simply had some intolerant streaks.

If churches want to teach that the Bible is not the perfect and unchanging word of God, good. If they lay aside the intolerant parts by acknowledging them—by saying that the Bible was written by human beings whose flawed ideas made it into the text and that we should take the good and leave the bad—wonderful! I wish every church was like this.

But we are not there yet. People are still growing up in and living in environments in which they think they need to figure out how the Bible commands them to live if they want to escape an eternity in hell. When these people encounter passages that say homosexuality is wrong and take these passages literally, they are acting under duress. This doesn't excuse their actions, but it means we need to recognize the roots of the problem—and one of these tangled roots is the fact that the Bible contains intolerant moral laws and threatens hell for those who don't keep them. Scripture itself needs to be held accountable for the part it plays in preserving a culture of intolerance.

I want more churches to focus on ethics first and preach that there is no condemnation for simply being yourself in ways that don't harm anyone. But I also want them to be honest about why we are free to say this. It's not because the Bible was written by people who got all the theological details perfect and yet somehow managed to mysteriously screw up the moral details. I hope the message doesn't end up being that you're free to be yourself within the correct religious tradition only and outside of it you're still going to hell. Instead, the reasons for the shortcomings of the Bible need to be fully acknowledged and followed to their conclusions.

1. My Testimony

I Corinthians 13:1–3 NKJV
Though I speak with the tongues of men and of angels, but have not love, I have become sounding brass or a clanging cymbal. And though I have the gift of prophecy, and understand all mysteries and all knowledge, and though I have all faith, so that I could remove mountains, but have not love, I am nothing. And though I bestow all my goods to feed the poor, and though I give my body to be burned, but have not love, it profits me nothing.

Love is arguably the greatest force in all of existence. Love is the answer. Love is all you need. And, according to what I believed for the first 27 years of my life, God is love. Of course. God is all you need. God is the answer. God is the greatest force in all of existence.

I grew up steeped in a message of passionate love sent from heaven to earth: love without limits, self-sacrificing love, love with the force of a hurricane, tenacious love that would pursue you when you thought you didn't deserve it and, if necessary, wait out your rejection without pressuring you. This was the love, this was the God, I was taught to believe in. And I believed, and, as best I could, I made some small effort to love back, for 27 years. Until suddenly one day I up and decided I wasn't so into passionate, personal, unconditional love and would rather be all alone in a purposeless and indifferent universe and so I became an atheist instead.

Wait... Does something about that last part seem a little off? I agree. What say you we go back over this story in a bit more detail?

Well, the love part and the belief part is all true. From the time I was old enough to remember, I attended Protestant Christian churches and schools and heard Christian radio stations playing in my parents' house and vehicles constantly. Orange County, California, was the world of my childhood: Beaches, palm trees, Disneyland. Sliding doors wide open to catch the breeze in the hot summer, letting snatches of mariachi drift in from the windows of passing cars. Pool parties, wealth gaps, freeways, freeways, freeways, Harvest Crusade bumper stickers, and Evangelical radio programs. Close to the entirety of my life centered around a spot in the heart of Orange County where I attended both church and a private school run by my church, and from which the same church broadcast a radio station that aired Bible studies and other informative Christian programming. In a typical week during the school year, I took in at least six sermons: one in person on Sunday and at least five on the radio while coming and going from school Monday through Friday, without even counting school chapels.

At this church–school complex my first understanding of almost everything in life was developed. I was there for the majority of my waking hours, a little brown-haired white girl, perpetually in a purple jacket, wandering the halls and blacktops or occupying the pews in the sanctuary or the classic plastic elementary chairs in the classrooms. Even when I was away from the place, the people who spent time there were my community, and I would think it should come as no surprise that I grew up sharing their view of life.

What I want to say next is that belief in God was foundational to my understanding of reality. But I almost feel that I can't communicate this point strongly enough. It seems weak to just say I believed in God growing up. Perhaps I can say that I took

God's existence for granted or that I believed in God just as much as I believed in the ground under my feet. Maybe those statements will convey the true force behind the idea. It's odd, because I can't say I ever experienced God in any supernatural way growing up, so some people might wonder why I believed at all. But I'd say God was like a relative who lived far away. I had never spoken to him or seen him, but everyone around me had always talked as if they knew him personally, so the idea that he might not be real never even crossed my mind.

When I say people around me talked as if they knew God, that's no exaggeration. They talked about all sorts of supernatural interactions, but most pervasively they mentioned the concept of *God speaking to them*. They mentioned it, I say. They didn't make a case for it. They didn't announce it. They didn't preface their comments with an expression of surprise that the creator of the universe had communicated with them. They just mentioned, offhand, as a matter of course, that God had spoken to them about various things.

I wasn't sure about taking this opportunity, but God said, "Just go for it."

Usually I would have gotten angry at my kids for acting that way, but I felt the Holy Spirit nudging me to just listen to their side of the story first.

I prayed about whether it was the right time to move or not, and I felt like God was saying, "Wait."

Remarks along these lines were simply part of daily life for me. Adults had always talked that way, and were never surprised to hear each other talking that way, so obviously they were all in constant communication with God. Now, if they were ever asked for details or were making an effort to explain the concept of hearing God's voice to someone who might be unfamiliar with it, they usually specified that it wasn't an audible voice they were talking about but more of a feeling inside themselves. It was, according to them, a form of supernatural communication, but not a shocking one.

When it came to tales of more shocking and miraculous experiences though, they were not in short supply. At the church I grew up in, stories of miraculous healings were fairly common. I specifically remember, for instance, stories of people being miraculously delivered from drug addiction and accompanying mental disorders. And while I didn't know anyone at this time who claimed to have experienced a more visually obvious case of healing, stories of people in faraway places getting out of wheelchairs, recovering their eyesight, or experiencing similarly dramatic instant improvements were circulated with confidence in their accuracy. Supernatural provision was also expected in realms outside of the medical, most commonly the financial. Over the years, I heard several stories of people who claimed to have taken some sort of financial risk because of the way they felt God was leading them (for example, donating money to a church even though they were worried about being able to pay their rent that month) and then received an unexpected check, usually said to have come in the mail from a stranger, that covered the expense they had been worried about. The network of mutually supportive stories of the supernatural was strengthened yet further by a wide variety of other accounts that sometimes cropped up, such as claims of people casting out demons, speaking in tongues, or being divinely warned of danger.

In this environment, it was completely unnecessary to teach a child that God existed. The idea was absorbed as naturally and unconsciously as the fact that a house is called a house. What I *was* purposely taught, and eventually believed just as strongly, were the specifics. The church I grew up in was a non-denominational Evangelical one with a strong focus on reading and teaching the Bible. Over time, I became familiar with the doctrines of heaven and hell, sin, grace, salvation, and so on. You could say my understanding of these concepts was fairly simplistic at first (though far more biblically accurate than the folk/Hollywood image of an old man in the sky and a devil in red tights)—it wouldn't be until college that I really got to know any Christians other than Catholics and non-denominational Evangelical Protestants. I wasn't aware of the more sophisticated side of the Protestant take on a lot of things yet, but that's a topic I'll return to later. For now, let's take things in chronological order, and I'll attempt to narrate my crisis of faith from the beginning.

The important thing to note, however, is that while this "crisis" started in the first decade of my life, it smoldered for 17 years before it ever led me to question God's existence. (It might be more accurate to refer to it as something other than a faith crisis at first, but that term is close enough. In fact, I suppose the bulk of what I experienced could be considered a crisis of having too much faith.)

Anyway, sticking to the point here, while I was surrounded by what seemed like abundant clear signs that God interacted with people, there came a time when I realized that none of the things people talked about had ever happened to me. I had never heard, seen, or felt God for myself, not even in that inside-your-own-heart sort of way. Instead, what I felt in my heart was a sort of emptiness and loneliness. Even before I began to become aware of my lack of connection with God, the problem had already manifested itself in a small way as a difficulty with believing in one of the specifics I had been taught.

I don't place much confidence in the accuracy of early memories, but in the absence of any other record to draw from here, I estimate that my first misgivings about a theological concept occurred sometime before I was in fourth grade and that fourth grade was when I began to feel real anxiety over the disconnect between what I naturally expected a relationship with God to consist of and what I found myself personally experiencing.

The first theological problem I seem to remember encountering, at some unknown early age, was my complete inability to believe in eternal life. At whatever point this struggle occurred I don't remember any thought of hell being involved in it. Perhaps I hadn't been asked to think much about hell at this point, although I can't say for sure. What I do remember is that I knew anyone who believed in Jesus went to heaven when they died but I also knew I had zero confidence in the reality of that scenario. I thought the people who had told me about heaven knew what they were talking about, but I just couldn't inspire myself to see this moment of waking up to the realization that I was in heaven, instead of dead, in my future.

Heaven was never described to me as a place full of angels playing harps or any of the other cartoony variations on the picture, but as a place where people could interact with God directly. I think this must have been part of the reason it was so difficult to believe in. I hadn't come to realize this consciously yet, but in my own personal experience I had never known any interaction with God, so I had no shred of familiarity on which to base a mental image of a place that was all about communion with God. The idea of breaking into a wonderful experience I had never had a taste of was beyond my ability to pound into my own head, but the idea of basically falling asleep and never ever waking up to realize you had been wrong about the whole afterlife thing seemed totally believable.

Somewhere along the line, I heard a pastor mention in a sermon that no one should feel too concerned over the fact that they sometimes doubt their beliefs because even among the great names in Christian theology there were people who experienced deep doubts even on their deathbeds. I thought, "Well, that just proves it. Someday I'm going to die, and I know I'm going to die feeling like there's no such thing as heaven." I found it utterly baffling that something I knew had to be real could feel so impossible—and that was the extent of my thoughts. I wondered at the strangeness of the disharmony between reality and perception and never asked myself whether the things I had been told about reality were actually true.

Fast forward to fourth grade and the start of all the real trouble: anxiety over whether or not I was "saved." In order for the question of salvation to have been as scary as it was, I assume the idea of an afterlife must have sunk into my mind and started to feel believable, and I was certainly well-acquainted with the concept of hell at this point. In fact, my understanding of hell might possibly have been what solidified my belief in an afterlife, since I've noticed how much more believable the terror inspired by a threat of eternal torment feels as compared to the unpredictable range of emotions that might be inspired by the promise of an often undefined eternal *something* sometimes known as heaven. As to why I'm pretty sure this all started in fourth grade, it's because I seem to remember my fears originally growing out of discussions surrounding a landmark event in the history of conservative Evangelical Christian film: the release of the first *Left Behind* movie.

In case you're not an expert on the art world of conservative Evangelical Christian circles, I'll elucidate the connection here. *Left Behind* is a film based on a series of novels by the same title that dramatizes a particular set of ideas about how the world might end. These ideas come from the way that certain churches, including the one I grew up attending, interpret Revelation, the last book of the Bible. Therefore, the effect of *Left Behind*'s popularity on my church community was that everyone suddenly had a lot of interest in discussing the end of the world. According to our church tradition, the end of the world would be signaled when, at some unknown point that could happen any day, God caused all the people who were truly living for him to suddenly disappear to heaven. After this, seven years of global catastrophes would follow, ending when Jesus returned to earth to rule over the entire world.

If you come from a similar church background to mine, you'll already know exactly what sort of neurosis tends to be produced by the ol' *Left Behind* effect. If you don't, allow me to elucidate once again: In the brief summary of end-time events I've just given, the most important phrases are "at some unknown point that could happen *any day*" and "all the people who were *truly* living for him." Why did our pastors and schoolteachers find discussions on the end of the world to be so important? Because they thought we needed to be prepared for it. Why did we need to be prepared? Because it could happen any day. How did we need to prepare? By making sure we were *really* living for God, not faking it. What would happen if we weren't prepared? We would go through seven years of terror and suffering. Looking back, I almost want to say, "What's the big deal about seven years if the world's about to end anyway?" But remembering how I felt as a ten-year-old, I couldn't say which was more frightening: the dramatized descriptions of famine, disease, and life on the run, or the imagined horror of realizing that all your friends and family had suddenly disappeared and that you were the only one left because you were actually a big fake. I'm pretty sure it was the second one. I seem to remember having a nightmare around this time about the fear and shame of being "left behind" and realizing that what I thought was good wasn't good enough, that if I thought I had been real with God, I hadn't been real enough.

From that point on, there wasn't a time for at least three years that I didn't worry about whether I was living this Christian life in a way that was good enough. I didn't know whether I was a real enough Christian to be taken to heaven with everyone else if the end of the world was about to happen. If I didn't know that, I also couldn't say I was sure I would go to heaven if I died either. Maybe I was fake. Maybe I did good things but didn't love God enough. Maybe I liked the idea of what I could get from God but didn't actively live for him well enough. Maybe I was one of the people Jesus had talked about who could live an entirely fake life, never really knowing God.

Matthew 7:21–23 NIV
"Not everyone who says to me, 'Lord, Lord,' will enter the kingdom of heaven, but only the one who does the will of my Father who is in heaven. Many will say to me on that day, 'Lord, Lord, did we not prophesy in your name and in your name drive out demons and in your name perform many miracles?' Then I will tell them plainly, 'I never knew you. Away from me, you evildoers!'"

I found it all too easy to believe that I didn't really know God because my life experience seemed to be nothing like that of the people around me. They heard God speaking to them, or at least they had a feeling they were able to recognize as his leading. They saw miracles. When they read the Bible, they felt as if certain verses were being highlighted just for them, like God was pointing out whatever message they needed to hear at the time. They felt God's presence around them. I felt absolutely nothing. I had been told that if you prayed to Jesus and told him you wanted to give your life to him, the Holy Spirit would come to live inside of you and you would have a relationship with God. But I had done that, and I had never experienced anything that I could identify as a relationship or a connection with a being who desired to communicate with me. When *Left Behind* came along and stirred up a storm of discussions about making sure you really had your heart in the right place, the realization that God seemed absent from my life dawned on me. God didn't talk to me, and I had never felt his presence. So what was I doing wrong?

Of course, the problem must be that I was doing something wrong. Just as always, the idea that God might not be real was unthinkable, so unthinkable that I never thought of it. Instead, I thought—I *knew*—that I was somehow telling God to stay back from my life. I wasn't trying to tell him that, but I must have been doing it because according to what everyone said, I should have been able to find him somewhere if I had asked him to come into my life and really meant it. People said that God was with me, that he was present all the time, even that I didn't have to be lonely because he was there. But if the creator of the universe was actually in the same room as me and actually wanted some sort of relationship with me, and I had done what everyone said you were supposed to do to initiate that relationship, then why did being alone still feel so lonely, and why did I feel so empty?

I find it necessary to emphasize again here that I really believed God was good, that, just like the Bible said, God was love. As I describe the different ways I tried to connect with God over the years, I want you to keep in mind exactly where I was coming from, no matter how ridiculous it seems to you. The way I responded to different ideas isn't going to make any sense if you don't remember that the foundational concept in my mind all along was that God was good, perfect, and ultimately the answer for everything, even at times when I couldn't understand how. I'm not sure if I can fully explain why I believed in that concept so firmly, although I assume the explanation is simply that I was exposed to it so early and so often, but it's not important to understand why I held the view as long as you remember that I did hold it.

And that's why the predicament I was beginning to find myself in was so terrible. I couldn't hear God speaking to me, but I *wanted* to. Intensely. And I couldn't figure out what was wrong. Since I felt so certain that God was perfect and that he wanted a relationship with me like everyone said, I could only conclude that the problem was on my end. At the same time, I didn't seem to be doing anything differently from the people who said they experienced relationship with God, so whatever the problem was, it had to be something buried, something that I wasn't allowing myself to see. This created anxiety over the question of what could be so bad about me that even God who loved everyone wouldn't intervene to shake me out of it and even I who was really making an effort to be honest with myself couldn't find the root of it. In this condition, I had no hope of any assurance of salvation.

These worries about my possible self-deception lasted until some point when I was in seventh grade. Over that period I prayed countless times that God would live in my heart, that he would forgive me, that he would show me if I was doing anything wrong. But there was never an answer or an indication that I had been heard, that my prayers had accomplished anything. If there was a relationship, it was one that somehow existed without communication. Since I didn't think such a thing was likely to be possible, I couldn't shake the dread that I might be one of those people who God would eventually declare he had never known. It persisted despite the fact that I had often been told faith had to be based on something other than feelings. On one hand, that concept made sense; faith was a choice to put confidence in someone, not a feeling. But on the other hand, without some indication that a relationship existed, how could I know if I was living the way I should? The Bible made it clear that doing good things wasn't enough and that love was necessary. If I had never sensed or felt God, how could I say I loved him rather than just wanting the good things I thought he would give me? How could I say I had anything other than head knowledge when the only way I knew anything about God was through third-party information and never through interaction?

In seventh grade, a small epiphany allowed me some peace for a short while. I managed to put the worries to rest temporarily thanks to a project we were assigned in Bible class (yes, our school had Bible class) requiring that we write out our testimony and give a brief presentation of what we'd written. Our teacher explained that each person's testimony could be the story of how they became a Christian or an account of how they had grown in their faith over the years. He also mentioned that if thinking about your history with God made you realize you'd never actually prayed specifically saying you wanted to live for

God, you might as well do it now, even though you were probably still "saved" in any case. As I write down that recollection, I have to say now it seems a little disturbing that we entertained even a small possibility of our eternal fate resting on a few words that we might have neglected to say without realizing it. Yet again though, at the time, I wasn't thinking about things in that way. I automatically agreed that of course it was better just to make sure—you could never be too sure about these things (as evidenced by the fact that I had been trying to find some sort of certainty for three years unsuccessfully).

In the course of thinking about what to say in my paper, I came to a decision. Everyone said that faith was a choice and that if you prayed to be saved you should just stop worrying about it. Well, I didn't feel what I wanted to feel, but I could choose to ignore that. I could choose to say everything was fine and stop worrying. So I did. I told God that I wanted to live for him and asked him to take away the doubts and fears over whether that was good enough, and from that day on, every time a feeling of doubt over whether I was saved came up, I ignored it. I considered that decision a turning point in my life and told people about it frequently over the next few years. I still remember the date even—March 31st—because every year when that date rolled around I would think back on the decision I'd made to put doubt in its place.

I had taken a step forward by choosing to ignore my worries about salvation, but while that problem was resolved, it wouldn't be long before others would arise. Perhaps a year or so later I began thinking seriously about the importance of evangelism and, once again, of hearing God's voice even though I was no longer looking for it as a proof of salvation. These concerns soon turned me even more neurotic than I had been before.

Underlying each worry was the straightforward belief that some choices are better than others. For one, if this future eternity with God people called heaven was so important, it seemed that choices that allowed one to know God better now must be far superior to those that didn't because they could in some way allow one to be happier for all eternity. The Bible seemed to be full of passages on the importance of putting God first in your life and not being distracted by other things. There was talk of receiving crowns, of running a race to win, of servants who are rewarded according to how well they invest their master's resources, and on and on with imagery that seemed to say the more you prioritize God now the more you'll enjoy being with him later.[3]

I'm aware that many people might say this isn't a correct understanding and would point to passages such as the parable in which workers who spend different amounts of time on a job are all paid the same at the end of the day,[4] and say that God doesn't play favorites, but the problem here is that while you can make a good case both for the claim that your efforts to live for God actually matter in some way and for the claim that they don't, there is no concrete proof of which claim is correct, so you are left taking chances with your eternity. And of course (more relevant to my current purpose, which is simply to recount my past experiences) whether or not my understanding was correct, it was still the understanding I had at the time, so of course it's what I acted on. I felt convinced that the way in which I lived my life did matter somehow and that there was some sort of greater

---

[3] Some of the Biblical inspiration for these ideas comes from I Corinthians 9:24–27 and Matthew 25:14–30.
[4] Matthew 20:1–16

closeness with God I could attain if I prioritized the correct things.

Now, this idea could be seen from a positive angle: My efforts to live for God would be rewarded. Good. But it could also be seen from a negative one: A relationship with God is the best thing that can be experienced, but only the best of the best get the full experience. Every moment I allowed my focus on this goal to relax, I might be missing out on something of eternal value.

In regards to evangelism, I was facing another situation in which it seemed clear that people had the ability to make some choices that were better than others, but this time the stakes didn't have to do with varying levels of a good thing but with the difference between heaven and hell. It was a simple case of putting two and two together. I had been taught that Christians were supposed to share what we knew about God with other people, and the reason why this was so important was clear: Without Jesus, people were headed for hell. As much as nobody liked saying it that way, that was the obvious bottom line.

Well, this was a terrible burden, wasn't it? Apparently there was something that all Christians including me could do, in fact had been called to do, that would turn people off of a course leading to hell. That idea naturally brought certain questions to mind: How much did my actions influence other people's eternal destinies? If I could produce any effect at all in this area, wasn't I obligated to pour all my time and resources into trying to point people towards God? Wouldn't it be despicably selfish to spend time on any other pursuit when nothing could even begin to match the importance of this one? Even if other people's salvation didn't actually depend on anything I could do, this command to spread the gospel had still been given, so wouldn't it be disobedient to ignore it, and wouldn't I miss out on something if I did?

It seemed that my actions were of horrific importance—because there was such a thing as eternity and the form it took could be influenced, whether to a small degree or an enormous one, by the way I lived now. The way I should live in light of the situation also seemed obvious, but I had a problem here, a big shameful problem: I couldn't make myself do the right thing.

With evangelism, despite the clearly desperate importance of the responsibility, I found myself hesitant to the point of paralysis when it came to carrying it out. Whether I was naïve, stupid, or simply trusting and earnest, it seemed to me that the people who spent time doing street evangelism were on the right track. If people all around us needed to know about Jesus, shouldn't we be telling them? The same reasoning applied to the idea of bringing God into my interpersonal interactions. If any given person who I happened to be having a conversation with didn't know about this most important of all subjects, didn't I owe it to them to at least mention that God cared about them before we parted ways? But I couldn't do it. On a visceral level I found any and all evangelism tactics revolting, and my instinct was to avoid them just as much as I avoided wearing clothes with obvious logos and hate them just as much as I hated cheesy advertisements.

I had a natural fear and disgust towards the idea of initiating any interaction that was intended to sell anyone on anything, but these feelings of mine seemed to stand in direct contradiction to the responsibility all Christians clearly had to tell people the truth. As usual, I concluded that my own feelings must be wrong. I interpreted them as cowardice: It wasn't that there was anything problematic about my understanding of evangelism; it was that I was too timid to do what I should do and too lazy to try to overcome my difficulty with it.

In regards to hearing God's voice, the problem was that, while I was now convinced that I didn't need to sense any connection with God in order to be saved, I knew that living daily with no awareness of God's presence couldn't be a good thing and was most likely a result of my failure to do something important. The Bible told the story of how Jesus had been willing to suffer and die in order to make sure anyone could have a relationship with God. Preachers and teachers had frequently expounded on this narrative by saying that Jesus didn't come to earth just to give you something that happens after you die but to transform your life right now. They proclaimed, as if it was the realest thing in the world, that God loved each and every person too much to put off this relationship until later and was eager to talk to any of us who would listen right now. If I wasn't hearing him, the only explanation I could think of was that on some level I was unwilling to hear what he had to say.

And then I drew a connection that would ensure I was absolutely miserable for the next six years: Maybe God *was* talking to me, and maybe one of the things he was saying was that I should tell people about him, and maybe because I hated trying to do evangelism so much I had constructed an elaborate deception to convince myself I couldn't hear God talking to me just so that I could deny having heard that one message. It would make sense, wouldn't it? I knew from general familiarity with the Bible that I should tell people about God, but I wasn't doing it. At the same time, I knew that God wanted to talk to everyone and that supposedly any roadblock to that communication would have to be on my end. It seemed plausible that the Holy Spirit would keep reminding me to do what was right and wouldn't barrel on with a bunch of lighthearted messages if I ignored the messages that carried a form of responsibility with them. The idea that I was actually deceiving myself this effectively was less plausible, but it seemed to be the only explanation that fit all the givens.

From some point during junior high until near the end of my first year of college, my existence was dominated by an exhausting cycle: First I would feel desire to avoid things I naturally found repulsive, then fear that something was wrong with me because I was actually supposed to like those things, then hope that perhaps those things were just good in general but not something I as an individual was required to enjoy or participate in, then fear again that I couldn't trust my perception of reality because clearly I was lying to myself in order to bend the rules so I could get out of something I didn't want to do, then shame that I could be so perverse as to not only disobey a command but then try to convince myself that the command didn't even apply to me, then hopelessness in knowing that, as the stubborn and selfish person I was, there was no way I would ever achieve the closeness with God that I wanted. And then it would all cycle around again. How could I want so badly to be close to God and yet hate the things I had been told he loved? And so on.

It wasn't just evangelism I disliked. It was just about everything I had been told would help me build a relationship with God. Church, singing praise songs, books on theology, prayer, reading the Bible. The more I worried about my inclinations and what they might mean, the more I realized I disliked everything I was supposed to enjoy. All of these bluntly Christian activities felt so lifeless or so forced: They weren't the types of pursuits I naturally enjoyed spending my time on, and they never delivered that relational element that was supposed to be at their heart.

I still made an effort to engage in them though. That's how powerfully I believed it was all worthwhile. No matter how difficult it was, throughout this period I poured hours and hours into the things I thought I was supposed to do, especially Bible reading. I had heard so often that God spoke to people through the Bible, and I felt certain that if I kept reading and kept praying, eventually I would feel him speaking to me. I read and read, through the entire Bible multiple times, when I had extra time and when I didn't, in my room, at school, in the back seats of cars, and in doctor's office waiting rooms. I prayed every which way I could think of, praying for people to be healed and for international conflicts to end, for my family, for myself, praying to give thanks or just to comment on life, praying a question and then listening silently for an answer, praying words directly from scripture, praying alone or with other people. I tried fasting. I fasted for one day at a time and worried about whether I had put enough effort in and whether I might finally hear God if I fasted longer. Maybe I didn't want to hear him enough. Maybe my heart was in the wrong place as long as I wanted to be comfortable more than I wanted to hear from God. I started fasting for multiple days and still didn't hear or feel anything other than worry that even now I might not be doing something right. At church, I tried to worship with my whole heart. I had heard so many people say that they felt God in this setting too, and scripture seemed to support the idea that singing in praise and worship was vital to a healthy spiritual life. I longed to experience God during worship like my friends did, and I tried to leave myself open to whatever form of interaction he might want. I tried to mean the words that I sang, to clear my mind of distractions, to ignore any worries about what others might think and simply put all my attention into showing God that I wanted more of him.

No matter what I did though, it all seemed empty. While I did learn information from the Bible and from sermons, as far as personal connection and communication went, I found nothing but silence. As the silence persisted and persisted, I knew more deeply that I was failing somewhere. Worse than failing. That I was purposely fighting everything God wanted for my life. There was no other way I could have managed to miss him time and time again in every place I was supposed to find him.

This was how I lived my life over those six years. I went to school and studied and in every spare moment worried feverishly about why I wasn't experiencing God and then beat myself up saying of course I already knew the reason and it was because I was disobedient to what God was saying. There wasn't much more going on. As far as hobbies, I did a bit of foreign language study. As far as relationships, they were practically nonexistent. I had the friends who I saw at school. I didn't put effort into anything beyond that because all my time outside of school went into Bible reading, praying, or having emotional breakdowns and hiding them from my parents. There were moments in abundance when the tension and despair built up to such a pitch that all I could do was cry, and I didn't want my parents to know that it was *this again*, so I would avoid being in the same room as them. Even though they were devoted Christians and had tried to make me feel better on several occasions, they didn't seem to understand why this all bothered me so much. I couldn't make them see what seemed obvious to me: that if a relationship with God was the most important thing in the world and I couldn't find any sign of such a relationship in my life, something had to be drastically wrong.

When I wasn't too embarrassed to talk about my spiritual problems with someone—I shared them with people like youth pastors or our Bible class teachers at school—I got one of two responses. Either the person believed everything I said as presented (including my evaluation of how lazy or cowardly I was being) and agreed that I was right to worry about what I might miss out on if I didn't make better choices, or they brushed off my concern saying that God loved me and couldn't be behind the harsh requirements I was imagining and that he was speaking to me just by letting good things happen in my life or in some other nondescript way. The first response didn't help me because I still wasn't able to go do the "right" thing after hearing it, and the second didn't comfort me because it seemed equivalent to saying, "God will never actually talk to you, so you might as well imagine that some ambiguous circumstance is a message from him just like how people read generically applicable horoscopes and feel as if they're getting something personalized."

So I was stuck. Stuck hating myself for not being able to do the one thing in life that mattered, stuck dreading the consequences, stuck begging someone who never answered for help. And it never once occurred to me to doubt this God who didn't answer. I knew too many people who heard him talking to them, not in an ambiguous way, but telling them specific things, anything from nudging them to start a conversation with a particular person to challenging them to move to another country. People all around me could repeat detailed things God had communicated to them and tell extremely convincing stories of how they knew they weren't just hearing their own thoughts. In some cases, before they had told anyone about what they thought God was saying to them, a spouse or spiritual leader had suggested the same idea to them, saying they felt like it was from God. In some cases, they had gone through a period of time where several different people had independently delivered the same message to them, as if God was making sure there was no way they could overlook it. In many cases they had felt like God was telling them to do something that seemed impossible, so they had told him they would do it only if all the necessary circumstances lined up, and then stood by in astonishment as all the things that seemed so unlikely proceeded to happen. These stories of dramatic confirmation usually related to big decisions, but even when it came to little things whose authenticity people didn't try to prove, they could still give details about what God seemed to have said to them. Even if it was just a feeling, that God loved them for instance, they described it as having so much strength and clarity. It was beyond obvious that someone was communicating with them all and that there was a lot more to it than a paltry awareness that sometimes good things happen in life.

In my desperation to hear something and my certainty that the real problem was my fear of doing things God might ask me to do, I started to imagine that any spiritual-seeming impulse might be God's voice, and eventually, as idiotic as it was, I started acting on what I thought I was hearing. When I could stomach it. This usually meant something along the lines of attempting to tell some random person that God loved them. Sometimes if I managed to overcome every fiber of natural resistance and do it, I felt momentary relief that I hadn't been a total coward for once. But this didn't stop more equally-as-difficult demands from popping into my mind relentlessly. Most of the time I couldn't bring myself to do what I thought I was being told, and my misery simply grew deeper day after day, year after year.

While I must have succeeded in putting on a normal face for people (No one ever remarked that I seemed wrong in the head), my true experience of those years was hell. I don't have much more to say about the time because it consisted of variations on the same scenario repeated incessantly.

I still don't know if you can understand or believe that I was so compulsively driven by this odd collection of impulses. Somehow the majority of people around me didn't experience the same fears that I did, at least not to my knowledge. (Thinking back, I feel like I could point out the ones who did, but who knows if the sense I have is really accurate or not.) My peers either felt like they did have a real relationship with God, or didn't think it mattered. But to me these harsh conclusions were the only way I could reconcile religious claims I thought were true with my own seemingly contradictory experiences.

I also want to emphasize that I'm not describing the unpleasantness of my past experiences for the purpose of showing how bad they were but for the purpose of illustrating that I wanted God badly enough to put myself through them. I certainly don't want anyone to feel sorry for me (I love the life I have now, and all this seems like forever ago), but I want people to understand that at this point I so sincerely believed everything I'd been told that years of unhappiness and fruitless prayers didn't deter me from doing whatever I thought might allow me to finally experience God.

It wasn't until near the end of my first year of college that I finally became convinced there were ways of living for God that didn't require me to be a fulltime street evangelist. When I realized this, everything about the quality of my life began to improve.

I had ended up in the thoroughly Christian Midwest at a Christian college where professors incorporated theology into many of the courses offered and students were required to take a handful of classes specifically about Christian philosophy and interpreting the Bible. The view of theology I got here took a different focus from what I had grown up with, and I found it freeing. Our professors heavily emphasized the subjects of grace and calling. Grace was a familiar concept, one I knew well on an intellectual level, but it would take several years for me to come to a more intuitive understanding of it. It meant that God loved me regardless of how good or bad a person I was, and regardless of whether I ever did anything for him. I knew that. I had heard it all my life. It hadn't stopped me from being troubled by cumbersome worries about whether I might be making choices I would regret eternally, but as I heard people stress over and over again that grace really meant I didn't need to feel personal guilt over how most things in the world turned out, I slowly started to worry a little less.[5] Calling was something new. It meant that there was something, or a range of things, in life that you were designed to do. God made every person different, and while some people were called to be pastors or missionaries, many people were not, and the world would not be a better place if every Christian tried to pursue this sort of path in life. Instead of identifying one across-the-board best lifestyle that every Christian should copy, each individual should

---

[5] The thing that really made a difference was that in college I was exposed to a heavily Reformed or Neo-Calvinist view of grace, which tended to highlight not only the concept of God's unchanging love that I already knew about but also, pivotally, the concept that other people's salvation was fully in the hands of God, given to them purely by God's grace, and not at all dependent on anything I could do for good or bad.

ask God to lead them to the specific work they were called to do.

This new focus changed everything for me. I finally understood that doing the right thing in life wasn't a question of calculating how to expose the largest number of people to the gospel. Over time, as I understood grace more deeply and became more familiar with the idea of calling, I came to realize that the most important thing of all was to cultivate a loving relationship with God because the more time I spent in God's presence, the more I would naturally act like him in every part of my life. God didn't need me to do anything for him. He hadn't saved me or anyone else because he needed a workforce to go do stuff for him. He simply loved people and wanted us to enjoy loving him. Yes, he would give us good and important things to do, but not so that we could earn his love, and not because he had no other way of getting them done. It certainly wasn't my responsibility to ensure the salvation of any other person. That was up to God. And I didn't even have to go into ministry as a profession. God had called his people to go into every sort of work and simply pursue it in a way that honored him. He didn't want a church made up entirely of people who knew how to give a good sermon, but also of people who enforced fair and honest business practices, encouraged children to explore the world, prevented crimes, wrote stories that touched people, challenged stagnant political norms, and a million other things. Tactics like street evangelism and handing out tracts might be effective at certain times in certain places, but clearly most people weren't going to be influenced by that sort of interaction anyway. Just as God called individuals to focus on one particular bit of work and do it well, he also called us to focus on the people around us and love them well. If he wanted us to eventually tell these people more about him, he would make the opportunities come up naturally.

After one school year of hearing these messages, I started to get it. I started to relax and realize that there was probably something worthwhile I could do with my life without hating it. Slowly, I started to become happier than I had been in a very long time. Worries about whether I was using every moment of time in the one and only best way started to fade, and for quite a while I was distracted from my search for interaction with God. Or rather, I thought I had found an answer to that too. Most of the people I was now spending time with weren't as "charismatic" as what I was used to. That is, they didn't talk much about miracles and striking supernatural experiences of God. Instead they were more intellectual, more focused on the idea that we could all learn things God wanted us to know partly by studying scripture and partly by observing nature and critiquing works of culture. In the Bible we could read God's unchanging and direct words to all humanity. In the natural world, which God had created, and society, which was made up of people created in God's image, we could pick up on other broad principles or currents of what God's Spirit was doing in the world today. To give a specific example, instead of being told that listening to Christian-label music was the best choice for everyone, I was now being told to listen to all kinds of music but to listen actively and think about what I was hearing, to break it down and decide for myself whether it was valuable and what I could learn from it.

I got into the habit of journaling about my thoughts and questions both while reading the Bible and while taking in various forms of secular art and communication, and for a while I felt that I had a relationship with God. He spoke to me through words that other people had written, and I answered by journaling about my thoughts in response, and I had some calling on my life to do some not unpleasant thing that would make the world a better place. Life was good. Or at least, better.

The fact is, I can't give an honest and complete account of this time without wrestling with contradictory memories. On one hand, I remember all the excitement of realizing I had options in life, enjoying new experiences, and making friends. On the other hand, I remember going to sleep most nights wishing I was dead and writing rambling stream-of-consciousness stories and poems about self-hatred and a desire that this good entity that made me would just destroy me since I was so repulsive to it.

In the process of writing the account you're reading now, I went back and reread my old journals from that time, and they confirmed the jumble of moods I remembered. I'm optimistic on one page and despairing on the next, sometimes going on happily for paragraphs about a science or entertainment topic that caught my interest and sometimes writing things like, "I feel like I'm only living out of obligation." Those latter three years of college were a strange time that I can only describe by saying I was pretty happy and pretty depressed all at once. I remember exhilarating conversations and fun-filled day trips with friends, and I remember nights when I was so sad I couldn't take it, walking to a friend's dorm room door and then leaving without being able to bring myself to knock. I remember playing in the snow and recruiting friends to help adorn a nude statue on campus with a coconut bra and grass skirt in the middle of winter. I remember learning to loosen up and dance for the first time at a Halloween party. And I remember walking across campus after one of my favorite classes on a beautiful day, noticing the sunlight on my skin, knowing that everything was perfect, and asking myself, "Why can't I feel anything about anything?"

With hindsight, I want to attribute a lot of the depression to lack of sleep, but there are clear reasons why negative emotions, regardless of their physical causes, formed themselves into the specific types of thoughts I kept having at that time. While I was relieved to know that God didn't expect me to be handing out tracts on the street corner, I still had wells of confusion about how anything in my life made sense if God was who people said he was, and in spite of all the myriad times I had heard people say that God loved me and despite the positivity that came along with feeling that I was learning something about God's ways by paying attention to the culture around me, the fear that had put down roots for six years or more prior to this—that my lack of connection with God as a personal being could only be explained by some unknown deeply wrong and twisted thing about me—never really disappeared. So while I was making progress at understanding ideas like grace on a deliberate, highly conscious level, when it came to the realms of habit and intuition, there were still entrenched problems that had never been addressed satisfactorily that led me to blame myself for everything in a hopeless, unconstructive way.

Still, at the time, feeling like I wanted to die whenever I had a spare moment to think was nothing compared to the years of acute condemnation that had come before. I remembered going to sleep sometimes during that earlier period with a fear that God would kill me for my disobedience (like Nadab and Abihu or Moses or Aaron or Uzzah or Ananias and Sapphira or the unnamed Corinthians who took communion in an "unworthy manner").[6] Having a take-it-or-leave-it sort of feeling towards being alive was much less terrible than fearing I was going to get myself killed by being such a bad person, so comparatively things were a cake walk. I also didn't realize at the time that my understanding of God was a major cause of my unhappiness; I attributed all the morbid thoughts and sadness to just hormones and told myself that everyone probably felt the same way. And while the life-draining sense that my very existence was problematic never really went away, there were so many good and promising things calling for my attention. All around me people were talking about finding God's beauty in paintings and symphonies, prairies and cities, cathedrals and tattoo parlors. They were abuzz with news on how the Holy Spirit was inspiring engineers to bring clean water to rural villages and scientists to develop safer energy sources and entrepreneurs to craft real paths out of poverty. With all these truly exciting things being opened up to me as part of the Christian life, the negative stuff at least had to take turns being at the forefront of my mind.

During this strange, contradictory time when I can't say I was making much progress on emotional maturity, the new information and experiences that came along with this community's passion for finding God everywhere did continue to open up important chapters in the development of my theological understanding.

For one, the exposure I was getting in my science classes to discussions on biological evolution was a big deal. You see, before getting to college, I had had only one or two brief

---

[6] Leviticus 10:1–3; Numbers 20:2–12, 22–29 & Deuteronomy 32:48–52 & Deuteronomy 34:1–5; II Samuel 6:1–11; Acts 5:1–11; I Corinthians 11:27–30

encounters with Christians who thought that the various species of life on earth had all evolved from a common ancestor. At church and school before college, every available opportunity was taken to promote young earth creationism with arguments that made it sound like all methods of determining the age of our planet were flawed beyond recovery and natural selection couldn't possibly result in an accumulation of useful genetic material over time. But once I had taken a genetics class that simply explained how things like DNA replication and mutations were observed to work in real life rather than picking out only creationism-related bits of information to cover, it seemed obvious to me that there was nothing spectacular or unbelievable about the idea that some mutations could be helpful and these helpful changes could accumulate over time.

My professors and classmates mostly came from the perspective that creationism and evolution had nothing to do with one's faith anyway. The Bible contained many different types of writing all inspired by God, and scripture itself never labeled Genesis 1 as literal history. If it was a metaphor, it still communicated all that humanity needed to know about God as creator, his meticulous care for his creation, and his plan for humanity. Did we really expect that God should have delivered a scientific treatise on how the creation and shaping of the world was physically carried out to his followers in the ancient world?

I liked this atmosphere in which science wasn't seen as a field in the grips of a vast anti-God conspiracy, and I didn't have to look far to find scores of people who in no way fit the stereotype I had been taught to expect of Christians who accepted mainstream theories on evolution. Creationists made it sound like if you didn't maintain with certainty that Genesis 1 was a literal historical account of how life came to be, your entire system of belief would be undermined and weak, but that wasn't what I saw at all. While the young earth creationist community I had come from seemed afraid of the secular world and talked about the gospel mostly in terms that T-shirts and bumper stickers almost did justice to, this community was engaging with the world, changing lives, and bringing hope. Their acknowledgement of the difficult-to-explain parts of life and faith only deepened their passion to know God's heart towards every issue and search out the creative resolutions his Spirit would guide them to.

My abandonment of the dichotomy that said either most of the world's scientists were lying to me or the entire Bible was junk, would bring about a couple notable steps in my ongoing search for closeness with God. The immediate effect was to make me ask a lot of questions about how God interacted with the physical world, which was a very good thing because it gave me something to talk to God about. I had to leave behind the oversimplified theology I had grown up with in which science obviously proved Christianity and anyone who said otherwise was lying, and in order to figure out what deserved to take its place, I had to do a lot of thinking, praying, and learning.

I wrote in my journal about all the questions I had for God, prayed about them throughout the day, sketched out my half-formed thoughts on their answers, and discussed them with Christian friends who shared my desire to bring God into every part of life. Some of the conclusions my changing views pointed to were immediately pleasant and in harmony with my existing beliefs, while others came with serious uncertainty and doubt. Even this was good though, since I took my doubts straight to God and discussed them, fully expecting that he would pick up the conversation, correct me anywhere I'd gone wrong, and introduce the sort of higher-level answers only he could provide that would end up strengthening my faith more than if I had never engaged with challenging ideas.

Did any of that happen? Well, at the time I did feel positively about the amount of subjects I talked to God about and the amount I learned about theological topics, but did God talk back? Was he an encouraging and involved father, guiding me in the right direction as I learned to challenge assumptions and step out for myself, or jumping in to warn me if I got too caught up in a faulty line of thought? Not quite. Although I was happy realizing how much time I spent talking to God, I can't honestly say I was talking *with* God. I was still plagued by loneliness and attempts at communication that died out into silence. I felt that whatever answers I came up with I had to find or make for myself because no voice from beyond me ever made itself heard: The process wasn't like having an informative discussion with a person; it was like researching, studying, and mulling things over to draw connections—that's exactly what it was. It was informative and invigorating, but it was no different from how people who never thought of God went about familiarizing themselves with big topics.

Regardless of the persistent unfulfilled longings though, on the whole these learning experiences made me feel more alive spiritually. As I developed nuances in understanding, Christianity seemed so much more vibrant and sensible than it had in the past.

In the midst of all this, I spent a semester in Central America, where I ended up encountering a jarring juxtaposition to the nuance I was learning to love. During the semester abroad I did almost everything with a local family day to day, including attending their charismatic and extremely conservative church. I had grown up in a church where people believed in supernatural experiences like speaking in tongues but didn't expect them to happen every day, I had started to get used to churches where such things were not expected to happen at all, and now I was at a church where supernatural manifestations were a normal part of every sermon.

It was an interesting experience to regularly witness the pastor of this church get fired up on a point, speaking with more and more passion until he launched into a cascade of incomprehensible syllables, a message delivered in "tongues." But I felt more concerned than interested on the whole: What people at this church believed about tongues was so different from what I had been taught in the church I grew up in that I had to wonder who was right.

What I had heard in the past was that the gift of tongues was mainly to be used in one's personal prayer life. It was like speaking a spiritual language to God, and since other people couldn't understand it, it shouldn't be made part of a church service unless someone was going to interpret what was said.[7]

I think I had heard someone speak in tongues twice before this, at two different churches, and never under circumstances that were conducive to my getting a good listen. Both were very short utterances given in front of a group of people and immediately followed up by an interpretation from another member of the group; both times the interpretation was a poetic verse of scripture. The first time I remember thinking, "That's familiar—It's from Psalms!" and the second time I can't remember if it was an excerpt from Psalms or one of the

---

[7] I Corinthians 14, especially verses 27–33, was the authoritative passage on the topic in the church I grew up in.

prophets. I couldn't recall later how the "spiritual" words had sounded—I probably hadn't even taken them in well to begin with, given that they were such short strings of sound that carried no meaning for me—but it definitely seemed to me that a heavenly language *should* sound beautiful and completely foreign, probably using sounds that didn't occur in any earthly language.

But now that I was spending time at a church where the pastor frequently spoke in tongues for comparatively extended periods of time, I was able to pay close attention, and I was surprised by what I heard. Instead of consisting of otherworldly sounds, the interjections of tongues sounded just like the Spanish the rest of the sermon was given in. What was more, they were made up of the same simple syllables repeated many times. While that part was at least unlike any earthly language, it also seemed simply unlike language. Frankly, it seemed made up, and the fact that no one present at the sermons ever claimed to have been given an interpretation of what was said added to my suspicion. In the past I had wondered many times how these fascinating heavenly languages might sound, but I had been caught off guard when I had a brief opportunity to hear them, and now that I was finally getting an ample chance, what I heard didn't sound as if the Holy Spirit were gifting a person with a complex, structured system of verbal communication at all; it was less interesting and less attractive than a plain old everyday non-spiritual language and too conspicuously exactly the sort of thing someone could come up with off the top of their head.

Other appearances of the supernatural raised red flags too. I couldn't help but feel uncomfortable and skeptical at one gathering together of several churches when an impassioned speaker blurted out that God was saying there were 20 people present who needed prayer for physical maladies. He kept repeating that there were 20, even after an awkward period of time had gone by with only 18 individuals having come forward. Eventually, two more sheepish volunteers agreed to be prayed for.

Outside of the time spent in church, everything about the semester abroad was wonderful, but church demanded such an inflated amount of my time that I came to resent it. Sunday mornings seemed to drag on forever, and the additional church meetings in between could be hours long. The strict standards of behavior this particular church expected also grated on me: We didn't get to celebrate most national holidays because they were "Catholic holidays." We weren't supposed to play cards or drink alcohol. No one specifically requested that we limit our music choices, but when my host mom stated that in their church they only listened to Christian music and then asked me what kind of music I liked, my momentary excitement that I could talk about all the Spanish-language artists I loved was quickly knocked out by the fear I might sound like a heathen if I let slip I was a fan of Juanes and La Oreja de Van Gogh, let alone Don Omar!

It was an odd back-and-forth to go from the Evangelical church that was all I knew, to the Reformed church where everything seemed so mature and enlightened in comparison, to this charismatic church where things that to me seemed to have little bearing on one's spiritual development were off limits and supposed manifestations of the supernatural were accepted without being scrutinized for validity. Overall, I felt disillusioned with church by the time I returned to the US.

At some point during my semester abroad I wrote what I felt was a scathing short story about a sincere Christian woman who had been diagnosed with cancer in high school and spent time in the hospital before eventually going into remission. The story consisted of her sharing just a few select memories about how uncanny it had felt for someone who had always been a bashful outsider at her Christian school, never knowing how to act around all the popular and confident students who everyone naturally perceived as also being the most spiritual, to suddenly hear those same peers holding her up as a beacon of faith as soon as she had gotten sick and not responded by angrily abandoning her beliefs. The fact that I had time to finish writing the story has a lot to do with why I felt disillusioned, I think: During the semester abroad, I had more time on my hands than usual, even with all the long church services. With fewer classes and less homework than I was used to, my mind was far too free to examine all the aspects of church life that didn't make sense.

Looking back on my own experiences at a Christian high school, why was it that the people who had done things like lead Bible studies or get accepted into the circles of confidence of extra-spiritual teachers had always come from the groups of most popular kids? Why hadn't God ever called any of the nerds who prayed and cared just as much to do things like share his words with their classmates? Why did cool godly kids still get to be looked at as godly even when they acted like jerks to the people around them while uncool godly kids were always suspected of teetering on the edge of leaving the faith because of the way they dressed or the fact that they liked anime or because of their reluctance to speak up about their opinions in front of others?

Why did people at the church I was temporarily taking part in not accept Catholics who believed in Jesus as being Christian? Why did they not seem to notice the suspiciousness of what they called speaking in tongues or of a speaker having to pressure people into making a message he supposedly heard from God come true? Why did people at the church I had grown up in expect to have a positive influence on non-Christians around them when they kept preaching the same black-and-white messages that had fallen out of touch with everyday life? Why did they talk as if conspiracies were everywhere—a liberal agenda trying to weaken Christian morals through movies and music, an atheist agenda trying to destroy faith through the theory of evolution—when the Christians around me who accepted secular entertainment and mainstream science lived with more of the unshakeable faith and radical love Jesus had embodied than anyone I knew?

I returned at the end of the semester feeling in need of some time away from churchiness, and when I attended my family's church with them over break, nothing seemed good enough. The sermons were all repeats; the atmosphere was unfriendly to people who didn't walk in already feeling like good Christians; the praise song lyrics were light on theology. How did churches go on like this year after year without hearing God challenge them to reconsider all the things that were done more because of tradition and politics than because they were beneficial? I was feeling jaded, and I knew it. Being able to point out how much other Christians were missing the point of everything almost made me feel like I was a good Christian comparatively, but it didn't make up for the fact that I had never stopped looking for some form of personal connection with God and had still never found it.

The rest of college wrapped up the same way—I continued to hear ideas that excited me at school and witness behavior that felt like a letdown at various churches.

Around the point where I seriously started to ask myself what I would do after graduating, people started to suggest that, since I liked language, I should try teaching English in a foreign country. I loved the idea of helping people learn a new language, so I looked into the options and ended up accepting a job in South Korea. The idea of living in another country was thrilling—the idea of having to control a class of kids, I have to admit, was terrifying. But this was an opportunity I couldn't pass up; I felt that the only responsible thing to do was overcome my fear and make it work.

So I got on a plane to cross the Pacific, taking my faith in God's good plans for this world and my disgruntled attitude towards church with me. I jumped into a busy life in Seoul, relishing the trains and the taxis, the café culture, the hiking spots right in the middle of the city, and the international vibe, but moving to a new country nevertheless brought with it the challenge of starting out, in some ways, all alone. I thought of all the theorizing I had heard about what church *should* be and hoped that I would be able to find a church community that would be like a family.

Lo and behold, one of my new coworkers soon informed me that her church was just what I was looking for, so I went along to a service on the fourth floor of a visibly aging building in a dingy part of town and discovered something that made me think God had brought me halfway around the world in order to get me to that very church: They were all about praying for Korean reunification. The people at this church, who came from many different countries, were convinced that God's plan for the world included reunification of North and South Korea, so convinced that they didn't pray things like, "Please bring these two countries back together," but instead things like, "Please prepare the South Korean economy for a smooth transition to reunification," or "Give us more TV shows that portray average North Koreans in a positive light so that they'll be accepted by their new neighbors when reunification happens."

Witnessing the depth of hope they had for this future made me look back on memories that hadn't seemed important before and see a pattern. I remembered noticing the names North and South Korea for the first time when I was a kid and wanting to know if the two countries used to be one and wondering to myself if they would be one again someday. I remembered sometimes praying for this to happen, now and again throughout the years when I thought of it, and asking a Korean exchange student at college what she thought about the idea. But until I went to that church, I had never met anyone who didn't think reunification was pie in the sky. The fact that I had always maintained an interest in the idea without it ever having been encouraged, and had then just happened to find a job opportunity in Korea and just happened to walk into a church where people felt certain that reunification was coming, had to mean that God had given me that interest and led me to a group of people he had called in the same way. Called to what, exactly, I never really found out. I lived in Korea for several years but never figured out what to do with my hope for reunification except to keep praying. With work and commutes taking up well over eight hours on weekdays and church involvement quickly growing to occupy most of the weekend, I never found time to get involved in too much else.

My hope of finding a church family was more than met though. At the church I attended in Seoul, I was privileged to be part of an international community of some of the most considerate and fun-loving people I've ever known, and I'll always be grateful to everyone who reached out to make me a part of their life.

Incidentally, I also found myself back in a charismatic-leaning environment in this community. The way the pastors told it, the church had been made up of people from various traditional, conservative denominations when it began, people who knew the Bible well and lived by it but found charismatic practices foreign. Then, at some point, supernatural things had started to happen at prayer meetings. People had started to speak in tongues or fall to the floor. At first the pastors had wanted to back away from whatever was going on, but after praying about it, they decided that they couldn't expect the Holy Spirit to remain exclusively within their denominations' ideas of a church service, and if these odd occurrences were how the Spirit wanted to let people know he was with them while they prayed, then so be it. They still abided by the biblical guideline to not let outbreaks of tongues and other behavior that newcomers wouldn't understand become a distraction at Sunday morning services, but at prayer meetings, where it was just the church family gathering together, supernatural displays were welcome.

In this church, I found people diligently seeking the balance between intellectual and spiritual I had been missing. Like the influences I had known in college, they placed a high value on thoughtful interpretation of scripture and welcomed the insights of many disciplines, like psychology and economics, when considering how to love people like Jesus loved them. But like the church I had grown up in, they were also open to the use of spiritual gifts and expected personal interaction with God to be part of life. This to me looked like what I saw modeled in the New Testament: a lifestyle in which powerful communication from God was key and people came to know Jesus through creative combinations of big ideas rather than through rigid traditions.

Here, I was surrounded again by stories of the supernatural. Over the time I was in Korea, several people I knew or had at least talked to claimed to have been healed from things like arthritis, back pain, digestive problems, and asthma, and I heard the stories of, or saw for myself, couples who had been trying to have children for years finally having a baby after a dramatic prayer from a charismatic speaker. At the frequent prayer meetings the church held, pastors and other speakers told us all to keep praying for the people around us with hope and fervor because we could see the prayers of the churches across Korea making a difference: Suicide rates were dropping, economic progress was advancing, the older and younger generations were finding reasons to reconcile their differences, all just as we had prayed for.

Most alluring to me, people in this church overflowed with information about how the Holy Spirit interacted with them personally, and they all assured me that God loved every individual human being more than what any of us could imagine and found his greatest joy in sharing a relationship with each of us. Every individual was God's beloved child, someone God would be sorry not to talk with every day, and the number one most important thing any Christian could do, more than preaching the gospel to others, more than doing charitable deeds, was to connect with God in whatever way allowed you to hear or feel the thoughts he wanted to share with you. That was the foundation from which everything else would grow. And the ways people spoke about finding this connection with God were numerous.

I knew people who said the time they spent praying was their favorite time in the day. They would talk to God about their lives, their families, the things they wanted to see change in the world, whatever was on their mind. Many of them would play praise music and feel like God was giving them a personal message through the lyrics of the songs or like the Holy Spirit was filling them with a sense of love or a concern for a particular group of people. While praying, some of them formed words silently within their mind; others spoke out loud; some prayed while sitting quietly, others while walking around their neighborhood; some journaled; some prayed in tongues. They would listen, and God would answer by placing new thoughts into their mind, by giving them a vision, by revealing direction in a dream that night, by providing clarity through a sermon or a conversation with a friend the next day. They would ask God how to pray for a particular topic and receive guidance. They would feel God nudge them about topics they had never thought to pray over, asking them why they never talked to him about those issues.

I knew people who genuinely preferred being in the front row of a church singing praise and worship songs to any other place or activity. During worship times I saw people dancing in the aisles and folding their hands over their hearts, overcome with emotion. When my friends talked about what worship meant to them, they described how close they felt to God during those times, like he was hugging them.

I knew people who fell to the floor after being prayed for and lay there motionless while worship and prayer times continued around them. When it came to this spiritual manifestation, I was skeptical at first; I had heard stories before from people who had felt pressured by those around them to get weak in the knees while being prayed for but simply never felt anything happen, so I thought the whole thing came down to a question of who tended to get caught up in hype and who didn't. But after I talked to friends at church who had this experience, I changed my mind. One person told me that she hadn't believed the Holy Spirit was really making anyone fall over until it unexpectedly happened to her and then she had been unable to deny that an outside force was behind the phenomenon. I asked another what she experienced, and she responded that she fell down because she felt a weight on her, pushing her down gently. I asked if she was awake while she lay on the ground, and she said that she was aware of what was going on around her but was focused on God telling her how much he loved her.

Even though these dramatic experiences never happened to me, at this church I certainly went through more periods of contentment than ever before. It helped that I usually didn't have trouble finding someone to talk with about difficulties I encountered now, and besides that, I felt like I was part of a team of people who were changing the world every day as they acted according to God's inspiration. There was still that one persistent problem though. As a part of a church like this, I knew that God wanted to communicate with me in a way that would be real enough for me to fall in love with him. I knew that he wanted me to find him in a way that was real enough that I would want to pray and sing and read the Bible, just like I wanted to spend time with my friends. It was possible for all those activities to lose their one-sidedness and become real interactions; I knew it was because of the thrilling testimonies that surrounded me on all sides. But it still never happened to me. Still, after all these years, God himself felt as far away as ever no matter what I did, even at points where people said that what had worked for them was not trying so hard—I took their advice, eased up, and waited for God to take the lead, and even that didn't change anything.

After I had been part of this church for a while, the consequences of my problem intensified when I was encouraged to join the church leadership program. It didn't seem like a huge deal; the program was just a higher level of involvement and responsibility many of the church members committed to in order to help keep things running smoothly and to foster their own spiritual growth. On one hand, it seemed like something I should do: The point was to challenge yourself to grow up spiritually and contribute to taking care of other, newer members of the community who were still getting their feet under them. It would be pretty selfish not to take part in that, wouldn't it? But on the other hand, committing to attend extra services and leadership meetings and to listen to extra sermons outside of church and even just accepting the responsibility of a small title that suggested people should look up to me as a spiritual role model was the absolute last thing I wanted to do. All these Christian things I did were still so empty, so unsatisfying, so draining because they were still all part of the charade of pretending that someone who, as far as I could tell firsthand, wasn't there, was actually my best friend.

Unfortunately, my feelings of guilt over not wanting to give back to the community won out. Joining the program seemed like such a natural step of spiritual growth. My resistance had to be just fear of responsibility, and I was afraid that I would fall farther away from the relationship God wanted to have with me if I continued to sit comfortably where I was at instead of putting in the work to spend a little more time at church. I joined and actually made it work for about a year, but after that time—a year of dragging myself to leadership meetings, hating every second of my responsibilities, and coming close to quitting several times—I finally gave up on it. It had been difficult putting my former amount of effort into things that lacked the relational element that was supposed to be at their heart, and generating this elevated amount of effort still with no payoff as far as closeness to God went was unsustainable.

Trying to force a change of heart on myself hadn't worked the way I had hoped it would, and I suppose the rest of my time in Korea after that was falling action, denouement. I had had everything anyone could ask for in the Christian life: a loving, Spirit-led community around me; an environment in which both heart and mind, charismatic experience and logical soundness were valued in the pursuit of God; a purpose to take part in that was beyond myself but close to my heart; understanding for my weaknesses and challenges to grow stronger. All that and more was available to me, and I thought I had taken advantage of it. I thought I had been diligent to look for God in all of it, and I knew I had been full of hope and expectation at some points and at least willing to ask God to take me back to that place of expectation at other points. Why at the end of the day did I still not have God here with me? Why did I still have no idea what other people could have possibly experienced that made them able to say without feeling dishonest that God was present with them and they loved to spend time with him?

What I perceived as progress in the Christian life for me looked like a graph that climbed for a bit, then fell abruptly to zero, then climbed again, higher this time, and then fell back to zero, then climbed again a little higher, but still fell back again to zero. I kept going through learning periods where I thought my problems would be solved, where I thought I was really going to find God: I would mature, I would gain confidence, and then the rush of new knowledge would start to wear off and I would realize that it was still just knowledge, just information taught to me by other people, and that I still hadn't caught that glimpse of God I was dying for, and I would fall back to that place of loneliness and despair.

After leaving the church leadership program, I started to talk more openly with some of my older, more spiritually mature friends about how far away God seemed, how it felt to me like he was a father I had only ever known through child support checks: Everyone kept pointing to his supposed provision in my life as proof of his love, but why wouldn't he *talk* to me or *be there* with me? Our pastors praised Jacob for wrestling with God for his blessing; why did my lifetime of refusing to accept anything less than God's presence keep leading to greater attrition instead of victory?

People shared encouraging words with me, and I refused as always to give up hope of one day walking into the Christian life I knew I was supposed to have, but nothing really changed. I fell into an uncomfortable rhythm of boldly declaring the idea of God I had faith in to myself and others while timidly asking God where and what he was and how I could still be missing him.

Eventually I moved back to the States. I hadn't continued teaching for very long, having opted to move into a position as an English textbook copy editor instead, but after a couple of years I decided I couldn't see myself staying in that career long-term either. (Despite my passion for the Oxford comma, I have to confess I sometimes found myself tired of being the resident grammar Nazi.) I wanted to be closer to family again and have the freedom of trying out other career fields without the complications of employer-sponsored work visas, so I moved home without much of a clear plan at all.

I teared up when they served us kimchi on the flight home. There was nothing special about popping the lids off the packaged meal and eating from the plastic compartments, but I had to look at the kimchi and think, "I wonder when the next time I'll eat this will be?"[8] It was a dish I hadn't tried before moving to Seoul but had eaten and enjoyed almost every day for the last four years, and it was one tiny piece of this whole life I'd built, this first independent life of my own outside of school, this life in which I knew how things worked, and now I didn't know what I was heading into or how much I might miss what I was leaving.

Just like when I had moved to Seoul though, I thought God was in the decision to go home. I had prayed about it and talked to the people at church, and everyone agreed it seemed like the right thing to do, so I knew it would work out. I never suspected that moving back to the States would actually begin a trickle of thoughts and circumstances that slowly and surely set up my dam of beliefs for catastrophic failure.

In Korea, everything was go, go, go! We got up early to catch the train; we worked overtime; we went out with coworkers and friends; we booked our weekends and midweeks with church services, prayer meetings, charity events; we squeezed in times to take Korean language classes and exercise and sightsee and call family back home and clean the house between it all.

Back in California, I was suddenly only working part time. Without having planned it purposely, I had reintroduced that dangerous element of having enough time to reflect, and I found myself naturally filling the schedule gaps with lots of thinking, reading, and journaling. My mind wandered back to

---

[8] Little did I know that by the time I got back to California in 2017, the foodies would have taken over and everything would have kimchi on it.

topics of interest left over from college, things I had never had the time to dig into like I wanted, and I realized that now I could finally devote myself to becoming as informed as I had been meaning to.

Being the kind of person who always feels a need to understand what fuels the intensity behind controversial issues, I was naturally drawn to hone in on the most debated issue I knew. At this point, that issue was still creationism. Disagreements over what biological evolution meant to the church had stayed fresh in my mind for the last handful of years partly because it still felt so strange to have experienced such a complete turnaround in my own views and partly because the church I attended in Korea had, here and there, displayed an odd attitude towards evolution: While the pastors of that church took the words of secular experts seriously on many scientific topics and had no problem incorporating them into sermons, the couple of times evolution happened to be mentioned, it was only to dismiss the theory apparently without having any understanding of it. I had been baffled the first time this happened, when a pastor had tossed out the comment that the theory of evolution was all wrong "because there are fossils at the top of the Grand Canyon." I just stared at the stage with the thought running through my head that that observation didn't contradict anything about accepted theories of evolution or geology; it was like saying that things couldn't be made up of atoms because some materials weigh more than others—there was no connection between observation and conclusion. I also heard evolution rejected as evil "because they want you to think you came from monkeys." But I didn't see how, when the Bible clearly said God had formed man from dust, it could be so dehumanizing to think that God wrote physical laws that formed dust into man via a natural process.

With those ideas swimming around in my mind, I simply had to know more. What was it about the topic of evolution that caused people who were thoughtful and detail-oriented when it came to other academic subjects to lower their standards so much? And what would I say to them in a conversation anyway? Did I really, really have good reasons for coming to the conclusions I had reached? I thought so, but there was always more to learn.

In the course of rounding out my understanding I read websites of creationist organizations, articles written by Christian biologists about the accuracy of evolutionary theories, forums on which various types of scientists discussed creationist claims, scholarly papers on genetic mutations and radiometric dating of rock layers, and Charles Darwin's book *Descent of Man*. I found that the issue was even more cut-and-dried than I had thought, and the new question that came to dominate my thinking on it grew out of frustration: Why were the people and organizations that promoted creationism so committed to preaching that if Genesis 1 wasn't history then none of the Bible could be trusted? As I knew from my own experience, there was no shortage of Christians who loved God and changed others' lives for the better without believing that the world was created in six days and who still saw Genesis 1 as a vital source of doctrine regardless of what type of writing it was, so why did these groups devote themselves to claiming that acceptance of biological evolution or an old earth invalidated Christianity? Did they *want* people to feel like they should walk away from the core teachings of their faith just because they had changed their mind on one non-vital question? I was sure that wasn't the case, but clearly they had gotten so caught up in the defense of a pet argument that they had let it eclipse the importance of everything else.

This frustrating circumstance led me to three important reflections. One, it was clear that many people who genuinely believed in young earth creationism could not allow themselves to consider information on evolution in the same way they considered information on other topics because they had been convinced by hyped-up arguments that the stakes were too high for that. Instead of being a question of how the physical world functioned, evolution had been turned into a question of salvation: If it was true, according to the defenders of creationism, Christianity was fake—and when you believe that your way of life and your confidence in things like eternal life could be threatened by an idea, you're unlikely to open your mind to even consider it. Thus, important reflection number one is that it's awfully hard to think with a level head about questions that threaten a belief of extreme importance.

Two, I wondered how difficult it would have been for the average Christian in the Victorian Era to see why the theory of evolution couldn't really be used to disprove the foundational doctrines of their faith. In the 21st century, with the benefit of a few generations of thinkers having pointed out reasons why reevaluating our interpretations of parts of the Bible in light of scientific discoveries isn't a catastrophe, it seemed obvious that God was talking to his people both through ancient scripture and through each generation's scientific advancements. But around the time Darwin lived, would people who had always assumed Genesis should be read just like a history book have been able to come to that conclusion themselves? When someone told them that scientific evidence disproved what they believed, it couldn't have been easy to recognize that the two options they were being presented with (*either* evolution is an accurate theory *or* God created the world) weren't necessarily incompatible with each other.

I wondered why God allowed the church to go through periods when missing pieces of information harmed their understanding of him or even made it seem as if he wasn't real. This was a concern that had also troubled me in the past when people talked about the Middle Ages, saying that low literacy rates and the absence of Bible translations into commonly spoken languages caused the church to go through a long period of superstition and error. I had always wondered why God found it in any way permissible for long stretches of history to leave the world with little to no true representation of himself and so many lies that would be all most people ever encountered.

I kept asking myself if there were people in Darwin's time who left their beliefs, thinking they had been shown false by science, who would have seen things differently today with the last 150 years' worth of theological development available to them. If humans didn't have infinite knowledge and God hadn't directed them in such a way that their finite knowledge would include the reasons why the Bible was correct, how could they be blamed for thinking it wasn't correct? To sum that all up, important reflection number two was that something didn't seem right about the idea that people might do their best to find the truth about God but come to the wrong conclusion because they didn't have access to some key information.

And finally, important reflection number three was that creationism as I knew it growing up had seemed factual largely because the people who promoted it truly believed it was factual. In the course of learning all I could on creation and evolution, I had started to discern the occult, ignored scaffolding that held the "scientific" creationism movement together, and it wasn't one of deliberate lies. If it had been, I don't think the movement would have enjoyed the success I had witnessed.

There would have been too many ulterior motives to pick up on and paper trails leading to less-than-holy inspirations for taking up the six-day cause. As it was, I found a different kind of paper trail, the kind left by people who have more need to deceive themselves than to deceive others: trails of unexamined citations.

Some of the most glaring instances were cases in which a critical reader of some article or book on creationism had pointed out that its author had included a "fact" cited from a work in which it was cited from a work in which it was cited from a work in which it turned out that the original author had made a mistake in their reporting of the information to begin with. And those indulgences in the deadly sins of poor scholarship were joined by numerous other, better known "facts" of creationism that recirculated and recirculated until they reached the status of folk wisdom: Just like the average American can tell you that time is money or vitamin C prevents colds, the average creationist can recite to you the thoroughly inaccurate claims that the principle of entropy shows evolution is impossible or that rapid snow accumulation in Greenland invalidates methods of identifying seasonal layers in polar ice cores. The ideas sound believable when a person first hears them, and they go uninvestigated.

There had been a time in my life when it looked to me like creationism was a viewpoint built on a wealth of data, and it took purposeful searching and evaluation of a variety of information to see that it was actually the result of people repeating each other's statements uncritically, building up a complex network of inaccuracies, each idea giving just enough support to its close neighbors to keep the whole thing from collapsing as long as you didn't subject it to any pressure.

My well-intentioned search for scientific information had ended up leading me to troublesome thoughts on human nature: It was clear that people could intend to find and tell the truth but could nevertheless end up adding to a web of errors instead simply because they were too afraid or not diligent enough to put ideas they accepted to the test. There was no turning back from realizing that. Now I couldn't stop myself from wondering if any other system of ideas I believed in had grown out of overenthusiastic acceptance of a few starting concepts and then anything that followed from them.

When I thought about the concept of a network of ideas with plenty of *internal* consistency but less consistency or ease of integration with principles from other spheres of life, the first belief that came to mind was the last—the very last—thing I ever wanted to question: I just couldn't ignore the fact that I had noticed hints of this type of problem surrounding the claim that Jesus had risen from the dead. This belief of supreme importance was one about which I'd had many uncomfortable thoughts in the past without ever having stopped to let them come to the top of my mind. Plus, the people who had taught me there was good historical evidence for the resurrection of Jesus were the same people who had taught me there was good scientific evidence for creationism.

Just as my school days had included many lectures, articles, and videos that argued in favor of creationism, they had included the same wealth of persuasive materials on the historicity of the resurrection. The formats of the presentations were similar, but the question of whether the resurrection had really happened was a much, much more important issue than that of evolution. (Even the people who spoke out strongly for creationism and made it sound a little too much like a question of salvation and damnation would have largely agreed in principle.) Jesus' resurrection was the proof of the faith, the reason we knew that the Gospels' claims of him being God incarnate and taking away the sins of the world were true. If Jesus had never actually come back to life, then there really was no reason in particular to be a Christian or to expect that there was a hope of eternal life for humanity either.

The original nagging question I had had about these lectures and presentations on the historicity of the resurrection was the question of whether they overlooked the source from which historical errors were most likely to come. Many of the first defenses of the resurrection account I was exposed to focused almost exclusively on proving that the manuscripts of the Gospels had been copied accurately over the centuries. This point was important since it showed that what we read in our Bibles today wasn't just a modern alteration of whatever the original writers had said, but it failed to address the more difficult question of how we could know if what the original authors recorded was accurate in the first place. Could the Gospel writers have been honest but mistaken in their tellings of events? Was it possible that embellishments had already become difficult to distinguish from facts in accounts of Jesus' life before the accounts were written down?

I had found the answer to those concerns of mine in arguments that focused on what could be discerned about the thinking of anyone who would have claimed to be a witness of the resurrection. Would it make sense, various apologists asked, for Jesus' disciples to maintain that he had risen from the dead even under threat of death if they knew the story was a lie? No, it wouldn't. I agreed with them that we had no reason to think

Christianity started with anything other than a group of sincere believers in the resurrection account.

But the one problem that kept returning now and again over the years to disrupt my peace of mind was the fact that I still saw too much room for inaccuracy to enter between the exact events that took place and the written accounts we had, and that problem was on my mind now more than ever. I now knew how easy it was for complex belief systems to grow out of a few mistakes as people who had no intention of lying engaged in the perfectly natural habit of holding on to bits of information they approved of without vetting their accuracy, and my fear was that the original kernel of pure sincerity that had catalyzed the birth of Christianity could have resulted from nothing more than a misunderstanding and that all the details could have developed in the retellings. Even with the sermons I had heard and material I had read about the accuracy of the resurrection account, I had never gotten ahold of enough information to rule out that possibility without feeling like I was shutting my eyes to something.

For example, what if it had all started with someone going to the wrong tomb or the authorities never having buried the body in the expected place to begin with or if the true first events in the chain were someone's dreams or visions of a resurrected Jesus? What if, for a reason like these or any other, someone had concluded that Jesus had risen from the dead without their conclusion being accurate? Other people who had been touched by the special insightfulness of Jesus' teachings then wholeheartedly believe the excited account, possibly with support from the same misinterpreted evidence if a missing body or empty grave was what had sparked it, and the story enters the community as fact. Then, over the next few decades, in the course of numerous retellings, all the details that make the story sound more airtight arise as answers to the questions of skeptics, given by different people at different times, probably with very little of anything that would have felt like lying to the person originally giving the answer on the fly—it would be so easy without even thinking to answer a challenge with a statement based on an obvious-seeming assumption or a quick synthesis of things you'd heard others speculate on. Finally, the Gospel writers, starting about 30 years later with the Gospel of Mark, begin to compile and compose their works, and might have introduced even more new material to fill in the gaps in ways that seemed sensible.

I didn't have an answer for these sorts of what-ifs because, to my discredit, I had always been too afraid to simply go look for information on what was known about historical events and the resurrection account. The arguments I knew that supported my beliefs had all been handed to me, and while I knew that the responsible thing to do would be to look up what the other side had to say too, I couldn't do it. I knew there were reasonable people out there who wanted to know what was true who didn't think there was good reason to believe that Jesus had risen from the dead, and I knew that when it came to any question that had reasonable people on both sides the only way to be sure of your own position was to look into both sides yourself, but the stakes were too high, and I was too afraid of what I might find out, so I had never so much as typed a related question into a search engine. I had grown too accustomed to life not working the way my beliefs predicted, so on some level I felt certain that whatever test of historical accuracy I came up with would only yield frustrating results.

It had occurred to me in the past, for instance, to see if any extrabiblical record existed of the striking events the Gospel of Matthew links to the crucifixion and resurrection: darkness covering the land (27:45), two earthquakes (27:51, 28:2), the veil of Jerusalem's temple being torn in half (27:51), and dead people buried around the city coming back to life (27:52–53). If I looked for historical mentions of an earthquake corresponding to the time and place, or of an eclipse or other unusual spell of darkness, would I find anything? Would there be any comment from a Jewish historian about shocking destruction of temple property or even anything that looked like a cover-up story for the unexplainable event? Or would I simply find a lot of modern people asking why these and other hard-to-miss events hadn't been recorded? The latter seemed more in keeping with that just-out-of-reach feeling I always had when it came to searching for God, so I had never tried it. I didn't need more sources of disappointment.

And now, going back to the present, I was still too scared to go looking for more information to convince myself that Christianity hadn't arisen from mistakes and wishful thinking. I was still too afraid that in the process of looking I would come across something that made belief even harder than it already was. So instead of searching for something to put my fears about the origins of Christianity to rest, I added those fears to the growing list of long-unsolved problems. There was my lifelong inability to find God's presence, the suspicions raised by how easy it seemed for serious errors to be taken in as important points of doctrine, and now the terrifying realization that I didn't really have good proof that my religion hadn't originated from one of these errors.

Being reminded of the fact that the event my entire worldview was built on was the one thing I couldn't allow myself to subject to a normal level of critical evaluation left me sad and restless. I couldn't honestly say that I had a better reason for my beliefs than conspiracy theorists had for theirs: I didn't know if my standards of evaluating truth were higher or more refined than theirs because I was too afraid to put them to the test, and I had no personal reason to believe in God because the relationship he supposedly wanted with me remained elusive.

Still, I continued to pray through even my strongest doubt. Whatever question arose, I talked to God about it. Whatever issue of theology seemed problematic, I told God why I had a problem with it. I knew that burying misgivings and negative feelings only weakened a relationship, so through prayer and journaling I told God all the things that made it so hard to believe in him and waited for some kind of answer. I thought that in some way he would show me what I was overlooking. He would correct me on what I was getting wrong; he would open up a new understanding that would show me how he had been with me all along; *something* would happen to make life worthwhile, to turn my mourning into dancing, to give me a heart of flesh instead of stone, to bring the dry bones of trust back to life. If I at least kept coming to God and saying, "Help my unbelief!" he would answer, wouldn't he? He would do the miracle only he could do and talk to me in a way I could understand, a way that I could tell was his communication, an aspect of his soul-satisfying presence, and not just a coincidence or an unremarkable thought of my own that I felt pressured into saying *might* have come from God because the possibility technically couldn't be ruled out.

The period during which all this uncomfortable thinking and desperate praying went on lasted about a year, from the middle of 2017 to the middle of 2018. At a couple points during that time, a favorable turn of events did make me say that perhaps God was talking to me by doing nice things for me. Whenever circumstances beyond my control lined up in a way that benefited me, I told myself that maybe it was God causing things to work out so that I could see he loved me. However, that idea never held up for long because these nice coincidences brought with them nothing of God's presence. They didn't lift the feeling that God was an absentee dad who thought gifts or checks were a fitting substitute for real, satisfying, two-way conversations. I knew I would choose in an instant to be poor and underprivileged if I could at the same time tell that God was with me and talk to him in a way that was intrinsically satisfying, rather than to have all the resources and opportunities in the world but maintain only the phantasmal level of interaction I already knew.

During this same time, I had also gotten involved in a new church and was regularly spending time with a group of friends I had met there. In addition to reaching out to God for help almost daily in prayer, I turned to my church family as another source of support. Looking for anything that could help me get back to a better place spiritually, I started to ask people at church about how God communicated with them. The answers, though, were less than encouraging. Some people asked if while reading the Bible I had ever felt like something was being "highlighted just for me" or "jumping off the page" and then seemed incredulous when I said no. They would ask a couple times if I was sure that didn't happen and then say they didn't know what to recommend.

Other people took an approach that was even worse. If I mentioned that I couldn't seem to hear from God and asked them what their experience was like, they would quickly start to explain that they could be imagining the whole thing really; they didn't want to say strongly it was God; it wasn't exactly supernatural; the messages they heard from God might have been just their own thoughts and feelings; the significant events might have been just coincidences. This signaled a big problem to me: I wasn't pushing anyone to say these things—even if I had intended to challenge their claims of supernatural experiences, I wouldn't have gotten the chance because they started with explanations like these from the beginning. It gave me the impression that they had thought before about the details of their spiritual experiences and felt that there wasn't really anything solidly supernatural about them.

This reminded me too closely of the nebula of false claims that had bolstered up confidence in creationism. The impression I got when people talked spontaneously about hearing God's voice was that many people had experienced supernatural things; but as soon as the context was shifted to one in which people anticipated that they might be questioned on the exact nature of their experiences, suddenly it seemed that very few people had experienced something supernatural and most people had only experienced hopeful interpretations of average events. Could it be that the confidence individuals expressed in other contexts was inflated by a certainty that *other* people had had undeniably supernatural experiences? I had been depending on the reliability of the supernatural my whole life (sometimes speaking of my own experiences as if I fully believed they were supernatural when in fact I wasn't sure) because I had heard so many other people share experiences they *knew* were supernatural. Had they actually been going through their lives the same way I had, drawing their certainty from the certainty of others around them, feigning it if they didn't possess it because their doubt *had* to be just an anomaly? In the course of trying to build up my faith through all these miniature interviews of fellow Christians, I had only succeeded in adding another worry to my list.

At this point, I decided to try talking to a professional. I found a Christian counselor and told him everything I was wrestling with—how I felt like I had no real reason to believe, that I couldn't find God in my life, that I didn't enjoy any of the Christian things I was supposed to enjoy. I confessed to him that I was afraid to look into whether we really had good reason to think Jesus had come back to life from the dead, that the proof I'd been offered for thinking the resurrection had really happened was the main thing keeping my beliefs intact and that I was too afraid to challenge it but never satisfied building my life around a "fact" that had to be kept insulated and handled delicately.

Even the counselor had nothing substantial to offer me. He told me I was asking questions that had no answers and focused mostly on how I shouldn't feel obligated to take part in church activities. While feelings of obligation were part of the problem, techniques for handling that emotion didn't address the foundational issue, which was that no combination of caring and not caring about various church activities and spiritual disciplines had brought me to God and the true obligation I felt was to keep trying until I found him. If that problem wasn't solved, it didn't matter much that I no longer felt guilty about missing a day of Bible reading. The counselor simply had no hints of solutions for these larger underlying problems and seemed a little annoyed that I insisted solutions other than lowering my standards for what counts as true existed.

Come the middle of 2018, I was now 27 years old, and I felt like I had passed through countless days of empty longing, of imagining a joyful moment in which I encountered any shred of God's presence. It had been years and years now too since the longing had become tainted with hatred for this existence of mine which somehow blocked itself from God. With all the drawbacks that came with my way of life, you might think I would be happy at the idea of finding out my views were wrong, but on the contrary as the problems I couldn't ignore began to increase even more rapidly that summer, I felt a stronger and stronger sense of dread. I couldn't imagine living without … not without God, since I'd been forced to go without him all this time … but without the hope of eventually finding God and without all that came along with belief that he existed.

Reality, of course, wasn't paying attention to my fears, and unpleasant realizations popped up rapidly over the next few months, beginning with one that leaped out at me when I happened to hear a celebrity talking about his Christian background.

I had had a conversation with someone who told me how much they liked the show *Queer Eye* for its theme of teaching people to live their best life with resources that were already available to them. One day, I wanted something to watch while exercising, remembered the recommendation, pulled up the show, and played what happened to be the first episode of the second season. It hit the ground running: Five gay men were on their way to help out the show's first gay guest in the town of Gay, Georgia, of all places. The atmosphere was lighthearted, but with serious touches, as the young man the episode centered around was struggling to relate to his family and the church he had grown up in.

In the course of the episode, one of the regular cast members, Bobby Berk, refuses to go into a church with the rest of the crew. Later, while talking with the young man's mother, Bobby chokes up telling her that church was his life when he was young and that he begged God constantly to make him straight, but with no result except that his church community eventually found out he was gay and turned their backs on him.

Bobby Berk's story wasn't surprising or unfamiliar to me; I had heard others like it many times before, but for some reason the theological problem it implied finally clicked with me this time. The churches I had been part of, with one possible exception, believed that same-sex relationships were wrong, and this wasn't, in most people's case, because of a dislike for gay people but because they had tried to understand to the best of their ability what the Bible taught about various moral questions and had come to the conclusion that this was what it taught. I had never been able to see a clear biblical case in favor of saying that God approved of same-sex relationships either (which had bothered me for quite a while because I could see no ethical reason why there should be anything wrong with same-sex relationships and didn't like that this biblical command had no discernible ethical backing).

But the churches I had attended also stressed that people didn't overcome sin and change their ways by willpower, no matter what the issue. No one was capable of reforming themselves. The only force that changed lives was God's grace, the free gift of the Holy Spirit living inside of you empowering you to live out God's will.

But considering the stories I had heard from people who loved God in their youth and felt abandoned when he never changed their heart or strengthened them to live a heterosexual lifestyle as his word seemed to command, it didn't look like the Holy Spirit was actually exercising transformative power. This, combined with all the other ways in which God never showed up and the fears I was feeling over whether I really had any sound logical reason to believe in him, shone a spotlight on a moral shortcoming of Christianity: How could God be just if he declared an action wrong in his law but didn't empower people to avoid it? It made no sense that the God I had been told of would leave people abandoned in their simple desire to do what he had commanded. Christianity claimed to offer a perfect moral standard given to man by a perfectly just God, and it didn't make sense to punish people for failings they couldn't prevent.

For this problem, I had no explanation. Except of course the explanation already embraced by many churches that the Bible wasn't really the unchanging word of God anyway so it didn't matter what it said about moral questions. This was a great explanation for allowing you to be accepting of people you clearly had no good reason to have a problem with anyway, but it had difficulties of its own. While some churches agreed with the idea and taught that those who rejected it were legalistic Pharisees, other churches were fully convinced that giving up the Bible as the ultimate authority on life was extremely dangerous, and they had a point: If the Bible wasn't really a message from God and its details didn't really matter, then how did we know the details about what made a person right with God were correct, or that anything about its presentation of God was correct for that matter? If some of it was made up, how did we know where the fiction ended and facts started? I saw no clear boundary lines. Churches disagreed about which parts of the Bible belonged in each category, and their opinions about what belonged in the fiction category seemed to be guided more than anything by what their own culture or peer-group found distasteful.

Best case scenario, all the intolerant and illogical stuff in the Bible had been made up by people, and yet, even though they had gotten that part all wrong, all the stuff that suggested I was right with God was actually spot on. Sure, that scenario was possible, technically. But it was so much more likely that Christianity had major faults with deep-reaching ramifications. Gosh *darn*, it was getting hard to maintain a positive attitude.

Unswerving, I continued to bring my concerns to God and to my church family. From God, I still heard and felt nothing. At church, I had a couple meetings with a pastor set up for me. He came highly recommended as someone who knew a lot about the logic and theology side of things, and I told myself that here, finally, I would find my answers, having full access to someone who wanted to think and understand and had chosen to make Christian ministry his career.

In the days leading up to the meetings I made notes of all my problems and concerns, everything a pastor might be able to help set straight, and when the time arrived, I showed up to the café we had agreed on early and excited. The conversations went well: The pastor didn't shy away from or seem annoyed by any of my questions, and he didn't give canned answers; I could see that the evaluation I had been given of him was correct. But his answers, enthusiastic and personal as they were, still didn't resolve the problem I was facing. I had never experienced God, so I had no personal reason to think he was real, and my search into logic, history, and so on for reasons outside of personal experience to think God was real had resulted in more cause for doubt instead. This was the problem. Anyone could say anything was real, and as much as I madly wanted God to be real, I needed reasons to think he was and answers to the observations that suggested he wasn't. In this area, the most important area, this pastor too had nothing of substance to offer.

His defense of God's existence came down to the following: He began by describing a scenario from a TV show in which a few coincidences make a girl think she has a secret admirer when she actually doesn't. Picture the two things that could go wrong in this hypothetical situation, the pastor said. The girl thinks there's someone out there who loves her, but there isn't; or she thinks there's not someone out there who loves her, but there is. It's difficult to find a truly satisfying answer to the question of whether God exists, he said, so which mistake is sadder in your mind? Isn't it sadder for the girl to overlook the signs of love a real person is sending her than for her to believe she's loved even if it's a mistake?

While I saw the attraction in the idea of making sure people at least *think* they are loved, I couldn't agree with his assessment. Yes, you could say that for a short time it could be more pleasant to let someone think they had a secret admirer than not to think they had one, regardless of what the truth was. But not for long. You could say that for a person who had no hope of ever *meeting* or *knowing* someone who loved them it would be better to let them believe in the fantasy that they were loved. But the second that that girl's inaccurate belief stops her from looking for or accepting a chance at *real* love, a daydream has turned into a tragedy.

That was the real problem I was facing when I looked for a good solid reason to believe that God existed: If my current belief was wrong, I wasn't left with a pleasant fantasy, free from negative effects on the rest of my life. I was left continuing to pour everything into the hope that I would finally encounter God, when I could have laid that hope to rest, accepted that I wasn't evil or rejected, left behind the laws and requirements that refused to make sense ethically, and stopped worrying so much. If I was wrong, I didn't want to waste my whole life being wrong; I wanted to find the truth.

Besides, God wasn't supposed to be a secret admirer at all. He was spoken of as a father, a best friend, even a husband to his people. He was supposed to be our most important confidante, not a shadowy figure who left us ambiguous signs suggesting he *might* exist. Having been a Christian for this long and still being stuck on the question of whether God was even *real* was comparable to saying I was married to someone who I had only ever gotten a couple text messages from. I ought to have been looking back on years of shared history by this point, not *still* standing at the altar after having made all the preparations I could in any way discover were needed, saying day in day out that I'm sure God will show up for me if I can find one more detail to tweak or one more part of my heart in which to feel more certain he's on his way.

The most helpful, most practical advice I received from this pastor was a little contradictory to the "believe if it makes you happy" approach. When I confessed my fear of researching what was known about the resurrection, he encouraged me to ask the truly difficult questions. It was better to know what you believed thoroughly he said than to be left with any seeds of doubt to grow back later. Hearing someone who cared say that searching for truth was still good and right, not something to run from or feel bad about, gave me a measure of peace. But even so, it still wasn't enough to convince me I should find out what the other side had to say. The nightmare of unearthing some insurmountable piece of evidence against the resurrection account was still too menacing.

Little nibbling suspicions that something wasn't right with the resources I did feel safe turning to, though, proved unavoidable. During this year of intensified searching for truth, I did read an article and a book about the resurrection of Jesus, assuming that because they were written by believers they would certainly be helpful in my efforts to believe.

The article came from a blog on which a former creationist from a scientific career field had written many detailed, citation-heavy essays about why the theory of evolution was both accurate and consistent with Christian beliefs. Since the author had engaged in enough unfettered critical thinking to change his views on science, I originally took his post on the resurrection as proof that it was a subject far different from creationism: A person who had a history of vigilance against poorly-supported conclusions could still conclude that the resurrection had happened.

However, I found his defense of the resurrection so comforting that I re-read it a couple of times as the months went on, and in re-reading, I ended up noticing that the types of sources cited in this article were different from those in the other posts of his I had read. Instead of his usual scholarly sources with no religious affiliation, these sources leaned rather heavily towards conservative Christianity and even included an author whose name I was surprised to see as I would have thought he tended towards too much bias for this writer to trust.

It would be dishonest to claim that this detail of citation proves anything about the resurrection of Jesus. It doesn't. But it made me uneasy. Did it mean that there was nothing in the works of secular expert historians that could deliver that knock-out punch of higher level scholarship? No pro-Christian smoking gun that any of them had to grudgingly mention or reinterpret or that they had accidentally revealed between the lines of other discussions? Since we had extrabiblical sources that mentioned the *death* of Jesus, it just didn't sit well that nothing more directly related to the resurrection had been brought up from outside of strictly Christian sources. A gem like that, ancient or modern, would surely be well-known by Christian history scholars, and I would have expected it to show up here. Or at least, I would have felt better if the list of works cited hadn't made it seem that belief in a historical resurrection might be limited not just to Christians but to certain groups of Christians, particularly the same groups who I knew to have lax critical standards when it came to science.[9]

The book I read about the resurrection raised the same fears more strongly, since it included a chapter on intelligent design and the inherently illogical nature of an atheistic worldview. While I believed in God and didn't want that to change, I couldn't help but feel put-off by the poor nature of the arguments the authors made. They clearly didn't see the flaws with intelligent design that seemed obvious to me, and if the attacks on atheism they had outlined were really the best they could do, I was worried—I could think of counterarguments that made more sense than their claims off the top of my head.

---

[9] I'd like to emphasize that point. You can say of course the sources talking about the resurrection were Christian sources because why would a historian accept this miraculous event and not become Christian? But my uneasiness was not so much over the fact that the sources were Christian as over the fact that they came from the specific Christian circles I had reason to mistrust.

Because of their poor treatment of the subjects I was most familiar with, I didn't feel much confidence in the rest of the book.

Again, for the sake of clarity and forthrightness, I have to stress that none of that proves anything one way or another about the historical nature of the resurrection. I've only included it to show how things looked from the perspective of someone who wanted to believe and was too afraid to go looking for hostile viewpoints. I just want to illustrate how unnerving it was to think you were hedged in safely, only exposed to information that had passed the filters of Christian thinkers, and still find these details that suggested something was wrong.[10]

By the fall of 2018, all the many somethings that seemed wrong had stacked up to a catastrophic level. After all this time of reaching out for God every day and grasping nothing, I didn't even realize how close I was now to simply losing the ability to keep believing. I'd like, for the sake of telling a good story, to have some dramatic event to point back to as a breaking point,

---

[10] Only after I had left Christianity and become accustomed to being out of it did I finally look for works that addressed the resurrection of Jesus from a nonbeliever's perspective, and I found that they did in fact exist and more than confirmed the types of fears I hadn't been able to find resolutions for as a Christian. I want to recommend one book as an excellent summary of the topic: *How Jesus Became God* by Bart D. Ehrman (HarperCollins 2015). It isn't primarily about the resurrection but addresses it in its Chapter 4 "The Resurrection of Jesus: What We Cannot Know" and Chapter 5 "The Resurrection of Jesus: What We Can Know," and the historical development of ideas traced throughout the entire book is fascinating in itself.

The reason I left Christianity without already having come to a conclusion about whether the resurrection story was easy or very difficult to explain without appeal to a miracle is discussed at length in Chapter 2, Section #1.

some definitive moment revealing the secret of what finally turns a relentless believer into a defector, but it wasn't like that. When the collapse finally started, it included nothing grander than a few more realizations in quick succession that swept away the last remaining filaments of plausibility.

On an unremarkable day sometime in October, the first fateful epiphany hit me: In the Bible, people who ask for a tangible experience of God get it. Scripture contains stories of people witnessing God's supernatural intervention in the world and rejecting it, but not stories of people who want to believe yet are plagued with uncertainty because God makes sure to only reach out to them in ways that are very difficult to distinguish from coincidences.

I had always heard that God wouldn't respond when anyone asked for proof of his existence because this would mean he was allowing human beings to manipulate his actions. Some people seemed to apply this principle only to hostile skeptics: God isn't going to do increasingly more impressive works to satisfy the demands of anyone who intends to reject the proof anyway. Some people seemed to apply it to everyone: The reason why God hasn't done anything in your life that you can recognize as him is that any sort of proof would remove the need for faith. I had agreed with that sentiment in the past despite how frustrating it was. I agreed that it sounded ridiculous to think God would drop some flash-bang miracle out of the sky every time someone dared him to, and I extrapolated from that idea that anything I hoped to experience for the purpose of feeling confident God was real and not having to wonder anymore probably wouldn't happen.

But on that unremarkable day, I realized that this claim contradicted the picture of God given in the Bible. In the Bible,

God doesn't hesitate to use supernatural answers to establish that he is the one speaking to someone. He answers supernaturally both to confirm the faith of those who want to obey him and to take away every excuse from those who have no intention of honoring him.

Taking some notable stories of faith and doubt in order, we see that the Bible begins with stories in which God is portrayed as communicating in great detail to figures like Noah and Abraham (for example, Genesis 6:13–21, Genesis 12:1–3, 18:17–33). When God asks Noah to build a giant boat or Abraham to trust that he will have a child of his own someday, he has credibility with these men. He has been conversing with them for years as a friend, and they have no doubt about what he is saying to them. They never find themselves in a situation in which they are unsure of whether a message was from God or from their own imagination, just as none of us wonder if we're imagining things when we have a face-to-face conversation with a friend.

Next, we come to the book of Exodus and meet Moses, an individual who has no doubt he's talking to God but is reluctant to obey what God says. When God first speaks to Moses from the mysteriously burning bush, he begins by clearly identifying himself (Exodus 3:6) and explaining the reason why he is sending Moses on a mission (verses 7–10). Moses then asks three questions (3:11, 3:13, 4:1) which are partly requests for information and partly suggestions that God has made a mistake in his plans. God responds by answering the questions with encouragement, with detailed and thorough information, and finally with miraculous signs given to Moses to convince others that God is with him. When Moses resorts to simply asking God to please send anyone else on this mission, God finishes the conversation by saying that his brother Aaron can partner with him to take the dreaded public speaking component off his plate. Displaying the common sense you would expect from a divine being, God combats Moses' reluctance with encouragement, explanation, and rebuke when necessary, not with ambiguity or silence.

Moses is sent to confront the pharaoh, a character who has become a symbol of stubborn defiance, but even this committed enemy of God is given a wealth of supernatural interaction (Exodus 7:8–12:32). It is harsh and gruesome, but undeniably supernatural. If God's interaction with Moses was a heated conversation, his interaction with Pharaoh might be comparable to a fist-fight or to a beating over the head with a megaphone, but certainly not to silence, not to ambiguity, not to a fastidious avoidance of demonstrating one's power.

Fast-forward to the book of Judges and the story of the notoriously doubtful Gideon (Judges 6:11–7:25). Similarly to Moses, when God appears to Gideon instructing him to save Israel from invaders, Gideon responds with questions that imply God's estimation of his abilities is all wrong, and as with Moses, God answers with words of encouragement (6:11–16). Unconvinced, Gideon asks for a sign to prove it is really God speaking to him, and God answers by making fire come out of a rock, which finally convinces Gideon of the speaker's identity (6:17–24). Later though, feeling he needs more proof of the message that God will use him to save his people, he asks for another sign, this time dictating what it should be. He asks God to make dew appear on a wool fleece on the ground, but not on the ground itself. God obliges and does just as Gideon has asked. Finally, Gideon asks for one more sign, this time for dew to appear on the ground but not on the fleece, and again, God answers with the requested sign (6:36–40). As in the other stories, here too there is no silence and no ambiguity. God employs precision, clarity, and communication to lead Gideon and treats Gideon's tests as an opportunity to win his trust.

Even in situations where the reason for compliance with someone's request is unclear, God is portrayed as having no hesitation to supernaturally prove that a message comes from him. In II Kings 20:1–11 for instance, we see King Hezekiah of Israel receive an outpouring of supernatural activity. First, the ailing king prays that God will spare his life from a deadly illness, which God agrees to do. Not satisfied, Hezekiah asks for a sign that he will really recover, and God, through a prophet, offers him a choice of two signs. He chooses the more difficult, asking for the shadow on a sundial to turn backward ten degrees, and God performs this feat for him.

Moving to the New Testament, we do find the closest thing to the claim that God won't satisfy a skeptic, but even here we see that the skeptics have not been denied a personal and supernatural encounter with God. In the Gospels, when certain religious teachers ask Jesus for a sign, he says they will be given no sign except for "the sign of the prophet Jonah" (Matthew 12:38–40), and similarly Jesus works comparatively few miracles in his hometown because of the incredulous and offended attitude people there harbor towards a local boy claiming to be someone special (Matthew 13:54–58). While Jesus doesn't jump to please his critics, he is still present with them (They get to interact with God incarnate!) and apparently showing signs of his supernatural abilities even in his hometown although the number of miracles done there is described as "not many." The sign he offers the religious teachers is no small thing either. As explained in that passage, it refers to his death and resurrection, which means that if the story of the Gospels is true, "not being given a sign" actually means getting to witness a roughly three-year ministry rife with supernatural healings and other miracles and on top of that witnessing Jesus predict his resurrection and fulfill his prediction in your lifetime.

When telling the stories of individuals, the New Testament follows the pattern set in the Old of God reaching out to people to answer their doubts just as anyone would make an effort to clarify their identity and intentions to others.

In John 1:43–51, a man named Nathanael is told by his companion Philip that Jesus of Nazareth is the Messiah predicted in scripture and that he needs to come meet him. Nathanael apparently expects nothing of the sort to be true since his only response is to ask, "Can anything good come out of Nazareth?" (v. 46), but he agrees to come along with Philip. Upon meeting Nathanael, Jesus tells him that he saw him sitting under a fig tree before Philip talked to him. Nathanael is deeply impressed by this supernatural knowledge of his whereabouts and professes belief in Jesus as the Messiah. The story shows Nathanael's dismissive attitude being met with a display of supernatural ability calculated to overcome it. The display isn't particularly grand, but Jesus knows it will be convincing to the person it is intended to reach.

At the end of the same book (John 20:24–29) we come to the story of the most famous doubting disciple of Jesus. After some of Jesus' followers claim to have seen him risen from the dead, Thomas states that he will not believe unless he is given the opportunity to see and touch the wounds he knows Jesus' body would bear. A few days later, Jesus appears to him and invites him to touch the very wounds he mentioned, causing Thomas to immediately declare Jesus his Lord and God. Jesus' attitude again is just what one would expect of a God who views human beings as his children or his friends. Although Jesus tells Thomas, "Blessed are those who have not seen and yet have believed," (v. 29) he also has grace and understanding for the needs of his children who aren't yet fully convinced. Instead of hiding himself from the person asking for extra assurance, Jesus gives Thomas exactly the experience that will convince him to have faith from that point on.

Finally, we have Paul/Saul, a particularly striking example because he begins proud and hostile but is completely changed by his supernatural encounter. His conversion story is found in Acts 9:1–22 and referred to in his letters, which make up several books of the New Testament, as well. Paul, being a devoted student of Jewish law, naturally starts off viewing anyone who says Jesus is God as a heretic. He is so impassioned against this heresy that he gets the religious leaders of his nation to give him permission to arrest anyone who professes it. (This is actually pretty understandable behavior when you look at all the commands given by God throughout the Old Testament to kill off false prophets and anyone who practiced "foreign" religions among his people.) But then Jesus bursts into his life: While a light shines down from heaven, Paul falls to the ground, hears Jesus identify himself as the one Paul has been persecuting with his actions, and is left temporarily blind by the event. After God sends someone to heal him of his blindness, he immediately starts to preach in favor of Jesus.

Because part of Jesus' message to Paul at his conversion is, "It is hard for you to kick against the goads" (v. 5), it is taught that Paul felt God "goading" him towards faith in Jesus but resisted. Whether Paul was fully convinced that scripture left no room for Jesus to be the Messiah or whether he "knew" in his heart he was wrong, the part Acts leaves no question about is that God does not remain in the background saying, "You should have known better," and leaving Paul to be condemned because the witness of scripture and of believers around him should have been enough. In this account, we see, just as in all the previous stories, that God does the sensible thing and exerts extra effort to get someone's attention when needed.

The evidence of all these stories of the supernatural showed me that something was up with the modern idea that God doesn't prove himself. I was so used to the stock characters of the bitter skeptic and the afflicted believer who persistently chooses faith without understanding, that I had never wondered before where the idea that belief should work this way came from. But now it suddenly seemed clear to me that it didn't come from the Bible. Where, then, did it originate? It certainly seemed that it had come about only because so many people in modern times asked God to show them he was real and never got any answer. In order to avoid the catastrophe of a reverse Mount Carmel (I Kings 18:20–40), those who already felt convinced God was real had to explain away his lack of action, and the unbiblical claim that God will never prove himself was invented.

Once this glaring discrepancy was added to my list of unanswered difficulties, my approach in trying to find a reason to believe shifted from just asking people how they heard from God to trying to find an answer to this problem as well. But when I explained to people that it didn't make sense for God to snub truth-seekers and skeptics today when the Bible set a different precedent, they responded with an answer that was as good as putting a nail in the coffin of my beliefs: They said that that was a nice logical approach but logic wasn't always a valid way of finding truth. In one case, I was told by the leader of a home church group I was visiting that I didn't need logic, I needed "spiritual knowledge," and that since God *always* answered people who asked him to speak, I must have been ignoring him, and that the doubts I thought came from my own thoughts were actually the words of the devil.

Whether the answer was extreme like that one or more subdued, it planted the same gigantic red flag: People attack the validity of logic itself when they encounter an argument they can't counter logically, and attacking the validity of logic should make no sense for someone who thinks that God created the world. Sure they could claim that our ability to reason was damaged by sin, but if it was damaged so badly that we couldn't tell whether a perfectly logical conclusion was actually true or false, then how could we know whether anything was true?

I started thinking about how much this dismissal of logic bothered me and how poorly it fit with Christian beliefs, and after having just been told that my reluctance to accept misty half-answers as a good foundation for belief came from the devil, it was hard for me to overlook another pattern of behavior that suggested believers were on shaky ground: What I perceived as honest questions that I had to ask in order to find God and live a Christian life with confidence, others saw as having negative and even evil motivations. Yet another terrible sign. If a person searches for information about something that is real and good, how can that search be evil? Even if my motivations had been bad, how can searching and asking be worse than not searching or asking? If my motivations were good, why should it be so hard for others who loved the same good, real thing to see that the search was good and beneficial? It all made much more sense if the thing being looked into couldn't stand up to honest investigation. Only then would a believer be forced to warn that investigating was evil, instead of standing back and watching as the most honestly skeptical investigators were routinely convinced by the evidence.

This correlated suggestively with something I had come to realize from asking people how God talked to them, both the acquaintances I had spoken with recently and the friends and church-mates I had questioned over the years. Among all the people I had talked to who said they heard or felt God communicating with them and all the people who had told me about clearly supernatural experiences of God, there was no trend that explained what I was missing. There was nothing that they shared that I lacked, no pattern that revealed the answer to the question of what I could do differently in order to hear from God. Some of them had invested less effort than me into prayer to hear from God. Some had invested more. Some had never made any effort at all; they said God had talked to them for as long as they could remember. Some of them had more faith than me: more of a sense of certainty that God would communicate with them. Some had less; they had started hearing from God after simply asking him to speak to them without actually expecting anything to happen. Some of them were more theologically conservative than me and some more theologically liberal. Some cared deeply about living ethically; some might have used the "God will forgive me" pass a couple times too many. Some followed biblical moral standards closely; others thought the Holy Spirit would show them which moral rules really mattered as they went.

This group, people who heard from God, didn't consistently share any particular quality that seemed important to hearing from God. They didn't all care more than I did about knowing the person of Christ. They didn't all have a more charismatic outlook or a more theologically sound outlook. They didn't ask

God to search their hearts and reveal their shortcomings more often than I did. They didn't all start with more faith. None of them had ever had to ask with persistence over such a long period of time before they found God's communication with them. It was infuriating.

Was I failing to hear from God because the secret was to have a C in your middle name or be born on a Tuesday or wear sandals on weekends or some other random detail I and all the pastors, speakers, and writers who covered the subject had never realized was important? Why should there be any secret at all? Didn't God want a relationship with me? Why should anyone have to do anything other than ask for his presence? If I was doing something wrong, why wouldn't he just let me know? Everything in my life had always been fine. I had always had a good family and enough money, and I had always been able to attend good churches and study the Bible. But I wanted *him*. I wanted his presence. I wanted to know what this love that made people willing to die for him after they'd tasted it was like.

Although I might have started earlier, I knew I had been looking for God's presence at least since I was ten years old, and that meant my fruitless search had now been going on for 17 years. In that time, the investigations I had made into history, theology, and science hoping to strengthen my faith had turned up no evidence for God's existence, and lately had left me doubting it instead. I couldn't keep waiting, worrying my life away. Something *had* to change. It simply wasn't possible any longer to keep a cold belief on life support just because God might be out there *somewhere*. I had to have him or abandon all these fatiguing attempts at getting him.

Taking a sober look at just how difficult I was finding it to keep believing in God and how many reasons I had found not to, I did wonder for a few days that fall if perhaps I should kill myself. I don't say that to be melodramatic; that was the cool-headed solution I arrived at as a way to minimize risk. If I was barely able to believe in God still, and truly losing my faith meant going to hell, and this life was of little value compared to eternity with God, then wasn't it safest to do anything and everything possible to make sure I never got the chance to stop believing in God? I couldn't see myself being happy having to live without everything I'd always believed in anyway.

Thankfully, I did also realize how little sense that made. If the God I had always believed in was real, there was no way that choosing to do something generally agreed to be wrong like killing myself could end up having a better outcome than choosing to do something right like continuing to search for him. If he had let me get to this place of unbelief for whatever reason, whatever he intended to happen next had to have some sort of purpose.

But my ability to believe *was* wearing dangerously thin nevertheless, and in a final attempt to save it I ended up trying the very last thing I could think of trying, the thing I'd been too afraid to do as long as I could see any other option. I decided to get angry. Just for a very brief time in a very confined way: a short letter of grievances that took something like 15 minutes to write. But within that defined space I didn't hold back. I said the terrible things that 17 years of unexplained rejection make you want to say to someone.

I tried to be crude and defiant, to act out as much as I could in a few paragraphs, because it was the only way of getting someone's attention I hadn't already tried. I had always expected that God would talk to me simply because I was his child asking him to, or if it wasn't that simple, that I could get myself to an optimal place for hearing him by living a pure and humble life as best as I could according to scripture and asking him to make up for my shortcomings. But since all that had never gotten me anywhere, there was only this avenue left. People had told me now and again that I shouldn't worry if God didn't seem to be leading me all the time because most of the time I was probably going in the right direction anyway, and if I started to get off track, God would be sure to warn me back to where I should be. Since nothing else had worked, maybe doing what seemed wrong and disrespectful would at least draw some form of correction or even punishment, anything I could hold onto as a sign God was really there.

So I wrote my angry, offensive little letter to God, the negative version of all the prayer-journaling I had done, the heated tirade that in any tangible relationship would certainly have led to consequences of some sort. But still nothing happened. Absolutely nothing.

That was it then. That was ... really it. Either God was a father who didn't even care enough to discipline his children—or to hug them after an emotional outburst or to cheer them on to speak their mind or whatever the appropriate response to my action would have been—or he just wasn't there. I was out of options. Love, devotion, and obedience hadn't worked. Looking for intellectual answers had led me to lots of perfectly sensible reasons why you didn't actually need God to explain anything about life, the very opposite of what I had hoped to find. And rebellion seemed off to just as lackluster a start as the other avenues. I'd tried it all; I'd reached the end. With my last drop of hope that God might show up exhausted, I had finally reached the point where I couldn't believe anymore. God wasn't coming for me. Not to encourage; not even to punish.

This was the worst that could happen. After such a long search, I could no longer escape the fact that everything added up to the conclusion I had feared. Everything I had lived and hoped for was apparently fake; I had been wrong about it all. For a few days, I lingered in a sort of half-belief, not allowing myself to be sure of the unavoidable, but as time went on it only became more obvious that God still wasn't going to intervene, even to keep someone from reluctantly walking away from him, and that wasn't the God I had thought I knew. If in order to believe in God I would have to believe he didn't care, then belief was even more impossible.

Just as I had held on to belief in shades that grew dimmer and dimmer, full unbelief too only came on in waves. The first was this dead-end of all my searching for God's presence, when I had to admit that the statement, "God is here," couldn't be true without a radical alteration of the meaning of at least one of the words "God," "is," or "here." The next two waves are covered in depth in Chapters 2 and 3, so I'll leave out the details here, but compared to the first they were rapid and far more intellectual—basically they were the result of me continuing to work through all my thoughts in writing after having to admit my beliefs were flawed. I spent hours journaling about the ideas rushing through my mind on most days, and it was all over within a few weeks. As I worked through my theology questions from the perspective of having given up, it was like I was allowed to think things that were forbidden before, and all the remaining pieces started to fall together.

For much of 2018 I had been despondent as my uncertainty in cherished beliefs grew, and finally arriving at a place of unbelief meant that everything was lost: I had built my life around one all-consuming desire, and its object wasn't real.

But having to confront the reality of such a resounding failure as this brought about the most unexpected results.

One day, not long after I'd come to the decision that I would have to leave Christianity behind, I was walking down a sidewalk, looking at a row of trees with leaves streaked yellow and red in our modestly crisp California winter, watching sparrows flit between the branches, and I became aware of an odd phenomenon: I was happy, *just* happy. I was looking at the scenery and enjoying it, and that's *all* I was doing.

I walked frequently and had been up and down all the sidewalks around where I lived and looked at all the scenery, but it had never been just that simple before. This experience of having my mind only on what I was doing and of feeling only one unmixed positive feeling was unfamiliar—and it was the best thing I had ever felt. Before I had given up on God, any and every time I did something, like walking, that allowed me to think and reflect, there was a part of me that was busy asking where God was, if I might hear him, if I might feel him, if today would be the day something changed. Whenever I was alone, a part of me was straining to find him—scanning every channel, sliding in and out of focus, ever alert for the smallest anomaly that could point me to him. I had never had a walk that was so peaceful. I had never been alone with my thoughts under circumstances that made it truly alright to be alone. Aloneness, until now, had always meant failure or rejection or oversight; I was never sure which.

Never in all my life had I dreamed how wonderful it was to be content with what was in front of me. A walk was a walk, not another event in the saga of a failing search for God, and the same dawning realization began to apply to everything. Everything I did was for the first time unclouded by fear and guilt and frustration, and I was able to be fully present instead of perpetually reserving a part of my mind for the task of asking God to show up. I hadn't even realized how constantly I had been calling out to God until I stopped: There had been very few moments for the last many years that I hadn't been thinking about and talking to God, and I certainly hadn't gone through one single full day without doing so.

Now I thought back on a wish that had passed through my mind many times and that I'd been ashamed of: As a Christian, I had sometimes reflected on how people in stories woke up thinking about the day ahead of them and set to work on what they intended to accomplish. I wanted to be like these fictional people. I wanted to wake up one day excited about a task ahead of me and start doing it without worrying about where God was or if I was acting in the best way to invite him in. I wanted to have a day of doing things for their own sake. And I always felt bad about it, for wishing that I could clear God from my mind.

But now that I was experiencing it, I knew I had been right to wish for it all along. I had never known before what it was like to be myself and let the world be itself and just live. As Christian as ever in my literary influences, I kept thinking of a Bible verse: "I will restore to you the years the locusts have eaten." Within a couple of weeks of becoming certain of my decision to leave Christianity, I felt like every day of peace and relief was making up for years of time eaten up by fearful religious compulsions.

A couple months had gone by before I realized with a jolt one night that I wasn't thinking about wanting to die anymore. This was another problem I hadn't fully understood until it was gone. For a few years before this point, I suppose I had thought I was better because I didn't feel unmanageably miserable all the time, but I hadn't noticed how often I imagined being done with everything in life, being nothing. I loved the perfect, compassionate God I imagined so much, and I hated myself so deeply for being unable to find him; I just wanted some resolution that forever took away all the problems Christianity was supposed to have solved but hadn't. Now it had been a couple of months since a thought or a wish like that had passed through my mind at all, and when I stopped to consider that, I realized that I felt excited about life in a way I hadn't experienced before.

Who I was, what I was, my existence, was not a problem to be solved. I wasn't a fundamentally flawed sinner in need of reconciliation with God. I was no longer that unhappy person who couldn't figure out why the reconciliation I had accepted through Jesus felt no different from rejection. I was free. Free to call a goddamn spade a spade for the first time in my life. Injustice was injustice, even when it carried a biblical stamp of approval. I could say that now. Truth was truth, even when it contradicted what many people wanted to keep believing. I could say that and not quail in fear when a pastor told me God would judge me for "sowing division" or "disrespecting authority." If God had never followed through with any of his other promises of interaction, why should judgment be the exception?

Finally, I wasn't crazy. Finally, I wasn't evil. Finally, I could admit that when someone gave no indication of being there, it was because they weren't there. Finally, all the good people who sincerely found another worldview to be more accurate than Christianity weren't condemned to hell. It was for all these reasons that I finally loved being alive.

From there, the positive developments continued to amaze me. Coming in right after the shock of discovering what it was like to truly be happy, the second biggest surprise was discovering what non-Christian human beings were actually like. One of my biggest fears as I had lost reasons to keep believing was how I would get on in a world of heathens. I knew, thanks to the impeccable studies of human nature which preachers had instructed me in over the years, that life among unbelievers would be unpleasant. The secular masses were bullying and disrespectful, sure to treat differences of opinion with ridicule and pressure to conform. Yes, one was sure to lead a lessened existence among these hopeless, amoral destitutes, but what alternative did one have?

Ever since I'd decided to settle down back in the US, I had gone on dates with several nice Christian guys, but never anything long-term; things had never clicked for both parties. I was still interested in looking for a relationship, but the grim picture I'd been painted of the secular world had me worried about my prospects. I wondered for a while if it would still be realistic to try to end up with a Christian. If only I could find a Christian guy who would also pretend I was Christian to my parents so that they never had to face the thought of their child being a hell-bound unbeliever, that would be perfect. But the more I thought about it, the more ridiculous the idea was. In all the Christian communities I had been part of, it had always been clear that dating or marrying a non-Christian was wrong. Could I really see myself being very attracted to someone who would compromise a principle like that, not to mention be fine with dishonesty like pretending I believed what my parents would have wanted? Probably not. It was a brief, silly dream to think of finding that puzzle piece. Anyway, it made more sense to at least be open to the idea of meeting non-Christians: If Christianity really wasn't true, as all avenues of reasoning seemed to suggest, then was there really, truly a good reason to want a relationship with a Christian guy, or was it just preference for the familiar?

In the end, tentatively, I removed my Christian-only filters, and, to my surprise, proceeded to meet a series of perfect gentlemen. The conversations all started online, just like they had with the Christian guys, and I followed the same habit I always had of only meeting someone in person if I could see potential for a good intellectual connection, and just as always that principle kept me from ever having a bad experience. These infidels were considerate, candid, fun, and not at all crude, pushy, or any of the negative things I'd been led to expect from non-Christian men.

Since my recent change of beliefs was such a gigantic part of everything that was on my mind, it came up in conversation frequently, and I learned things that fascinated me from these first interactions with nonreligious people in which I had nothing to prove or defend. Several of them had stories similar to mine of coming from Christian families and realizing that their beliefs seemed inaccurate, and I picked up on a pattern among both those who had come from religious backgrounds and those who hadn't: The comment kept turning up here and there that they tended to keep quiet about their thoughts on religion around people who wouldn't agree with them. They didn't want to offend anyone or make anyone uncomfortable. It was just too troublesome of a topic to get into. So they did things like say a prayer when asked to rather than make waves. From one angle this should have been exactly what I expected to hear since I myself was agonizing over the question of how I could ever let my family know that I couldn't believe what they believed when that would mean they were losing a child to something worse than death. But the angle that prevailed in my mind at the time was that this was a remarkable discovery indeed, since I had always been bombarded in Christian circles with descriptions of how arrogant, outspoken, and interfering the nonreligious person could be.

In the narrative I was used to, Christians were always the ones who felt pressured to keep quiet, while everyone else was respected for sharing their thoughts, but apparently that wasn't how things always worked in the real world. Apparently, there were plenty of nonreligious people who simply went along with an expectation to act Christian (or some other religion) too. I was flabbergasted to discover that Evangelical preachers had been wrong not only about cosmology but also about sociology. Who could have guessed the two things might go together?

In the interest of showing how similar the experiences of conversion and "deconversion" can be, I think it's worth mentioning that I'm now married to one of the dashing young non-believing gentlemen I met soon after changing my views. I know from my years in Evangelical settings that Christian conversion testimonies often end with two elements meant to show how real the positive transformation Jesus effects in a person's life is: a description of a sense of wellbeing or improved mental health and an account of how things in life started to fall together in a tangible way, such as an account of meeting a spouse or discovering an ideal career field. Right up until the moment I couldn't believe any longer, I thought my life was about to go backwards in both of those areas. I was sure I would be depressed without the hope of God and struggle to find happy relationships among people I had little in common with. Instead, once I was no longer fighting to make a broken belief system mesh with reality, I discovered the peace and joy Jesus had never delivered, and once I started interacting with people who were free to follow observations of life to their natural conclusions, it wasn't long before I met someone who truly shared my deepest values.

It's funny, really, how closely my experiences mirrored those I'd heard about in conversion stories, right down to the "and God brought my husband into my life" detail. But look at the irony of this with me. The only type of story I knew was the one in which Jesus saved the day. People without Jesus were lost, and they found their way in life when they found him. I only found satisfaction in life when I finally decided God was not the answer, and that decision became the foundation for other wonderful experiences. I had never agreed with the people who told me that "blessings" were the sign of God's favor or presence in my life, but if all the people who had made that claim had been correct, this would be a real conundrum for them. Within a couple weeks, the mental and emotional positives of my existential crisis had already started to outweigh the negatives; within a few months, my life circumstances were visibly changing for the better, for instance, when I started dating the man I'm now married to. A year after changing my beliefs, I could say with no hesitation that my life was better in every way, material and immaterial, than it was when I was a Christian. If God actually did use positive reinforcement of this sort to communicate with people, then I could only conclude that he was extremely pleased with my decision to become an atheist.

(Of course, I don't think the explanation for this turn of events has anything to do with a contradictory deity. It seems more likely that finding an answer for a longstanding question or problem simply provides direction that makes progress and growth easier. Once you can feel good about your understanding of the world, it's easier to meet likeminded people, discover where your passions truly lie, and so on.)

But there is a class of discomfort that comes along with a conversion of any sort, and that's the difficulty of knowing how to approach your old crowd. In this arena I can't claim that I've made particularly good choices. Since, at the point I left my beliefs, I was an ocean away from my old friends and only starting to make new ones, my instinct was to sever ties, for a few reasons. First, although I had come to terms with the problems in Christian beliefs and all the grief they'd caused me, I saw this story of freedom from God I now had to tell as a powerful instrument, capable of doing great harm if I wasn't careful with it. Unlike me, many of my friends and acquaintances said they had found everything that mattered to them through becoming Christian. Their belief in God was too precious to them, I thought, for me to risk ever bringing up my side of things. Losing my beliefs had felt like an unwilling confrontation with facts I couldn't fight, but at the same time my personality had never been well-suited to being religious anyway; Christianity was just part of what I was born into. I was afraid that these other people really were better suited to believe in the supernatural than not to and that they would have the same experience of coming up against information they couldn't defeat but with much sadder consequences.

I contacted a few particularly close friends and told them how my beliefs had changed, but without going into great detail about the reasons. I told them I would be happy to talk about the reasons if they wanted to know but that I had to warn them it might take them to uncomfortable places. The conversations didn't turn that way at the time, and I haven't made an effort to go back to the subject. As for those who I hadn't spent as much time with, and even for a couple close friends I was particularly afraid of hurting, I've let our efforts to stay in touch fall by the wayside. Perhaps I'm wrong in this approach—probably so.

And then there was the hairy subject of what to do about people who are a part of my daily life. Even here I ended up breaking ties with a friend, someone I was living with. I had started off as the person who always had Christian advice to give her when she asked, and when I really started questioning my beliefs, I had told her, but then the full change happened so fast, and no explanation I could put into words at the time seemed good enough to account for how I could have really stopped believing seemingly overnight and why I didn't want to go to church anymore, so I didn't really try to explain, and then I was dating a non-Christian and I couldn't get it out of my head that someone in her position would have to be thinking, "How did you go from the person who was helping me come up with strategies to live a good Christian life, to this?" and I knew at the same time I must have been misjudging her, but I didn't know how to sort it all out, so I stayed in my room or out of our place more and more, and by the time our lease was up we didn't keep in touch.

With family though, just disappearing wasn't an option, and they were the people I was most afraid of hurting. I'm still growing in my ideas about how to relate to them and my courage to go through with those ideas, and that's why there's a pen name on the cover of this book.

As I briefly mentioned, when I first changed my mind about everything, I entertained the idea that perhaps my parents would never have to know. At the start this seemed essential—I couldn't imagine how horrible it must be for someone to believe in heaven and hell with the force of conviction I had learned from our church and find out someone they loved no longer believed in God. According to our church, all people were without excuse for their unbelief; all rejection of God was willful rebellion; no one was going to avoid hell by saying they hadn't known any better. While I knew that my conclusions were the only ones I could honestly come to, I didn't think my parents could see it that way, not according to the teachings they were surrounded with. I certainly wouldn't have been able to see things that way in the past when my thinking was more closely aligned to that of my home church. To talk about my lack of belief to them, I was sure, would sound like a confession that I was purposely putting myself in terrible danger, like announcing I had resolved to become a heroin addict.

Things would have been simple if I had had no qualms about trying to convince them to change their minds in the same way I had. If that was my goal, then I wouldn't worry about any negativity they might initially experience. But this prospect was frightening too. Knowing their histories, where they were coming from, I was afraid that losing the idea of God and all that came with it would be terrible for them. Perhaps I underestimated or misunderstood them, but I didn't want to take the chance of possibly ruining their happiness. I really felt like I could allow them to live in a better world if I could stop them from realizing anything that damaged their beliefs or their hopes for the future. It appeared to me that so much of what they did had always been done for their faith and for their children, and I thought they deserved to live in that better world where things worked the way they wanted, where things like heaven, and the hope of meeting family there, existed.

But in a community where religion is everything, it would take an elaborate work of ongoing deception to keep a secret like mine, and that was never a realistic option. For a short while, I avoided bringing up the change and continued to talk as if I still saw things as I always had, but eventually I had to introduce my family to my boyfriend, so they got a hasty and awkward rundown of how some things I felt bad telling them about had changed. (If I hadn't started with that, they would have immediately asked what church he went to, which would have been an even more awkward way to find out.) And then I avoided the subject afterwards. I didn't want to leave them without hope, so I never specifically said I didn't believe in God. I knew they were probably stronger than I gave them credit for, that they deserved to hear the truth, that their happiness wasn't that dependent on what I did anyway, that I wouldn't advise someone else to hide part of their life from their family, but in my mind reality was a world in which they didn't have to worry about me, and I wasn't ready to completely abandon caution when it came to breaking reality.

In spite of the behind the scenes awkwardness though, we were all able to get along. They accepted and enjoyed spending time with the new addition to the family even though they knew he "didn't believe in anything supernatural" as I had put it. In that I could see some of their best characteristics coming through—their tendency to just be welcoming and waste no time feeling bothered over the way others lived their own lives. I wish religion had never touched any part of that, never pushed them to see other decent people as sinful or doomed. It's such a shame that the same thing that had brought them together and given them purpose had to include those aspects that opposed their innate propensity towards being accepting of others. And I know it's a shame too that I let any of this come between us and that I'm still wrestling with the question of how to interact with a handful of individuals who I'm (probably unreasonably) afraid of hurting.

Perhaps it hasn't been all that long when it comes to the time scales of adjusting to major life changes, and perhaps my trial and error at how to balance truth and love in these delicate situations will eventually bring me to a place where I'm satisfied that I'm doing the right thing. As I'm writing the end of this chapter, it's been a little over two years since I had to walk away from my old beliefs, and this span of time feels simultaneously much longer than it is and almost vanishingly insignificant. It feels long because all the sadness and desperation that were woven through my Christian experience have become nothing but distant memories, things I can hardly believe I felt for so long. But it still feels like yesterday that I was in church or praying with family. Already over these two years there have been countless times at which I've been overwhelmed with gladness that I'm free of the anxiety that used to follow me everywhere. It happens when I meet new people without worrying what sort of "Christian witness" I'm supposed to be to them, when I turn on the radio without worrying if the music is the type I should be listening to at the moment, when I sit quietly without worrying that silence means I've done something wrong, when I write without worrying that I've let time spent doing what I love eat into time I should have been praying, and when I realize I've gone through another day without hating myself.

In two years I've grown completely accustomed to not going to church and don't understand how I used to put up with having *six* scheduled days a week. I've committed wild acts of godless rebellion like taking a puff of someone's weed once or twice and calling people by the pronouns they prefer. Strangely enough though, in the midst of this hedonistic existence I've descended to, there's one prayer I've never stopped saying. It's, "If you're real, I still want you." At the very beginning, I said this prayer daily, hoping that maybe, *maybe* I had missed something. As time went on and I became more sure and felt more positive about the conclusion I had come to, I said it a little less often and mainly for the possible benefit of others. I had started to write down the material that would become chapters 2 and 3 of this book and then to think about sharing it with other people, and I really didn't want that to happen if my search for God had gone all wrong somewhere. If God actually was real and I had missed that, even though I didn't see a fraction of a percent of likelihood that that was the case, I certainly didn't want to tell other people anything that would put them on the wrong track too. But like I said, I had no reason to think that was the case and very good reason to think that sharing my experiences with others would be helpful, so I proceeded according to logic but always with that kill-switch prayer in place.

Today I still say that prayer whenever I'm hit with a particularly strong realization of how unfair or unintuitive the world can be. That shadow of a hope that maybe a perfect solution to everyone's problems is out there somewhere, no matter how well hidden, is always ready to jump to my lips, even though I know how little sense it makes that a loving higher power should be hidden at all. The majority of the time, I focus on the imperfect but tangible solutions to life's problems that I get to be a part of, and it's been much more enjoyable and rewarding than my old search ever was. The persistence of that one prayer is the continuing echo of an intense sincerity of belief that went supernova. My passion for God began so hot that it burned up everything standing in its way—relationships, goals, ethical convictions—nothing was spared. But it was so truly sincere, and my need to interact with God was so driving, that in the end it destroyed itself: I couldn't stop looking for God even as it became clear that my search was only illuminating all the murky areas I could have assumed he was hiding in if I'd been able to hold back from investigating them.

If you share that same perilous sincerity and you've found my story compelling, I invite you to read the next two chapters, where I discuss what to me is the truly interesting stuff: In between the terrible moment when I had to admit belief was gone and the happy series of slow awakenings to a calmer, lighter world without it, there was a period of concentrated reflection that helped make the transition possible. During that time, I started to make some sense of how God could have seemed so good and so bad simultaneously throughout my life. While I would have said that I loved God, clearly I hadn't actually met God and couldn't have said a single thing about him that approached the level of detail with which I could talk about any human being, from someone I'd known all my life to someone I'd met in passing.

It wasn't actually God I was drawn to, I realized. My church community had taught me that God was love and God was truth, and those were the things that had attracted me all along. I knew what those values were. They didn't shapeshift or contradict themselves or dance around the edges of comprehension. I was familiar with them. I interacted with them daily. And I would certainly always pursue them gladly. As long as I believed that God was synonymous with love and truth, I had thought I could do the same with him. But at every instance throughout my life when push came to shove, loyalty to God had to be enforced through fear and by blurring the meanings of things so badly that they couldn't be identified as true or false.

The chapters that follow detail how I chose the substance of what I had believed God to be over the label my church had told me to give that substance and why I think other unhappy zealots out there can find freedom by doing the same.

2. Love & Personhood vs. Fear & Abstraction

John 3:16–21 NIV
… God so loved the world that he gave his one and only Son, that whoever believes in him shall not perish but have eternal life. For God did not send his Son into the world to condemn the world, but to save the world through him. Whoever believes in him is not condemned, but whoever does not believe stands condemned already because they have not believed in the name of God's one and only Son. This is the verdict: Light has come into the world, but people loved darkness instead of light because their deeds were evil. Everyone who does evil hates the light, and will not come into the light for fear that their deeds will be exposed. But whoever lives by the truth comes into the light, so that it may be seen plainly that what they have done has been done in the sight of God.

This chapter and the next record the ideas that turned my loss of belief from a tragedy to a change I enthusiastically accepted. Once my search for a personal, experiential reason to believe in God had finally come up empty, it became easier for me to see the problems I cover here. These are problems of theology and logic as well as personal observations of ways that Christianity just doesn't work the way it claims to in real life.

If, instead of being myself, I were an acquaintance of mine—if instead of being the person who wrote this book I was someone who knew that person before and after their "conversion" experience, I think I would be baffled. "How could someone who was so serious about God and what he wanted have ended up concluding that he doesn't exist?" I would wonder. But that's just it. The people who are most sincere in their loyalties can be the people who will reject the object of their loyalty most strongly when they realize its identity has been misrepresented.

The God I had been in pursuit of all my life was supposed to be a loving person, and one of the things that easily swept away any regret I felt over my loss of belief was the realization that when people like me ask in all earnestness why they can't find their loving father anywhere, they are answered with arguments that substitute fear for love and an abstract, undefined force for a person.

Although what I wanted was to *know* God, I was told to just keep believing in spite of his absence for reasons such as that it's difficult to *absolutely* rule out the possibility of the universe having been created by *some* higher power or that if I didn't believe and was wrong I might end up in hell. Yes, I was passionately sincere in my desire to believe in the God who inspired the statement, "God is love,"[11] but that desire sickened at the thought of having him replaced by a silent, far-off mystery felt only through the threat of punishment.

The first two sections of this chapter discuss theological problems surrounding the idea of hell and its use as negative motivation for belief. If I could have a conversation with every person who has been where I was, it would be on this topic because the anguish people are put through by trying to become whatever it is they need to become to escape hell is nothing short of cruel. There is also a nonsensical side to the idea—It's absurd to think that the God spoken of in the Bible would ever want people to live in a state of uncertainty over his existence, their life choices dictated by fear, when all that would be needed to inspire their joyful lifelong loyalty would be for

---

[11] I John 4:8, NKJV

him to drop in and say hi in a way that makes sense to them once in a while. But the strength of the fear can be so great that it's impossible to see how ridiculous the premise is; I know that firsthand. And that's why it's important for people to understand the severe theological flaws inherent to these fear-based arguments.

The second two sections of this chapter cover areas of church life in which we should expect to see evidence of human interaction with a divine personhood who would exhibit the personality traits ascribed to him in the Bible. What we actually see, these sections explain, is the absence of such interactions and many excuses made by people that try to replace God as a knowable being with God as an unknowable, unfalsifiable possibility.

In short, the point of this chapter is that people who can't find and fall in love with God by meeting him are under no obligation to call themselves Christians for fear that somewhere out there punishment might await them if they don't—and that people who do claim to have a relationship with God have an odd idea of what it means for one being to relate to another.

#1 The doctrines of hell and salvation only make sense if access to and understanding of information is more important than love.

If Christianity were presented merely as an option, a system you can take part in if you like, it would be the subject of far less controversy and the source of much less grief. But in many churches and many passages of the Bible, it is portrayed as the only alternative to a destiny of unending torment in hell. According to the Sunday-school story that has shaped so much of American history, the whole world is condemned to hell and only those who believe in Jesus and ask him to be their lord (meaning the authority to whom they give their allegiance) will escape this condemnation.

In church, the ultimatum between salvation and hell is spoken of as if God's love and personhood played into the picture. Everyone who does not come to believe in Jesus as God is said to have "rejected" him, as if they knew exactly who he was and just didn't like him. This might all make sense in a world where God was sure to interact with people, but it simply does not work in real life. We live in a world where people like me exist, along with all sorts of other people who want to know what is true and have never encountered God.

The problem with the familiar presentation of salvation first struck me as I thought about the importance given to the idea of Jesus' resurrection. "Why do apologists write books intended to convince people that Jesus rose from the dead?" I asked myself. Well, presumably because they think their words can change people's lives. If they present historical data that convinces someone the story of the Gospels is accurate, this person might come to believe in Jesus as God and thus be "saved." But we haven't always had eye-catching popular-level writing to hand a historical argument for a supernatural resurrection to people on a platter. Were people in the past who weren't history scholars out of luck? If they heard an educated figure they trusted say the Gospel accounts weren't true and believed what was said, were they condemned for their lack of expertise? And what about people today who are focused primarily on higher-level academic treatment of this topic? In that body of work there exist plenty of hard-to-dismiss reasons *not* to take the Gospels at face value,[12] and if a person is truly convinced by these reasons, truly finds them more accurate than the others, should this person end up in hell for doing their best to understand history and getting it wrong?

If you live in a world in which God interacts with every individual, gets to know them, and tells them what information to put their trust in, then things are simple. But without this supernatural interaction, we are left with a picture in which people's eternity hangs on their ability to reconstruct the likeliest chain of events behind a collection of ancient documents whose factual correctness is debatable and debated. If people who don't believe Jesus is God go to hell, and if God doesn't tell people what to believe in a way they are sure to understand, then it would seem there are all kinds of reasons a person could end up in hell other than willful rejection of God.

Even people who feel certain that their beliefs are correct should be able to see that it isn't evil for others to come to different conclusions, even if those conclusions are actually inaccurate. Imagine, for the sake of example, the best case scenario for those who claim the resurrection is a historically documented

---

[12] As mentioned earlier, see *How Jesus Became God* by Bart D. Ehrman (HarperCollins 2015), especially chapters 4 and 5, for a good summary of this type of information.

supernatural event. Imagine that this event is beautifully supported by clear, readily accessible historical data. Imagine that you would have to be stupid not to see it was true. Well, what if someone really is that stupid? What if they're too stupid to put two and two together and realize that Jesus is God? Is stupidity a sin deserving of hell?

Far more common than actual stupidity of course is a combined lack of education and lack of interest. There are all sorts of historical and scientific facts that masses of people consider basic, everyday knowledge but that many others are ignorant of. Whether this is because they've never tried to learn about anything beyond their own personal experiences, or because they're too busy thinking about celebrity gossip to think about history, or for any other reason, it's hard to make a case that people should go to hell for ignorance. Even in a society where most people know something about Christianity, many people weren't raised in a context in which any religion was considered true or important, and with all the religions out there claiming to be the one and only key to everything, is it really a sin for these people never to have realized that they *should* have embarked on an academic quest to evaluate the historical claims behind all of them?

Even if a person is quite studious and well-informed historically, they could still make a logic error when thinking over the case of the resurrection and so never conclude that Jesus was God even if that was the correct conclusion. It could be that there was one brilliant theological argument out there that, if they had encountered it, would have caused them to see things differently. But if they do their best to interpret the data they have access to accurately and happen to get off track, by a little or a lot, are they condemned to hell for making a mistake?

If, as many of us learned in church, a person is saved by believing in Jesus as God and acting on that belief, then salvation is largely determined by luck. If a person doesn't happen to have access to the right information or to be in the correct frame of mind, they will apparently end up in hell for the egregious sins of being unintelligent, misunderstanding something, not realizing they had been lied to by someone, not realizing the full importance of something, failing to give proper thought to an argument, being too intelligent so that they find flaws with claims of apologists that the apologists don't have an answer to yet, and other similarly evil behaviors.

This same problem applies to people raised in other religions as well. For instance, what would convince a Jew or a Muslim to become Christian? All three religions claim to have the correct view of following "God," and each one claims that the other two have severe problems in their theology that are displeasing to "God." Let's say in a hypothetical situation that Christian missionaries go to a Muslim town and preach that Jesus is God. The Muslims aren't won over by this because they've been told all their lives that Jesus was a prophet who some people wrongly worship as God. The Christians offer some arguments to support their position, and the Muslims offer some counterarguments, and in the end nothing changes because it's all my-book-against-yours.

Are these people now condemned because they've heard the Christian gospel and rejected it? To them, it didn't appear true. It didn't satisfy the requirements they thought were necessary when making a good theological case. Perhaps this is the fault of the missionaries. Perhaps there were better arguments that would have demonstrated clearly that Christian theology made more sense than Islamic theology. Perhaps this is the fault of some past generation of Muslims who set up unreasonable expectations about how to approach theology. Regardless, the question remains: Are these people condemned for not accepting something that, as far as they knew, was false?

Keeping all these various scenarios in mind, let's think about what the Bible says. Does it support the idea that salvation begins with achieving a particular mental state, the state in which one is convinced that Jesus is God?

Perhaps unsurprisingly the answer is both yes and no. The Bible contains passages which say that a person must declare Jesus their lord in order to be saved, but it also contains passages which suggest that it is more important for a person to respond well to whatever knowledge and understanding they have than for them to attain a specific piece of knowledge or a specific state of understanding.[13] In the churches I have been part of, only the first type of teaching was acknowledged, and sermons on salvation began with the assumption that no one could hear Christian claims about Jesus being God and honestly fail to conclude they were true. But if teachings of the second type, and the experience of all of us who cannot honestly claim Christianity is true, are taken into account, you would have to conclude that people won't be punished for not being Christian

---

[13] A famous literary example of the idea that it's not what knowledge you have that matters but how you respond to whatever knowledge you do have, is the passage in C. S. Lewis's *The Chronicles of Narnia: The Last Battle* where the God-like character Aslan tells a man who had only ever heard of Tash, a false deity worshiped in his nation, "[...] all the service thou hast done to Tash, I account as service done to me." Lewis presents his allegory for God as a being who is pleased by anyone who lived to do what was right even if their understanding of right was not well informed.

if they didn't have a good, convincing reason to think that being Christian was the right thing to do.

When you come across two seemingly contradictory ideas such as these, there are a variety of ways to understand what might be going on. For example, both ideas might be wrong. Or one might be wrong while one is right. Or the apparent contradiction might harmonize in some way that shows both ideas to be right. Let's examine what these scenarios would mean in this context.

One, both ideas are wrong, which means that the Bible has a serious error in it or that our understanding of what the Bible says is in serious error. The idea that salvation comes from belief in Jesus is wrong; the idea that God cares more about how a person responds to the understanding they do have than about what that understanding happens to be is also wrong. If both of these ideas are wrong, this could lead down a variety of paths, for example, both claims could be wrong because God isn't real and so the very concept of salvation is imaginary, or both claims could be wrong because there is a God who bases salvation on people's understanding of information but the understanding people need to reach in order to be saved is not that Jesus is God, or both claims could be wrong because everyone goes to hell or everyone goes to heaven or for a number of other reasons. This all most likely means that it doesn't matter what you believe because God is not real or has not revealed to humanity how to be saved or because you have no control over your eternity.

Two, the idea that salvation comes from belief in Jesus as God is correct, and the other is wrong. This means that a person's eternal destiny is decided by factors such as their intelligence and their access to information. (Some Christians try to avoid this problem by claiming that all non-Christians who know about Christianity have willfully rejected it, but because my own life experience contradicts this claim, I can't take it seriously.)

Three, the idea that salvation is based on whether a person responds well to the understanding of the world they do possess is correct, and the other is wrong. This means that if you are convinced Christianity is true, you should live accordingly, and if you are convinced some other worldview is true, then you should live accordingly; you aren't going to hell just for not finding Christianity convincing.

Four, both ideas can be harmonized in some way. If both ideas are correct, we arrive at the same result as in option three. You are saved by correctly responding to whatever understanding of life you are convinced by, and if this understanding is that Jesus is God, then you need to live for him, but if you are convinced of some other worldview, then you need to live by it instead. Neither honest response leads to hell.

With these four options (or three results) in mind, let's examine some biblical passages that present the possible contradiction between the two ideas (the idea that a necessary step on the road to salvation is to achieve a mental state in which you are convinced Jesus is God vs. the idea that what matters isn't the knowledge you have but what you do with it).

On the one hand, we have passages such as these two from the book of Romans, which describe an information-based salvation (emphasis added).

Romans 10:9–10 NIV
If you declare with your mouth, "Jesus is Lord," and believe in your heart that God raised him from the dead, you will be saved.

*For it is with your heart that **you believe and are justified**, and it is with your mouth that **you profess your faith and are saved**.*

Romans 10:14, 17 NKJV
*How then shall they call on Him in whom they have not believed? And **how shall they believe in Him of whom they have not heard?** And how shall they hear without a preacher? [...] So then **faith comes by hearing**, and hearing by the word of God.*

And on the other hand, we have passages such as these, which describe how people's state of guilt or innocence before God is decided by whether or not they follow their conscience (emphasis added).

Romans 2:12–16 NKJV
*For as many as have sinned without law will also perish without law, and as many as have sinned in the law will be judged by the law (for not the hearers of the law are just in the sight of God, but the doers of the law will be justified; for when Gentiles, who do not have the law, by nature do the things in the law, these, although not having the law, are a law to themselves, who show the work of the law written in their hearts, **their conscience also bearing witness, and between themselves their thoughts accusing or else excusing them**) in the day when God will judge the secrets of men by Jesus Christ, according to my gospel.*

Romans 7:7–9 NKJV
*[...] I would not have known sin except through the law. For **I would not have known covetousness unless the law had said, "You shall not covet."** But sin, taking opportunity by the commandment, produced in me all manner of evil desire. For apart from the law sin was dead. **I was alive once without the law**, but when the commandment came, sin revived and I died.*

These two quotes from earlier in the book of Romans are talking about the moral laws that, according to the claims of the Old Testament, were given by God to the Jewish people. (For example, the Ten Commandments are a part of what these passages call "the law.") The book of Romans is a letter written by the Apostle Paul to a church in Rome in the middle of the first century A.D., and in it Paul develops his views on salvation at length. The message of the letter is that everyone is considered guilty before God because no one can keep God's law perfectly. Because of this, Jesus became human, lived a life in which he kept the law perfectly, and then suffered a punishment of death and separation from God the Father as if he had been just as guilty as the rest of us. By undergoing a punishment he didn't deserve, Jesus fulfilled the demands of God's legal code and gained the ability to transfer his status of innocence to anyone who asks him to do so.

The interesting thing about these two passages is that Paul says the original guilty status doesn't apply to people who don't know about the existence of this law in the first place. The passage from Romans 2 says that people who have never heard of the law are accused or excused by their own conscience—since conscience is the highest moral law they have, they will be judged according to whether they obeyed or disobeyed it. In the passage from Romans 7, Paul says that before he learned from the law that some things were wrong, he did those things without them being sinful. Because he didn't know any better, he wasn't guilty.

In the book of I Corinthians, another letter written by the Apostle Paul, he applies the same principle to Christians. (Emphasis has been added to outline the main points.)

I Corinthians 8 NIV
Now about food sacrificed to idols: We know that "We all possess knowledge." But knowledge puffs up while love builds up. Those who think they know something do not yet know as they ought to know. But whoever loves God is known by God. So then, about eating food sacrificed to idols: **We know that "An idol is nothing at all in the world" and that "There is no God but one."** *For even if there are so-called gods, whether in heaven or on earth (as indeed there are many "gods" and many "lords"), yet for us there is but one God, the Father, from whom all things came and for whom we live; and there is but one Lord, Jesus Christ, through whom all things came and through whom we live.* **But not everyone possesses this knowledge. Some people are still so accustomed to idols that when they eat sacrificial food they think of it as having been sacrificed to a god, and since their conscience is weak, it is defiled.** *But food does not bring us near to God; we are no worse if we do not eat, and no better if we do. Be careful, however, that the exercise of your rights does not become a stumbling block to the weak. For* **if someone with a weak conscience sees you, with all your knowledge, eating in an idol's temple, won't that person be emboldened to eat what is sacrificed to idols? So this weak brother or sister, for whom Christ died, is destroyed by your knowledge.** *When you sin against them in this way and wound their weak conscience, you sin against Christ. Therefore, if* **what I eat causes my brother or sister to fall into sin***, I will never eat meat again, so that I will not cause them to fall.*

In this passage, Paul clearly teaches that a person's mental state can determine whether what they do is right or wrong and that following the dictates of conscience is more important than possessing correct information about the situation. He explains that idols of pagan gods have no power and therefore if a Christian feels no qualms about eating food that was sacrificed to them, they are free to do so. However, some Christians might have incorrect information. They might think that pagan gods are actually real and that by eating food offered to them they are participating in something wrong. If they hold this belief and eat this food while believing it is wrong to do so, then they "fall into sin" and are "destroyed."

So, what are we to make of the fact that Paul teaches that salvation results from hearing and believing a specific piece of information but also teaches that a person's guilt or innocence before God depends on whether they did what they thought was right or what they thought was wrong according to their best understanding, regardless of the existence of some more complete level of understanding they were unaware of? Is a vital tenet of Christian doctrine hopelessly self-contradictory? Is salvation a matter of who's smart and fortunate enough to process all the data correctly? Or is our highest responsibility ultimately to conscience?

In my opinion, the first option, the one that sees true contradiction, is most likely to be correct. I think that Paul spoke of following one's conscience as being more important than possessing perfect knowledge of a situation when he wrote about situations in which it was obvious that some people lacked knowledge. But I think he failed to see that people could be presented with the gospel message he held so dear and honestly disbelieve it, and because of that he wrote as if human limitations no longer factored into things at this point.

Paul, according to what the New Testament tells us, was devoted to the study of Jewish scripture and at first viewed claims of Jesus' divinity as heresy, but after experiencing what he believed was the voice of Jesus speaking to him from heaven, he spent the rest of his life preaching and writing about how scripture actually contained prophetic elements that foretold Jesus as the savior of the world. When the New Testament speaks of Paul interacting with people whose beliefs are specified as being different from his own, these people are either Jews who don't accept his view of Jesus or adherents of polytheistic religions.

We have no inkling of a suggestion that Paul ever had to seriously consider the idea that God might not exist. He had always viewed the world from a Jewish perspective, which, with its coherent picture of a single omnipotent creator God beyond human imagination and its clearly stated laws, must have seemed superior to the chaos of pagan pantheons. In the scriptures we today call the Old Testament, he would have seen the concept of disbelief in God equated with the idea that one can get away with wrongdoing (e.g. Psalm 14), never with a logical search for truth. His primary theological concern was to show that the Jewish scriptures pointed towards Jesus as Messiah and Son of God. We can tell from the way he writes that he didn't feel his backdrop of Jewish beliefs needed to be proven. For instance, take a close look at another excerpt from Romans:

Romans 3:5–6 NIV
But if our unrighteousness brings out God's righteousness more clearly, what shall we say? That God is unjust in bringing his wrath on us? (I am using a human argument.) Certainly not! If that were so, how could God judge the world?

Without getting into what Paul is explaining here in the first place, notice that to answer a challenge to his explanation it is enough for him to say, "That argument can't be true because if it was, it would disprove the idea that God can judge the world."

In his mind, and presumably the minds of his audience, God's judgment of the world is an indisputable fact, and anything that contradicts the idea must be false.

In Acts chapter 17:22–31, we see Paul giving a speech in Athens specifically to Greeks who are unlikely to be familiar with Judaism. His approach with them is to point out sayings about divinity that they are familiar with (*"For in him we live and move and have our being.' As some of your own poets have said, 'We are his offspring.'"* Acts 17:28 NIV) and extrapolate from their conception of divine power to say that his idea of an all-powerful God makes more sense than their idea of limited gods.

Paul lived in a time and place where the existence of the divine could be taken for granted, and all he felt he needed to do was clarify what God's true nature was. He thought that his reasoning was built on scriptures that recorded an ancient tradition of contract-making between God and humanity stretching back to the creation of the world. He never had to wonder whether he could maintain his beliefs with integrity after encountering challenges that are common today, such as being given convincing non-supernatural explanations for why the world works the way it does. He had no way of knowing about modern factual obstacles to accepting the existence of God, and so he could not offer any advice on the problem to the modern well-meaning truth seeker.

Similarly, since Paul had begun as such a passionately traditional follower of Jewish law and then become so utterly convinced that Jesus was actually at the heart of it all, it's not difficult to understand that he would have seen other Jews' disagreement with his conviction as a rejection of something obvious, especially when the Old Testament already contains the motif of God's people rejecting vital principles of his laws over and over again. In his mind, there was no reasonable room for doubt or confusion on this topic, and his zeal to show that his reinterpreting of the Old Testament was correct has shaped the course of history.

Now, as I said, this is my opinion, my best guess, on why the contradictory teachings on salvation exist. I think Paul was just a well-meaning human being who didn't realize he had failed to account for the phenomenon of people hearing the gospel and honestly thinking it was incorrect information. If this explanation is correct or if the teachings can be harmonized, either way the practical result is that it doesn't matter what you believe as long as you live according to your convictions. Clearly, this is a desirable way for things to end up, as it removes the worry that you or others could end up going to hell despite having lived to do what was right. But what if the harsh option is actually the correct one? What if there really is a God who will allow everyone to go to hell unless they declare their allegiance to Jesus?

Well, if this is true, it leaves much of the world in a sorry state. And also an ambiguous one: Many churches teach that people who have never heard of the Christian gospel won't be judged as if they had and neither will people who were too young to understand it—a great teaching all around since no one likes to think of hell being full of babies. But if that immunity for ignorance doesn't extend all the way up to adults who know the details of the Christian gospel yet also know it can't be true, then where does it stop? What level of exposure and understanding makes someone fully responsible, and why in the name of all that is sacred does the Bible contain detailed passages on things like genealogies and not on the epistemology of salvation?

But more important than the frustrating nature of this belief is the fact that it opens up more room for contradictions. Consider biblical teachings such as the following, which states that salvation won't result from saying the right words without living the right life.

James 2:14–19 NKJV
What does it profit, my brethren, if someone says he has faith but does not have works? Can faith save him? If a brother or sister is naked and destitute of daily food, and one of you says to them, "Depart in peace, be warmed and filled," but you do not give them the things which are needed for the body, what does it profit? Thus also faith by itself, if it does not have works, is dead. But someone will say, "You have faith, and I have works." Show me your faith without your works, and I will show you my faith by my works. You believe that there is one God. You do well. Even the demons believe—and tremble!

This well-known selection from the book of James highlights the problem of knowledge without action. According to James, belief in God or profession of Christian faith, if it is not accompanied by proper actions, is no more effective in leading to salvation than nice words are effective in filling a hungry person's belly. As long as the only possible application of this teaching is that belief and works need to occur together, we haven't introduced any new contradictions yet, but the fact is that in real life the requirement to hold Christian beliefs can come into conflict with the requirement to do what is right.

Imagine for the sake of example an uneducated peasant man in a past century who spends almost all his time working to keep himself and his family alive. He knows from church that God made everything, that God is good, that participating in church sacraments puts him in good standing with God, and perhaps a handful of other spiritual claims, but he doesn't have the luxury of time or energy to think over these things much.

One winter, marauders attack the village he lives in, murder anyone in their path, and plunder the stores of food. Even though he fights back and prays for God to come to his aid, men, women, and children are left dead all around him and soon more begin to die from malnourishment despite his prayers for God to send help and the best efforts of the survivors who are strong enough to bring in additional food sources. He can't make sense of how God could allow any of this to happen.

Although there are theological arguments that might have answered this question for him satisfactorily, he doesn't know them and doesn't have anyone around who is able to articulate them in a way he can understand. All he knows is that he's been told that God is good and powerful, but God seems to have abandoned him. In his mind, the problem is simple: The church claimed that an all-powerful and compassionate God existed, but life has disproven that idea, so the church's claims are lies. For a year he lives a mostly isolated life, bitter at the church that failed him. The next winter, the marauders return, and this time he is among those killed.

Does this man belong in hell? To him, it was clear that God couldn't be real. His understanding might have been overly simplistic. There might have been explanations that could have caused him to see things differently. He might have missed something that was right in front of his face. But regardless, in his mind he saw a choice between claiming to still believe in something he had just seen exposed as a lie or openly calling it false. His conscience demanded a simple and truthful response to his life experience.

Now, picture a slightly different situation. Say that the man from our example jumps to a different conclusion. After experiencing tragedy, it doesn't occur to him that God is a made-up idea. Instead, he "realizes" that God is actually cruel or cold-hearted. He refuses to continue praying to or attending the church of this cruel God because his conscience demands that he only give his allegiance to a good and just authority.

Again, does he belong in hell for this? If he had continued to practice Christianity at this point, he would have done so believing that he was serving a deity that was cruel. If the Christian God is not cruel, he would have been in effect serving the wrong God with the right name.

The point that I eventually came to in my search for God was one at which I had to say either God is not real or he is deceptive. Everything I had experienced and discovered seemed to be pointing towards the conclusion that God didn't exist. I had no encounter with him. The encounters others claimed to see in my life and even in their own lives turned out to be indistinguishable from natural events. There was no logical reason God had to exist and no experiential reason showing that God was likely to exist. And the more I examined what I really knew about the Bible, the more problems I found there too. The only way I could have continued to assert that the God of the Bible was real would be to say that he purposely made it seem as if he wasn't. And I couldn't do that. I couldn't believe in a deceptive God. I had to choose truth, as best as I could discern it.

If a profession of Christian faith is a requirement for salvation (Romans 10:9–10) and doing what is right is also a requirement for salvation (James 2:14–19) and your actions are not right before God if you believe they are wrong when you take them (I Corinthians 8), then people like me who can't call themselves

Christians without feeling that they're lying to themselves or supporting an unjust institution are definitely going to hell—and I see more difficulties lying in the course of someone who is resolved to find harmony between that catch-22 and the concept of God's deep love for all people than in the course of someone resolved to show, for example, that the verses which describe salvation by verbal profession of allegiance to Jesus never say that this is an "if and only if" situation and therefore are not in contradiction with more lenient-sounding passages. Of course, as I've already explained, I think that the reason why this theological dilemma that many people find themselves in is not discussed or accounted for in the Bible is because Christian doctrine is not a carefully crafted set of instructions given to us by God to bring us to him; it is a collection of human ideas that are not above contradicting each other.

But if the difficulty that comes with fitting these teachings into real life is not enough, there is still another related collection of ideas that needs to be considered: Since one of the primary aspects of salvation people are concerned with is salvation from hell, it seems to me instructive to consider what hell is, why it is bad, and how people might end up there. When we dissect this topic, what we find is revealingly similar to what our study of New Testament scripture has suggested—that either hell is a place where people are punished for their lack of knowledge and understanding or it is a place you don't need to worry about ending up in. Consider with me a few different ideas of what hell is and their implications.

One: Hell is a place where people are punished for rejecting God. According to this view, people who end up in hell will realize they were wrong and wish they had chosen differently during their life. (Interestingly, the Bible seems to provide some support for this idea, but it was not a popular view at the churches I attended. In Luke 16:19–31 Jesus tells a parable that involves a man in hell begging for someone to warn his surviving family to change their ways so they won't end up like him. Understandably, the churches I was familiar with didn't like what this suggests about God *sending* people to hell or of regretful people being punished eternally for wrong choices made in life.) In this view, hell is bad because it is a place of torment and people end up there because they are not allowed to enter heaven.

Two: Hell is separation from God. Because God is the source of everything good, complete separation from him would be miserable. On earth, no one is ever completely out of God's presence because God is everywhere, but he won't force anyone to spend eternity with him if they don't want to. Instead of being sent to hell unwillingly, people choose hell to avoid being with God.

Three: Hell is the experience of being with God and hating it. No one will ever be separated from God, and at some point in an afterlife or in the future everyone will have perfect communion with him instead of the imperfect interaction we experience now. Those who love God will experience this as heaven while those who hate him will experience it as hell.

Now, let's think about what these three understandings of hell mean for us as human beings. Do we need to worry about ending up in hell despite our best efforts to find and live by the truth?

According to the harshest version of the first view, the answer is yes, and I'm alright with people claiming this as their view as long as they're also willing to admit that it means salvation is a matter of processing information about God and not a matter of loving God. According to this harshest version I'm referring to, people realize they've been wrong all along only when it's too late (just like the man in the parable in Luke 16). This means that information that could have convinced them of the truth did exist but they weren't given access to it until this point. Whether that information was a more obvious type of proof that God was real or an understanding of what God's character actually is or just the realization that the choices they had been making really weren't worth the consequences, if people don't realize their approach to religion is wrong in this life and do realize it in the afterlife, then their eternal fate is being determined by choices they made without the benefit of having all the facts.

Remember, if everyone who doesn't profess faith in Jesus goes to hell, this means that the kindest, most altruistic people will go to hell if they were devoted Buddhists their whole lives or if they were so busy juggling jobs to feed their kids that they never stopped to think much about religion. According to the harshest idea of what hell is, these people will realize after they die that they missed the most important part of life—that they should have acted just as they acted throughout their lives but doing it in Jesus' name instead of in the name of Buddha or common decency, that God so wanted to have a relationship with them during that brief span of life on earth but that he'll have to deny them an eternity with him now that they actually understand how things work. They'll realize that what mattered wasn't whether their character aligned with God's character but whether they were smart enough to solve the puzzle of which of the many ideologies that claim to be absolute truth was actually correct. To many Christians, this is of course unpalatable, and I don't know if I've met anyone in person who held to that exact view. Perhaps more common when people are pressed for details is a softer version of the idea, which says people can still choose heaven or hell after they die and gain full knowledge of both, and that some people will still choose hell because they will do anything to remain the ruler of their own life rather than acknowledging God as their authority. I've even heard people specify that those in hell could leave at any time but they stay because they're unwilling to submit to God.

Anyone who believes in the harshest version of hell has to admit that salvation is not about loving God, that if God is truth and a person loves truth, if God is justice and a person loves justice, and so on, none of that matters—if a person sees God for who he truly is with clearer faculties than they had on earth and wants to be with him, none of that matters. All that matters is whether that person gathered and processed information during their mortal life in such a way that they put the proper name to what they loved. And anyone who believes in the less harsh version has to admit that none of us really has to worry about ending up in hell. We will only end up there if we actually prefer it to the alternative.

Similarly, if hell is separation from God or the state of being with God and hating it, we must arrive either at the conclusion that salvation is for the smart and lucky or at the conclusion that none of us has to worry about ending up in hell.

If hell is separation from God and only people who would rather suffer than be with God end up there, then you have nothing to worry about. You will only go to hell if you actually find it to be the better option. If hell is separation from God and people can be sent there unwillingly, then this means that the people in hell actually loved and desired God all along. Separation from what you desire is painful; separation from what you hate is not.

When you think about it, wouldn't a human being have to be the most damaged sort of psychopath, someone whose desires and appetites were truly opposite from what is typical, in order to hate the source of all good, beautiful, enjoyable things? There are people who hate God because they think he is unjust or unloving, but I've never heard anyone state that God is the reason for everything good and the remedy for everything bad and that they hate him regardless. It would seem that any person who does not find their joy in life from experiencing or causing pain should have no fear of hell, unless salvation has nothing to do with your heart or desires and is only a prize for a few A+ students who manage to ace their metaphysics exam within the time limit.

Finally, if hell is being with God and hating it, this is the least worrying option of all. It certainly doesn't matter what you know during your time on earth. It only matters what you love.

The importance of all this (besides the point that some understandings of what hell could be imply that your religious position doesn't matter) is that the views that allow hell to work as a threat scary enough to make people change their beliefs require God to be a fantastically unpleasant character, and this just isn't the God many Christians would say they know. If you can preserve the assumption that all non-Christians are bad people or ignore the fact that most people in the world are just as strongly and honestly convinced of their religious beliefs as you are convinced of yours, then perhaps you can manage to mix the idea of a wildly compassionate God with the idea of a God who would turn people away once they realize they want him.

Despite all my mental contortions, those two ideas remained oil and water for me. People, and the Bible, said that God was love and that the position of the heart, more than words and knowledge, was what really mattered in salvation. But whenever doubt in the specifics arose, people said, and pointed to passages in the Bible that said, only those who came to the correct theological conclusion were saved. It was too obvious that the threat of punishment for wrong ideas was being used to compensate for the absence of the love and relationship that would have dispelled wrong ideas naturally. In order for the threat to carry any force, it required a different understanding of who God was and what salvation meant, a cold and elitist understanding and one that would do me no good anyway: If salvation depended upon processing information correctly, and my efforts to process information correctly kept leading me to the conclusion that God wasn't real, then what could I do? In the end, I took it as an added reason to leave my old beliefs behind. This odd religion I had lived in, in which love was everything but at the same time only those who said the right words went to heaven, didn't just fail for me—it could never have worked. It was inherently contradictory, inherently unable to hide that ill-fitting part of itself that had grown up as nothing more than a method of intimidation to scare people away from leaving.

(#1.1 Does predestination solve the problem?)

In the section above, I approach the problem from the viewpoint that to me seems most sound, a view that sees free will and determinism or predestination as basically indistinguishable. A person does not have unlimited free will to do just *anything*. For instance, a person who has never heard of Jesus or Christianity and has never received a divine revelation of these concepts might be perfectly free to become a Bible-believing, church-attending Christian, but unless they receive new information from either man or God, this is clearly never going to happen. The same could be said of a person who grew up in a Christian environment but was born with a severe mental disability that prevented them from ever developing their intellectual capacity past that of the average two-year-old. Because their physical circumstances have put them in a situation in which they are unable to understand some things about Christianity, their free will on this point has been heavily limited. When it comes to people who have access to identical information but come to different conclusions about it, my supposition is that if we knew everything, we could point to the exact circumstances of their lives that cause them to differ: Just as a complete ignorance of Christianity or an inability to understand its teachings would drastically limit the range of Christian activities a person is likely to engage in, so every person's genetics, brain development, life experiences, and numerous other factors will in a subtler way influence how they engage with any topic, including Christianity.

Because circumstances beyond an individual's control have some influence over that individual's choices, it seems necessary to acknowledge some level of determinism. But at the same time, even if an omniscient person could trace deterministic reasons behind all our choices, we would still have to be realistic about the fact that from our perspective it will always appear that we have power over our own choices. When we choose to take or not to take an action, what we feel is our own desire to accomplish a certain outcome. We aren't aware of some underlying history of chemical reactions that takes us to that point. And there is no practical way to live as if we didn't have free will. We have to exercise control over our choices and cannot escape the need to make choices. In effect, there is little difference between free will and determinism. Our choices are under our control, and yet we need to understand that we didn't make ourselves and that we cannot enter into any choice with perfect knowledge that would allow us to always identify the best decision.

So much for my understanding of how these questions should be approached, but I can imagine that someone might say my discussion in the previous section of love, knowledge, salvation, and hell is irrelevant to the question of whether God exists because it doesn't take into account the possibility of an extreme form of predestination. Perhaps neither love nor knowledge has anything to do with the question of who is saved from hell and the only deciding factor is God's choice of who to save.

I hardly know where to begin in addressing this point. For one thing, many Christians would find the idea of saying that predestination exists almost more unthinkable than saying that God doesn't exist. And the other side can feel just as strongly about the idea of free will. (Look up "Calvinism vs. Arminianism" if you aren't familiar with this debate already. I particularly recommend the jokes that each side tells about the other.) In Section #3 of this chapter, I'll spend more time discussing how this unresolved dispute over a vital point of doctrine, and other disputes like it, are difficult to reconcile with the idea of God's personhood, so for now let's limit ourselves to briefly answering the question "Does the suggestion that salvation could be determined by predestination change anything about what was said above?"

It might change something for people who currently have no trouble believing in God, but not for people who have been unable to convince themselves of God's existence. There may be some people who can honestly say, "I have no question that God is real, and I am certain that the way I live because of my belief in God is what's best for me and for others." If a person's convictions are such, then they could, if they wanted, dismiss all my arguments by saying that I wasn't predestined to salvation and that is why all my attempts to find God have failed. Of course, this would mean that God creates some unchosen people with a desire to find him, so that they suffer in this life as they are unable to find him, only to suffer eternally in hell afterwards—but if that's what you need to believe to stop your world from falling apart, well, you do what you gotta do. For a person like this, the idea of predestination could be useful in preserving mental peace.

However, for anyone who already has good reason to think that God is not real, the idea of this sort of extra-cruel predestination doesn't change anything about the way you should live your life. For one thing, it doesn't seem to have much biblical basis. It's true that the concept of God choosing who will find him is mentioned several times throughout the New Testament,[14] and in addition to this, there are Old Testament references to God

---

[14] Romans 8:29–30; Romans 9:10–25; Ephesians 1:4–5, 11; II Peter 8–9

hardening someone's heart or causing someone not to listen to the truth.[15] However, the people who are unchosen or turned away from truth are always spoken of as being hostile to God's ways. There is nothing anywhere in the Bible to give support to the idea that some people want God and search for him but can't find him because they weren't chosen. In fact, we see God telling his people in the Old Testament that they will find him if they search for him with all their heart and in the New Testament we are told that if we draw near to God he will draw near to us.[16] If your experience contradicts this message, this is just another example of a flaw in a religion you must already have found other flaws in if you are having this much trouble believing in it.

Another grim but nonetheless practical reason not to worry is that in the unlikely event this proposed theory of predestination were true, there would be absolutely nothing you could do about it. The entire point of the proposition is to say that sincere people's failure to find God can be explained away by the idea that these people weren't among those God chose to find him before the world began. If God's election is all that matters and our desire to find God doesn't matter, then there is absolutely no way we can escape hell. We might as well try to enjoy this life at least.

I hope that if you are one of these sincerely unsuccessful people you won't give this suggestion a second thought. It does nothing to prove God's existence and only works to give someone desperate to believe in God a last excuse not to address inconsistencies in their beliefs or the problems raised by other people's experiences.

---

[15] Exodus 4:21, 9:12; Joshua 11:18–20; Isaiah 6:8–10
[16] Jeremiah 29:13; James 4:8

#2 Pascal's Wager doesn't work.

There exists a proposition, which you may have heard referred to as Pascal's Wager, that says if you don't believe in God and you turn out to be wrong you've lost a lot because you go to hell, but if you do believe in God and you turn out to be wrong you haven't lost much because you won't be any more dead than anyone else. For a long time this idea convinced me that I had only two options: to believe in God (whether happily or unhappily) or to give up on believing and always live in fear of being wrong.

Since Christianity is supposedly a loving relationship with God, it's sad that when push comes to shove, this is the type of argument that's brought out to keep you believing. When comprehensible signs of God's love and presence are consistently absent, your growing doubts won't be answered by your heavenly father reaching out to assure you he's with you but instead by human beings telling you that you can't really know the truth about God's existence anyway so it's better to just make a bet that minimizes your risk of eternal suffering. What could be further from a relationship? Because of the prevalence of this argument and the power its fear-based reasoning has to lock people into a loveless religion, I think it's important to address its flaws.

As a Christian, I never thought that the reasoning of Pascal's Wager would be convincing enough to change the mind of someone who didn't believe in God, but for a long time I thought it was a good enough reason for me not to change my mind away from belief. However, there is actually more to the problem proposed in the wager than at first meets the eye. The course of action the wager suggests is both more distasteful and less logical than those who find it convincing probably realize.

First, let me address just what is so distasteful about the wager. This unpleasantness in itself doesn't undo the logical soundness of the argument, but it's a worthwhile thing to be aware of, and I'll get on with the logical undoing in a minute.

Let's say that I am a person who has made my best effort to understand life, and this effort has led me to the conclusion that God does not exist. Should I still try to believe in God just in case? If God isn't real, I won't regret having lived for a lie once I'm dead, and if he is real, I've escaped hell. Doesn't it make sense to make temporary sacrifices that I can't regret in order to keep the possibility of eternal gain open? Well, it might make sense, but in all its practical outworking it also turns out to be pretty selfish.

The Bible is clear that lip service isn't enough to put anyone in right standing with God. It won't make a bit of difference if I say "I believe in God" and don't mean it. Plus, even if I really do believe in God, that still won't make a difference unless I live out a relationship with him. A passage we've just seen in Section #1, James 2:19–20 NKJV, says, "You believe that there is one God. You do well. Even the demons believe—and tremble! But do you want to know, O foolish man, that faith without works is dead?" and the writer goes on to cite examples from the Old Testament to prove his point. This teaching implies that if I'm serious about doing what it takes to avoid the possibility of hell, I have to live a life in which my *actions* are based upon my best understanding of what God wants me to do. Now, determining what God wants one to do is another very difficult problem that I'll return to in the next section, but for now let's run with the assumption that a person needs to do their best to understand God's will and then act on that understanding.

Churches differ in their interpretations of the Bible, but any individual must do their best to live by the interpretation that convinces them. Unfortunately, when we make an honest effort to discern the best interpretation, the one that is most likely to be accurate, it's not always going to be the interpretation that we like best. Let's take an example that is frequently under discussion today: the biblical stance on same-sex relationships.

I'll quote two passages from Paul's letters that give straightforward commentary on the topic. There are other relevant passages in both the Old and New Testaments that address it with varying degrees of ambiguity, but these two rather unambiguous ones are enough to start with.

I Timothy 1:8–11 NIV
We know that the law is good if one uses it properly. We also know that the law is made not for the righteous but for lawbreakers and rebels, the ungodly and sinful, the unholy and irreligious, for those who kill their fathers or mothers, for murderers, for the sexually immoral, for those practicing homosexuality, for slave traders and liars and perjurers—and for whatever else is contrary to the sound doctrine that conforms to the gospel concerning the glory of the blessed God, which he entrusted to me.

This passage does not say that believers should condemn "those practicing homosexuality" but it does say that the practice of homosexuality is against God's law. The statement that "the law is made not for the righteous but for lawbreakers" should be understood in light of similar statements given in the Gospels and Paul's letters (e.g. Mark 2:15–17, Romans 7:7–9) to mean that the law exists to make people realize that their actions are wrong so that they will turn to God and ask for forgiveness.

I Corinthians 6:9–11 NIV
Do not be deceived: Neither the sexually immoral nor idolaters nor adulterers nor men who have sex with men nor thieves nor the greedy nor drunkards nor slanderers nor swindlers will inherit the kingdom of God. And that is what some of you were. But you were washed, you were sanctified, you were justified in the name of the Lord Jesus Christ and by the Spirit of our God.

There are two things worth noting in this passage, similar to the other. First, Paul puts homosexuality right in the middle of a list of sins, showing that he considers it to be just as obviously sinful as stealing or worshipping idols. Second, he clearly considers all these sins to be equally as bad and equally as forgivable, equally as much of a big deal for the unrepentant and equally as inconsequential for those who have left them behind and been "sanctified" and "justified." The rest of the passage in fact contains the famous statement "All things are lawful for me, but all things are not helpful" (NKJV), which suggests that none of these warnings against wrongdoing have anything to do with whether people get sent straight to hell for committing certain sins but more with whether they are living the full life God wants for them right now.

During the time that I sincerely believed the Bible was given to humanity by God, doing my best to understand what God's law said on this issue, I arrived at the following understanding: The Bible says that same-sex relationships are wrong just like it says gossip, theft, alcoholism, and a host of other undesirable behaviors are wrong. It also says that the most important virtue of all is love. It never says that you can change someone's heart just by telling them they are wrong. It does, however, say that it's not okay for a church to condone any of the behaviors that scripture points out as being wrong (I Corinthians 5:1–8). Taking all of this into account, the standard of action I think I will be held accountable for is to love gay people, not Bible-bash them, and support the creation of a church environment that will make them feel comfortable attending. However, the creation of a positive environment can't go so far as to say that same-sex relationships are not wrong. We have to be honest that the Bible says they are wrong, but we also have to admit that it is up to God to change people's hearts on the issue. We shouldn't be saying that gay people go to hell because the Bible doesn't say this, but we should encourage them to fight their predispositions if we can because their lives will be better overall if they do so. I also agree with my church's teaching that "all sin is idolatry," by which they mean that the biggest problem with any sinful action a person takes is that God told them not to do something but they did it because they loved that thing more than they loved God, essentially putting it in God's place. If the Bible says homosexuality is wrong, and people decide to live their lives in same-sex relationships, then they are engaging in life-long "idolatry" (showing more reverence/love for something that is not God than for God). If someone spends their whole life loving something more than they love God, perhaps they do end up in hell. I had better encourage gay people to try to overcome their same-sex attractions because that is what's most likely to be best for them overall. (However, I don't like this conclusion because my conscience tells me that same-sex dating and marriage couldn't be wrong because it doesn't hurt anyone, and some people are simply always going to be happier in these relationships than in heterosexual ones.)

Now, remember, we are talking about Pascal's Wager here. In our example, I am already at the point where I doubt God's existence because of a variety of difficulties unrelated to this question of homosexuality. I am considering the possibility that

I should try to convince myself to believe in God just to make sure I don't go to hell if there is such a place. However, there is more at stake here than my own temporary losses if I'm wrong. If I intend on really living for God, I am forced to take certain moral stances, such as in this case concluding that homosexuality is a sin and that the best thing I can do for gay people is to try to help them become straight.

The severity of the effect this attitude has on human rights is debatable since it doesn't obligate me to, for example, vote against legalizing same-sex marriage since that won't do anything to change people's hearts. But it does set up worrying scenarios such as the fact that, if I'm really consistent in this belief, I should hold to the idea that no matter what I know about the physical innateness and ethical innocence of same-sex attractions, I have to believe that if a gay person really wants to live for God, they'll find a way to overcome their nature.

If God is not real, anyone who spends their life fighting their attractions will gain nothing from their efforts. Knowing this, if I try to believe in and live for God in order to save myself from a hell that might exist, this means that in order to secure my own possible future benefit, I have thrown my support behind the idea that others should be asked to sacrifice relationships that would have drastically increased their quality of life. And that's just the conclusion that I personally reached on that topic while trying my best to interpret scripture objectively. It's easily possible that people may reach harsher conclusions on various questions as they attempt to flesh out the true moral standard they will be held to.

Another of the many ways my own wager influences others has to do with tithing. Say my best understanding of scripture is that I should donate at least ten percent of my income to the church, which is a common understanding that Christians of many denominations hold. This means that in order to possibly save myself from hell, I am funding an organization devoted to spreading the very message that I'm not sure I believe in. If I'm wrong, my donations will probably have helped to put others into the unpleasant situation I am currently experiencing of having to give up a level of autonomy in life under duress of the threat of hell. The same could be said about evangelism, whether my conviction is that I should be handing out tracts on a street corner, funding missionaries, or simply encouraging friends to believe in God if the subject comes up. If I have children, this wager also obligates me to raise them as Christians. Faith without works is dead, and if I don't believe in Christianity sincerely enough to think my children will benefit from sharing my beliefs, I don't believe in it sincerely enough period.

As I've said, these scenarios and the many other similar ones that could be listed don't undo the logic of Pascal's Wager. If God is real, my actions will probably have benefited the people influenced by them in the long run, and if God is not real these people's increased suffering will be just as inconsequential after they're dead as mine was. But I think that the consideration of how my beliefs influence the lives of others should take away the cavalier attitude that sometimes accompanies this argument. I'm not only gambling with my own feelings but with the quality of the lives of others, and if I'm wrong I will have helped to ensure that they spent the only moments of existence they would ever know subordinating their happiness to a lie.

To some degree, the distastefulness of this situation itself poses a logical problem. If God is truly loving, if he truly understands the human condition, if he is truly merciful, if passages of scripture such as Jesus' claim that he came to give abundant life

(John 10:10) are truly accurate, then why would God leave an honest seeker of truth in such a position that the choice to follow him has to be accompanied by this uncertainty over whether one is helping or harming others? Why wouldn't he provide this person with some other sound logical reason or some personal encounter so that they could follow him willingly, knowing that he was really there? The apparent cruelty of giving someone nothing but a fear of hell to work with suggests that the situation is more likely to have come about by the unfortunate accumulation of contradictory ideas on relationship and judgment than by the design of a loving God.

And this leads into even clearer flaws in the logic of Pascal's Wager. Once again, let me reiterate: The wager isn't addressing people who already believe in God and just aren't sure whether they can get over their laziness and actually live for him. It is addressing people who feel truly unconvinced that God could be real but still fear hell because there's always a chance they may have come to the wrong conclusion. Speaking as someone who has been one of these people, I'll tell you that for anyone in this position there's bad news and there's good news. The bad news is that your chances of figuring out what needs to be done in order to avoid hell are even worse than they might seem. The good news is that they're actually so bad, you're screwed no matter what you do.

The flaw in Pascal's Wager is that it assumes a person who is afraid of a hell they have no concrete reason to believe in will also know a course of action that can be taken to avoid hell. This cannot be assumed. I've been talking about Christianity this whole time, but the fact is that if you don't know whether Christianity is true, then that's just it: You don't know whether Christianity is true. If nothing has convinced you that it is true so far, why assume that its claims about hell and how to avoid hell are the ones that need to be followed?

Look at my case again. I've discovered flaws (listed throughout this book) in Christian theology that make it seem very unlikely the religion is true, and now I find myself in a situation that adds yet another contradiction on top of the rest: I was told, and I read in the Bible, that the Christian God is full of love and doesn't desire that anyone would end up in hell, and yet I find myself in the cruel situation of having no certainty and fearing that even if I make what seems to be a safe bet for myself I might hurt someone else. There is no particular reason that I should assume the best failsafe against hell is to follow Christian practices. Do the other religions of the world actually contain any more problems and contradictions than Christianity does? Maybe yes, maybe no, but they all have problems and contradictions. If I currently feel that Christianity is the religion I need to focus on, chances are that this is simply because it is the religion I am most familiar with and that forms the largest part of my cultural background.

The only perfect way to reduce my chances of ending up in hell to zero would be to satisfy the requirements of all religions, but this isn't possible since many of them require that their followers not practice the others. This is why my situation is so hopeless. If fear of hell is the only thing pointing me to believe in any religion, it just doesn't provide the information I need in order to do anything about the fear. Maybe the best way to make sense of the tragedy of wanting to do the right thing and not knowing what it is, is to conclude that whatever God or gods exist are actually cruel beings who like to deceive and confuse humanity. If this is the case, there is nothing I can do. I might as well forget about it and try to enjoy my life now.

Or maybe the safest thing to do is to try to live by underlying principles shared by many religions and pray that if a higher power exists my desire to do what is right won't go unnoticed. The heart of most religious practices seems to be doing good for others, so perhaps what I should do is focus on helping the most people and hurting the fewest. And since religions differ in their claims about what exactly is good for people and what is bad for them, the most objective way to figure out what is most helpful to others would be to rely on fields of investigation rooted in empirical studies on how various actions affect people, such as psychology, sociology, biology, medicine, economics, political science, and so on. While doing this, there's no real reason to practice anything particularly religious other than perhaps saying some generic prayers now and again to whoever might be out there to help me do what's right. As long as I'm not hurting anyone, once again, I might as well try to enjoy my life without further worry since I have no reason to think worry will help me.

And if for some reason, logical or illogical, I continue to feel that my paranoia over hell can only be put to rest by trying to be Christian, there is still the problem of love. Remember, Paul said, "... though I have all faith, so that I could remove mountains, but have not love, I am nothing. And though I bestow all my goods to feed the poor, and though I give my body to be burned, but have not love, it profits me nothing" (I Corinthians 13:2–3). I find that living for God in order to escape the possibility of hell causes me to resent him rather than love him. I'm forcing myself to give advice to my gay friends that contradicts my understanding of what is best for them. I'm forcing myself to donate to a cause whose merits I'm not sure of. I'm forcing myself to direct people towards God in their times of need even though I don't know whether this will ultimately be more helpful or harmful for them. I'm doing all these things because of what I might eventually get out of the deal, and this violates my conscience. I resent that God would allow the human conscience to develop in a way that wasn't in line with his laws, that he would leave me without any convincing evidence of his existence and only the threat of hell to get me to believe his laws were even real, and that he hasn't provided me with whatever experience I need to fall in love with him so that right now I would already be living for him out of gratitude instead of forcing myself to live for him so that I might possibly someday be glad I did.

It's always possible that a person could come to Christianity in this unpleasant way and then encounter God, truly fall in love with him, and have the problem resolved. But if their efforts drag on for years with no intervention on God's part, then it can't really be concluded that their attempt at Christianity is getting them any farther from hell. In fact, the longer they make themselves available to connect with God's love and nothing happens, the more evidence of Christian claims falling short they accumulate. What are we to make of the general picture painted by statements such as, "Draw near to God and He will draw near to you," (James 4:8 NKJV) or claims of Jesus like, "'He who has My commandments and keeps them, it is he who loves Me. And he who loves Me will be loved by My Father, and I will love him and manifest Myself to him'" (John 14:21 NKJV)? Does God draw near to and manifest, that is *show*, himself to people who draw near to him and keep his commandments, or doesn't he?

I propose that Pascal's Wager makes no sense: A person who continues to be motived by nothing more than a fear of hell cannot have discovered the right way to live. The wager should never have been presented as, "Trade your life now, get insurance against hell later." It should have been presented as, "Trade your life now, get a wild stab in the dark with a very low probability of happening upon something that might keep you out of hell later." It makes far more sense for a person who already finds religious claims unconvincing to accept the conclusion that they are all false. The more aware a person is of difficulties and contradictions within and between religions, the more this makes sense.

I'll end here with a personal observation on this topic. I have been a part of conversations in which someone communicated that they grew up Christian but later discovered flaws in the belief system and could no longer hold to it, and yet even though they found its teachings untrustworthy, their fear of hell remained so strong that they couldn't stop inventing new and terrible ideas of what God might be to explain it. Maybe God was the sort of person who would hide all sign of himself, even allow evidence to point away from him, and still condemn anyone who didn't show blind, senseless loyalty. This idea is completely at odds with orthodox Christian teachings, and also makes you ask yourself whether you would really want to cooperate with and spend an eternity with a being like that, but it was compulsively persistent.

Fear of hell is a powerful psychological vice, the perfect invincible monster. When you cause someone to picture the worst thing they can imagine and convince them from childhood that they are in danger of it and then situate it in the world of the afterlife, a place no one can go and explore and come back from to tell you firsthand there's nothing to be afraid of, you create a state of psychological conditioning that, in many cases, can't be resolved with logic. Just like someone suffering from PTSD might feel afraid even when they can see with their own eyes that the things they are afraid of aren't around, fear of hell doesn't necessarily go away when reasons to believe in hell disappear. If it wasn't for this powerful force of conditioning, ideas along the lines of Pascal's Wager probably wouldn't be influential enough to be worth discussing.

#3 There is no Christian consensus on foundational spiritual questions.

Christianity claims to be the one and only true path of reconciliation between humanity and God. People who adhere to it expect it to answer certain questions, such as "How can I be in right standing with God?" "How should I live?" and "How can I feel secure about my eternal destiny?" If Christian beliefs were given to humanity by God and the answers to these questions are found through relationship with God, we would expect the answers to be clear. As different people interacted with God and came to know him and his will, we would expect that their understanding of Christianity's foundational requirements would become more similar. Unfortunately, this doesn't seem to be the case. What we actually find is that various groups of Christians (who to me all appear to be honestly pursuing God through their study of scripture and openness to God's voice) cannot agree on issues of vital importance.

The way ideas are formed within Christian communities does not display the pattern of information flow we would expect to see if all Christians were getting to know the same perfect and loving being. It more closely resembles what we would expect if people were coming to a consensus by exchanging their own thoughts on an ambiguous topic. Different communities develop different and often contradictory doctrines, which show signs of being influenced by the culture each community lives in and the standards each community typically uses to evaluate orthodoxy. What I mean by this is that churches in more conservative or more liberal times and places for the most part end up developing more conservative or more liberal doctrines in accordance with their cultural influences, and churches who lean more towards literal interpretations of the Bible will fairly consistently end up with doctrines shaped by this standard while those who focus more on adopting whatever teaching seems to affect outreach most positively will end up with a set of doctrines influenced by that standard. If God were really communicating with his followers about important teachings, it would seem that some trend distinguishable from purely naturalistic cultural influence should show up.

As things stand, we have churches that disagree on almost all important topics and who all claim that they have developed their views through prayerful communion with God by way of scripture, the leading of the Holy Spirit, application of foundational Christian principles, and so on.

One topic that doesn't seem nearly as straightforward as it should given its importance is that of salvation itself. As I discuss in Section #1 of this chapter, there are various ideas about what hell really is, and besides the three I discussed there, there is also the idea that no one actually goes to hell, at least not eternally. Then, in addition to this disagreement about what people need to be saved from and whether we actually need to be saved from anything, there is further disagreement about how we can be saved. As I briefly mentioned in Section #1.1, some churches believe that people choose to follow God for themselves, while others believe that God has already determined who will choose to follow him. The understanding of the interplay between grace, faith, love, obedience, relationship, good works, and other concepts is also complicated, so complicated that I doubt heavily that anyone could give clear answers about whether various combinations of actions and intentions result in a person being saved or not. It's even more doubtful that different people asked to answer the same list of questions of this type would come up with the same answers. Even certainty of one's own salvation is often left up to vague assurances such as a feeling that everything is okay or the conviction that "God knows my heart," implying that love and good intentions are what matter. And then of course there are the people who just don't know whether they are saved or not. Related, although possibly less important in determining everyday decisions, is the ambiguity over what salvation means. Has a person who does whatever it is people need to do to be saved gained just a better life now or also something eternal? If the result is something eternal, what is it? Do people go to heaven, live on an improved earth, or something else? And what will any of these experiences actually be like?

The first two questions at least (What do we need to be saved from, and how can we be saved?) can't be dismissed as unimportant since their answers determine whether being Christian actually matters. If there is something terrible to be saved from and people do need to hear the Christian gospel to be saved from it, and the ability to accept salvation is within their power, then outreach and evangelism should be prioritized much more heavily than they would need to be if the "unsaved" are not actually that badly off or their exposure to the gospel won't change anything. For a religion that claims to exist for the purpose of connecting people to God, it's very strange that so much about this connection and its importance should be left open to interpretation.

Before we take a deeper look at other topics within Christianity that seem to merit more clarification than they've been given, let's use this one to pull out some principles that will apply to each of the others.

(1) There are a variety of ways to explain why we lack certainty on these important topics.

For whatever unresolved question we discuss, such as the question of how a person is saved, we can explain the lack of agreement between churches in many ways, including the following: (a) There is a correct answer, God communicates clearly about what it is, and people who claim that a different answer is correct are lying to themselves. (b) There is a correct answer, God doesn't tell us what it is, but it's important that we figure out what it is. (c) There are different correct answers for different people. (d) God doesn't care what you do, or God isn't real and people are unknowingly inventing what they think he is saying.

Now, if Christians are actually in communication with God, and God actually wants people to know things such as what they need to do to be saved, then it's odd that different people who make an effort to discern God's communication with them come up with contradictory ideas about what he's saying. To me, the only satisfying explanation of this phenomenon is (d). I think Christianity actually originates from well-meaning people doing their best to figure out what is true rather than from a source beyond humanity, but I can't really disprove the idea that there might be some higher power who just doesn't care about communicating or interacting with humanity, which is why that possibility is included in (d) as well. I have difficulty seeing how explanations (a) through (c) could be correct for the following reasons.

Explanation (a)—that God makes the correct answer clear to people and self-deception is the reason why other answers exist—contradicts my personal experiences. A couple of the unresolved disagreements I'll go on to mention here are ones that I first learned about in the church I grew up in. For years, I agreed with the views that that church took and thought their reasons for seeing things as they did made sense, but later on, after being exposed to other communities and hearing why they held other views, I decided that their explanations made more sense and changed my mind. Before changing my mind, I wasn't lying to myself. I just didn't know any better than what I had been told. And after changing my mind I still wasn't lying to myself. I was honestly convinced that the new explanations I had heard were more consistent and complete than the old ones. I also didn't see any sign that people in either of the two communities were lying to themselves. They seemed to all be looking for truth and defending the answers that made the most sense to them.

Explanation (b)—that there is a correct answer and God does not make it clear but it's important that we figure it out—isn't satisfying to me because it raises the same problem I addressed in Section #1 about salvation or, in the examples that will follow, right living, being based on understanding of information and therefore only being achievable by the smart or lucky.

Explanation (c)—that there are different correct answers for different people—might technically be defensible, but certain telltale signs make the chances of its being correct seem very low to me. The primary difficulty is that if there are different correct understandings of Christianity's core teachings for different people, it can't also be true that there is only one correct answer for all people, but many people seem to be under the impression that there is only one correct answer out there. It's not impossible that God could have given different people different correct answers about most Christian beliefs but chosen not to communicate with them about the fact that this is how things work, therefore leaving that question itself open to confusion. But it seems unlikely. For one thing, that question itself is important. If God wants people to know their own path to finding him, it seems unlikely that he wouldn't also want everyone to know that others have different paths so that no one would feel that part of their own path was to help others by converting them out of the form of Christianity that was actually best for them.

To me, explanation (d)—that God either isn't real or doesn't care what people do—appears to have fewer difficulties than the others. Both scenarios would explain why the ranges of answers to the questions I'll list below seem human in origin. In either case, people have been left to invent their own ideas on each topic and won't be rewarded or punished for coming up with certain answers.

(2) The feeling that the correct answer to the question is obvious can blind people to the level of uncertainty that actually exists.

Both for the topic of salvation that I've briefly covered and for the others that I'll introduce below, people who feel sure of their own understanding of the subject could easily say that God hasn't been unclear at all and I'm the one trying to introduce doubt about what the correct answer is. However, what I'm trying to do here is simply to point out that for every answer one church feels certain of, there is a contradictory answer that another church feels equally as certain of, and both churches think they are hearing from God. I'm not trying to make either church doubt their answer. I'm trying to explain to people who wonder whether Christianity has divine origins that this situation suggests it doesn't.

Some people might say that the answer to such-and-such a question is obvious because the Bible explains it. For example, "The way to be saved is obvious. The Bible clearly says that everyone is condemned to hell unless they ask Jesus to save them." My problem is not that I disagree with their way of reaching certainty. It's that I don't see how another Christian who pursues a relationship with God just as sincerely could reach a contradictory conclusion if both are talking to the same God. Another person might say, "The idea that everyone is condemned to hell unless they make a specific profession of faith is obviously wrong. When interpreting scripture, you have to prioritize strongly supported core principles over specific details. The principle of God's love for us and the importance of our love for each other is clearly one of the most important messages in all of scripture and makes it obvious that those who live a life of love don't end up in hell."

The person with the more sophisticated answer and the one with the more direct answer each feel as if they have taken the steps God wanted them to take in order to discern the best viewpoint to hold. Neither person is likely to wonder why God doesn't help us all out by communicating with humanity in a way that makes such a vital question clear to us all. They both feel certain that their view is correct, so they wonder instead what agenda or deception is causing the other person to turn a blind eye to such an obvious fact. The one who focuses on the threat of hell should just think more about what God is really like and the answer would be clear. The one who focuses on the principle of love should stop prioritizing their own feelings over things directly stated in the Bible and the answer would become apparent.

This type of certainty is probably the reason why more people don't see a problem with the lack of communication and clarity coming from God to the church. In their eyes, there is plenty of clarity and others just miss it. If the church is missing this much though, we still have a problem. People are looking for truth and trying to live the way God wants. The only one in this situation who has the ability to make sure that someone encounters a message about the truth in a way they understand is God. A person with the best of intentions is still imperfect and prone to misunderstanding scripture or any other form of communication, but God who is perfect could reach out to people with a message he knows they will understand in the intended way. If this isn't happening, we still have to wonder if God is absent or uncaring.

Now, keeping those principles in mind, let's take a closer look at some new examples of disagreements, the lines of thought that go into supporting both sides, and the reasons why the confusion seems to indicate a lack of divine communication.

First, let's talk about the issue of women in ministry. Out of the churches I've attended, there were two that held strong opposing views on the subject. One took the official position that women should not be placed in positions of spiritual authority over men. This meant that while a woman could be a pastor who ministered only to other women or to children, she should not hold a position such as head pastor that would make her a spiritual leader in the lives of adult men. It was fine for women to have authority over men in business or politics, but not in the church. The other church believed that men and women were equal in their capacity to handle spiritual authority over others. They employed both male and female pastors and gave equal weight to the input of all pastors to the church.

The reasoning of the first church was based on biblical passages such as the following:

I Corinthians 14:34–38 NKJV
Let your women keep silent in the churches, for they are not permitted to speak; but they are to be submissive, as the law also says. And if they want to learn something, let them ask their own husbands at home; for it is shameful for women to speak in church. Or did the word of God come originally from you? Or was it you only that it reached? If anyone thinks himself to be a prophet or spiritual, let him acknowledge that the things which I write to you are the commandments of the Lord. But if anyone is ignorant, let him be ignorant.

I Timothy 2:11–14 NKJV
Let a woman learn in silence with all submission. And I do not permit a woman to teach or to have authority over a man, but to be in silence. For Adam was formed first, then Eve. And Adam was not deceived, but the woman being deceived, fell into transgression.

The verses from I Corinthians come directly after Paul has been giving instructions about how to preserve order in a church meeting. He gives instructions about prophesying and speaking in tongues to allow church gatherings to run smoothly and ends the list of instructions with this section about women keeping silent.

The verses from I Timothy are part of a passage in which the author begins by encouraging Christians to pray for people in authority and continues to call out the men specifically to pray and the women to be modest and excel in good works. From that encouragement, he runs directly into the command for women to learn in silence.

The first church that I attended thought that these commands were meant as general instructions to the church as a whole, just like the other instructions in the passages they come from seem to be. This church believed that it would be irresponsible for them to employ female lead pastors because the Bible says in these passages that women are not suited for this type of role and are actually more prone than men to being deceived on spiritual topics and thus misleading others as the passage from I Timothy indicates.

Based on my own observations, I can't conclude that this was some sort of plot to maintain male dominance. What I saw was one of two things happening in regards to this teaching: (1) Men and women who had been steeped their whole lives in the idea that the sexes have different roles in the world saw nothing wrong with saying that church leadership just wasn't a strength or a role for women. (2) Men and women who believed in equality in most or all other areas had to say with some embarrassment that this must be the best way to run a church otherwise the Bible wouldn't say so and that if it seemed to go against our values today we must be missing something because God doesn't make mistakes and we do.

In contrast to this, the second church was aware of these passages but said that because the Holy Spirit was so clearly working through female pastors to accomplish great things, they had concluded that those passages of scripture were given as commands to specific churches at specific times, not as a guide to all churches at all times. They also pointed to cases in the Bible in which women have authority, such as Deborah, a spiritual leader of ancient Israel (Judges 4), and Priscilla, a woman described as playing a role equal to her husband in instructing a young dynamic male preacher (Acts 18:24–26). According to this church, because God was working through women in their community and not communicating to anyone that anything was wrong, and because the Bible speaks positively of instances in which women held spiritual authority, the passages that seem to forbid female leadership couldn't actually be instructions for all churches.

At this church, based on my observations, I can't conclude that their openness to female leadership was a wishy-washy ploy to appear relevant or run away from the possibility of offending anyone. There were other issues on which they took stances that were offensive to the general secular population because they felt that scripture and the Holy Spirit had shown them that these stances were correct. For instance, they claimed that people can and should treat same-sex attraction as something to be overcome by prayer, loving support from Christian friends, and lifestyle choices. They felt that scripture left room for this interpretation and that they had seen it work by the power of the Holy Spirit, so they stuck by this message even though it sounds offensive to many people. I can only conclude that their views on both of these issues were sincere attempts to discern what God wanted without respect to how good or bad the conclusion sounded.

What we see here is that two churches hold opposing views on the subject of women in ministry and both believe that they are being true to God's will and faithfully interpreting what he has communicated with them. It would seem that God cared enough to raise this issue as a topic for discussion but not enough to let people know what he wants done. And this isn't some trivial anything-goes topic either. It's important to know whether certain people are doing wrong just by going into ministry or whether a church is doing wrong by keeping gifted people out of ministry on the basis of sex.

Just as with all the disagreements here, it would be extremely easy for the first church to say that the second has failed to give scripture its proper place of authority and is now being led by emotions, and it would be extremely easy for the second church to say that the first is overly simplistic in their interpretation of scripture and puts too much weight on human traditions. And each could so easily say that the other isn't listening closely to God's voice because they are distracted by some agenda or some inflexible expectation about how God should do things. These are exactly the types of things that are said in such situations that stop people from wondering why the low level of clarity and unity that exists between churches makes it seem almost like there is no one telling each church when they are getting off track.

Another disagreement that is perhaps of less direct importance, but still important, is the question of origins. Some Christian circles, including two of the three Christian communities I was part of over the years, insist that the first few chapters of Genesis are at least mostly historical when they describe the creation of the earth and mankind and therefore the vast majority of scientists must be wrong in their theories about things like solar system formation and biological evolution. Other groups insist that these theories are too well supported by evidence to be wrong and that the creation account is intended to teach important concepts, such as that God is the creator, but not to explain the actual physical mechanism by which creation happened.

Many of your average churchgoers could get away with saying this dispute doesn't matter and focusing on more pressing needs, but for some people, different understandings of origins strongly influence how they relate to God and others. For one, Christians who work or want to work in any field of scientific research concerned with anything that relates to a theory of origins are being told by part of the Christian community that the only way to be responsible to others and pleasing to God in their work is to reject the prevailing theories. In order to explain why an overwhelming majority of their colleagues find these theories credible, they have to tell themselves that these people are mistaken or biased. Another way that this issue quickly takes on importance is when Christians who were raised being told that the world was created miraculously in a short period of time look into scientific arguments for great age and evolution and find them convincing. Some of these people stop believing in God or the authority of scripture because it appears to them that science is directly opposed to what the Bible teaches.

Some Christians are sure to say, "Of course people should be listening to scientific findings first. Science is a search for truth, and God obviously wouldn't lie about the world he made, so there must be a different way to understand scripture so that it aligns with scientific findings." The trouble is, it's not that simple for people who feel deeply convicted that God has led them to interpret scripture in a particular way and be faithful to it. The very reason that they don't listen to the claims of the scientific community is that in their minds, they *know* what God has said and they won't listen to anyone who contradicts it no matter how trustworthy they seem. The only person who could convince these Christians that their understanding is misguided is God himself, but it doesn't look as if he's intervening to communicate with them.

From the other perspective, Christians who think that the scientific community is wrong might dismiss the opposite view by saying that Christians who agree with theories like evolution are more willing to trust human ways of discovering truth than the direct explanation of truth God gave us in the Bible. Or they might say that these people have compromised their Christian views in order to not be called stupid or unscientific by others. But it doesn't seem this way to Christians who agree with mainstream theories on origins. Back when I was sure that Christianity was true, I eventually decided that these theories were as well supported as anything else I believed about how the physical world worked even though I had been taught differently in church. For me, this didn't mean getting greater acceptance or respect from people. It meant admitting that I had been wrong about something for my whole life and feeling stupid about things I had said in the past, and it meant adopting a view that I thought most of the people close to me either would not care about or would see as a sign that I was weak in my beliefs. I came to the conclusion I did because I wanted to know what was true, and when I made up my mind, it made me feel like my theology and reasons for believing in God were stronger than ever, even though others expected them to be weaker. I thought I had discovered new, encouraging ideas about how God related to humanity that I had been overlooking all my life. As far as I could tell, I was following what God would have wanted me to do, and he never communicated differently to me. I think that most Christians who agree with mainstream ideas on origins sincerely believe they are making the intellectual choices God wants them to make. They believe that if God made the world, their minds, logic, science, and so on, that he will speak to them through these things and not mislead them and that this is part of how he instructs them in the proper interpretation of scripture. If God clearly communicated to them, in whatever way he knew they would recognize as his voice, that something they believed was actually incorrect, I think they would listen.

We see again that two camps both want to know what is true but are using completely different criteria to figure out the answer. It seems unlikely that God would refuse to at least tell them which criteria to prioritize, and yet some feel that they have been led to prioritize a simple reading of scriptural texts while others feel they have been led to prioritize a larger logical framework or some other concept. Did God point different people to different answers, or did they all imagine that they were hearing from God at all?

Yet another controversy among Christians exists over whether Jesus will literally return to earth or not. Some churches take statements on the subject throughout the New Testament to mean that Jesus will physically return to earth someday and that his return will be accompanied by the ending of current human political structures and the destruction and recreation of the world.[17] Others do not think that the idea of Jesus' return is

---

[17] One example of this is Matthew chapter 24. I recommend reading the whole chapter, but here are some excerpts from the NKJV: *[...] the disciples came to Him privately, saying, "[...] what will be the sign of Your coming, and of the end of the age?" And Jesus answered and said to them: "[...] you will hear of wars and rumors of wars. [...] nation will rise against nation, and kingdom against kingdom. And there will be famines, pestilences, and earthquakes in various places. [...] And this gospel of the kingdom will be preached in all the world as a witness to all the nations, and then the end will come. [...] Immediately after the tribulation of those days the sun will be darkened, and the moon will not give its light; the stars will fall from heaven, and the powers of the*

meant to describe any literal events. While this dispute could easily be pushed aside as irrelevant to most daily choices, in practice it is not, at least in my experience. In the community I grew up in, many people believed that the world would end when Jesus returned, and I often heard people state that long-term environmental problems were nothing to worry about because God already knew when the world would end and things were bound to get worse up until that point. So, while it would be easy to say that without greater clarity on the topic we should err on the side of caution and avoid any actions that could make the world worse, in my experience an appreciable number of people tend to feel a sense of confidence in their understanding of end-times theology and therefore don't realize that they are gambling with the future when they act as if problems of global scope are all up to God to sort out.

At the two extremes of this scale, we have people who think that with enough bad choices humankind could destroy itself and people who think that no matter what we do God is going to keep the world going until he wants it to end. There are also people who fall somewhere in the middle with views such as that God has already determined when the world will end but humanity still has a large influence on what life will be like between now and then.

As with all these topics, there are many reasons why each group could say that the others are missing an obvious message or purposely refusing to listen to what God is saying, but if each group thinks they are hearing from God, then God is the only one who could resolve the confusion and bring unity.

---

heavens will be shaken. [...] But of that day and hour no one knows, not even the angels of heaven, but My Father only."

We could continue to list other disputes between opposing camps who can each provide scriptural support for their opinion and/or each believe that the Holy Spirit has led them to think as they do. For example: Is it sinful to be in a same-sex relationship? Should Christians be pacifists? Under what circumstances is divorce allowable? Are all forms of rebellion against government wrong? What is a spirit and a soul? The list could go on, highlighting all the things that seem to matter but must not if everyone who seeks to hear from God about them has been given a different answer or has been left to find their own answer.

To me, the explanation seems clear. People are left to develop their own answers according to their own means because that is all they have, and this is a good reason not to believe in God. While it's impossible to disprove the existence of a God who is undetectable and never interacts with people, this is not the God who most people are interested in. People love God because they think he has certain specific personality traits and ways of relating to humanity that are good (He acts in love, involves people in his story for the world, etc.) and they fear God because they think he requires them to live in a certain way and that their obedience or disobedience has consequences. If this specific personal being exists, then the church's striking amount of confusion over what he is saying about the most important of issues suggests that he is unable or, much more likely, unwilling to communicate.

For a long time I took the stories of fellow Christians about all the ways God had communicated with them as proof that God was real. People always seemed to be hearing his voice giving them encouragement, directing them to the best course of action, or reminding them of what was right when they wanted to compromise. And whenever an indication appeared that the information supposedly communicated by God might not have been the best, people always seemed so sure that it was their own fault—they had misheard because they hadn't invested the proper time into seeking God's will, because they had their priorities out of order, or because they were already so set on their own plans that they didn't really listen like they should have. It always seemed that the right answers were there, being offered by God to anyone who was willing to listen carefully and set their preconceived expectations aside, but of course it was all unverifiable. Maybe the people who heard God telling them to accept a particular job offer or reminding them that he loved them when they felt lonely really were hearing from God, but there was no way I could know whether that was true. Even if the job they thought God was directing them towards turned out not to be so great, there always seemed to be a reason to think the advice had been from God anyway—that job had caused the person to move to an area where they found what they actually wanted later perhaps, or it was meant to teach them patience. I couldn't really expect to see any noticeable difference between someone who was truly hearing from God and someone who imagined they were.

But as soon as I look to a situation in which people's claims of hearing from God should be verifiable, I find that they seem to be shown false. Does God actually care more about giving his people a little help in their career paths than about ensuring that they know whether certain actions are harmful to the church as a whole or how much their choices now influence their eternity? I think it's unlikely. Instead, both types of communication are equally as imagined.

#4 You're not supposed to act as if God were actually real.

This last point is going to be a catch-all for several minor observations of mine similar to the thoughts covered in Section #3. The lack of agreement on vital issues discussed in Section #3 gives a clear indication that Christian doctrine is being slowly invented and tweaked by humans rather than being received from a divine source. But that is not the only indication that God is suspiciously missing. Here I'll share some thoughts that add to the picture but are more specific to my own years of Christian life. The following are four lessons I learned well during my time in church that suddenly seemed problematic once I became aware of the inconsistencies I've discussed throughout the rest of this chapter.

(1) You're not supposed to actually follow God's commands unless your culture says it's okay.

> The churches I attended all made it clear that they believed the Bible was the word of God. They referred to it as "inspired," meaning that the thoughts it contains were given to the authors by God rather than invented by humans. And at least one of these churches referred to the Bible as "inerrant" as well, meaning that it contained no inaccuracies.
>
> These churches taught that the Bible provided a moral law that was superior to the legal codes of any nation, the norms of any society, and the direction of one's own conscience. And I believe it would be accurate to say that this is a typical stance among Evangelical churches. The message I got growing up from the pastors of my church and the creators of Christian media coming out of churches and organizations

around the world was that without the moral compass provided by God's law given through the Bible, people would have no good way of agreeing on what was right. Morality would shift over time, and right and wrong would be left up to each individual's opinion.

Another idea I often heard preached at the churches I attended was that Christians were called to be different from the world around them. Instead of following whatever the changing moral current of the culture we lived in happened to be, we were supposed to stick to biblical values, when they aligned with the values of our culture and when they contradicted them.

In light of all I was told about the Bible and the importance of the moral commands God had given us through it, I thought it was strange that Christian morality nevertheless seemed to be guided in some ways by the evolution of moral standards throughout history.

In an extreme case, we see that in Old Testament times God is portrayed as commanding things that would be unthinkable today. He tells his people to invade a new land and kill all the inhabitants of certain cities in order to avoid being influenced by their pagan traditions,[18] and there is also the story in which God tells Abraham to offer his son as a burnt sacrifice.[19] Today, we would say that the idea of killing people because God said to get rid of them so they wouldn't be a bad influence on us was pure evil. God would never say that. Just about anyone from any church would tell you in an

---

[18] For example, Numbers 31:12–18; Joshua 6:17; 8:2, 25–27; see also Deuteronomy 13:6–18.
[19] Genesis 22:1–14

instant that if you think God is telling you to kill someone, you don't know how to distinguish God's voice from other influences and you probably have other serious problems that need to be addressed as well. The situation surrounding the story of Abraham gives rise to an even more pronounced problem. Not only would we say that the idea of God asking someone to sacrifice their child today is horrific, but even within Old Testament times, we see that the law supposedly given by God to Moses forbids human sacrifice and that the practice of child sacrifice in pagan worship is called an abomination.[20]

When asked why God would tell his people to do things that he would later forbid, an answer that one might give is that these commands didn't violate the moral senses of the times. Abraham was asked to sacrifice his son in a time when sacrificing children to deities wasn't shocking and before God gave the law that specified which religious practices were acceptable and which weren't, and Israel was told to invade the Promised Land long before a social conscience against invasions and wars for profit was developed. God wouldn't tell people to do these things today because he has used the instruments of his direct commands and a natural refining of moral senses to bring people closer to what he always intended. Before this refining had happened, he sometimes worked through the moral shortcomings of the times to accomplish his purposes.

Now, we have a problem here. On one hand we're being told that the Bible gives us an unchanging moral law that we

---

[20] Exodus 13:11–15; Deuteronomy 12:29–31; II Kings 17:16–18, Jeremiah 7:30–31

should follow even when it disagrees with the moral law of our culture. But on the other hand we're being told that God can tell people to do things that directly contradict his own moral standards, such as telling Abraham to sacrifice his son when the law would later reveal that human sacrifice is unacceptable to God or telling Israel to wipe out the pagan nations around them when the New Testament would later introduce a completely nonviolent form of devotion and modern cultures would cement the taboo against religious violence. (And even if we argue that these particular stories are not historical anyway, we still run up against the problem that people believed they were historical for centuries so we still see God allowing people to believe he did things contrary to his nature as if this was good.)

It seems that the standards of morality that God held his people to changed over the course of the writing of the Bible. In light of this, it's a little strange that many churches claim our moral standard should remain the same as what was recorded in the New Testament two thousand years ago. After all, at the time Jesus lived, people who studied the Jewish scriptures and wanted to live by them were scandalized that anyone would suggest that the laws of ritual purity and animal sacrifice they contained were not important—God had specifically instructed Moses that these laws were very important. But New Testament writers would state that these laws were no longer a necessary part of life and had been "fulfilled" by Jesus, and today Christians rarely give them a second thought. The New Testament overturned centuries of devotion to scripture by claiming that God's people should continue to follow the spirit of these laws— love and justice—in a more intuitive and "Spirit led" way rather than maintaining that God required adherence to the specifics. Today, from what I can see, the church appears to be divided over the question of whether this principle of evolving moral standards ended with the New Testament or not.

The convolution of the issue gets deeper as well. As I mentioned, the churches I was part of took the stance that we should still live fairly literally by biblical morals today and claimed that the Bible's moral standard was perfect and unchanging, despite the problems I've just mentioned. But while claiming this, they simultaneously held views that are equivalent to saying that some commands, even those found in the New Testament, can be overlooked.

As Section #3 mentioned, one of these churches disregarded biblical instruction about the place of women in ministry because they felt it couldn't apply to them and that God was leading them in a different direction. They were able to justify the existence of the command by saying that it was meant only for a specific time and place and by citing examples of people in the Bible who seem to be spoken of positively while not following this command. But this sort of argument could be made about almost any command. For example, the Old Testament speaks positively of a widowed woman who seduces her father-in-law in order to become pregnant when he fails to provide her with another husband to give her children—because that's how strong the cultural importance of children and family lines was (Genesis 38). Could this perhaps be used to say that some laws of sexual conduct found in the Bible aren't really as important as the cultural values of the day?

A command that was more universally ignored among the churches I attended was the command to obey governments and view them as having received their authority from God (Romans 13:1–7; Matthew 22:15–22; I Peter 2:11–17). Even though this command is clearly stated, the general feeling seemed to be that it just couldn't be right, at least not all the time.

The conflict in my mind centered around the history of the American Revolution. I had heard many spiritual leaders say that you should always obey the government unless doing so would require going against God's laws. That seemed to line up with what the Bible said. Well, the Bible didn't specifically state the "unless..." part, but adding that condition seemed like a reasonable interpretation. But whether the command was to always obey or to obey unless told to do ungodly things, the fact was that the American Revolution would have to be viewed as unbiblical either way. It represented a case of people rebelling in armed conflict against their government because their interests weren't being fairly represented. Their desire for self-determination could hardly be played off as a refusal to comply with an unbiblical law, especially when the New Testament specifically told Christians to pay their taxes to the Roman Empire without listing any exceptions for cases in which they didn't benefit fairly from what was done with the money (Romans 13:1–7).

With the advantage of hindsight, I'd have to say that the American Revolution was a good thing, but if I had lived at the time it took place, could I have justified it according to the standards of biblical interpretation I was taught growing up? Probably not. I can only guess that the church that taught me these standards while also speaking of the American Revolution as if God were on the side of the revolutionaries simply overlooked the contradiction. The positive historical outcomes and generations of culture celebrating the effort to gain independence made this church unable to see the American Revolution as something that could contradict their values.

Another problematic command found in several places throughout the New Testament instructs slaves to obey their masters.

Ephesians 6:5–6 NIV
Slaves, obey your earthly masters with respect and fear, and with sincerity of heart, just as you would obey Christ. Obey them not only to win their favor when their eye is on you, but as slaves of Christ, doing the will of God from your heart.

Colossians 3:22 NIV
Slaves, obey your earthly masters in everything; and do it, not only when their eye is on you and to curry their favor, but with sincerity of heart and reverence for the Lord.

I Timothy 6:1–2 NIV
All who are under the yoke of slavery should consider their masters worthy of full respect, so that God's name and our teaching may not be slandered. Those who have believing masters should not show them disrespect just because they are fellow believers. Instead, they should serve them even better because their masters are dear to them as fellow believers and are devoted to the welfare of their slaves.

Titus 2:9–10 NIV
Teach slaves to be subject to their masters in everything, to try to please them, not to talk back to them, and not to steal from them, but to show that they can be fully trusted, so that

in every way they will make the teaching about God our Savior attractive.

I Peter 2:18–20 NIV
Slaves, in reverent fear of God submit yourselves to your masters, not only to those who are good and considerate, but also to those who are harsh. For it is commendable if someone bears up under the pain of unjust suffering because they are conscious of God. But how is it to your credit if you receive a beating for doing wrong and endure it? But if you suffer for doing good and you endure it, this is commendable before God.

Today it would be unthinkable to accept slavery even if slaves were treated well and the system was based on economic status instead of racial prejudice or sexual exploitation. In contrast to the modern view, the passages above instruct masters to treat their slaves well but do not introduce the idea that people shouldn't own other people.

To defend the existence of these passages, the argument will probably be made that slavery in the Roman Empire was much different from the abusive systems we think of first in modern times and, while it may not have been ideal, it was an established cultural institution that couldn't just be gotten rid of quickly, so giving these instructions was just as important then as telling employees to do their best at work is today; therefore, the Bible doesn't actually give any support for modern forms of slavery, which are completely different systems from the one it addressed.

However, in order to make an argument like this, one has to use a variety of tools to interpret the biblical command and decide whether it applies to a particular situation. To reach the conclusion that the Bible does not support modern slavery, the person making the argument has to bring in historical knowledge about what biblical authors would have meant when they talked about slavery and then employ their reasoning abilities to decide whether two situations described with similar language really are similar enough for this command to apply to both. Through the process of interpreting this command, they conclude that there are people called slaves who are fully justified in disobeying people called masters even though the explicitly stated command found in the Bible is for slaves to obey their masters.

This example demonstrates that, although people say that the Bible provides an unchanging moral standard, we can't assume that this standard is recorded to a level of detail that makes interpretation unnecessary. It is up to us to figure out just how similar our situation today must be to the situations that surrounded various biblical commands before the commands can be said to apply to us. In practice, this often means going with what feels right because, as the examples covered in Section #3 show, two people with opposing convictions can put together two opposing interpretations of the Bible that are both well supported by history, logic, other parts of the Bible, personal experience, and so on.[21]

---

[21] And before you go saying that the example I've just given seems like such a cut and dry way to figure out what a command means, consider that when people in the United States owned slaves there were some Christians who used parts of the Bible to justify modern slavery. For example, consider an argument mentioned by Frederick Douglass in his *Narrative of the Life of Frederick Douglass, an American Slave*: "[...] it is nevertheless plain that a very different-looking class of people are

Our decisions usually come down to saying that certain instructions aren't for us because how *could* they be—they just sound wrong.

Usually this is a decision that was made generations ago, probably not even deliberately, so that we today have grown up taking for granted the assumption that certain commands are not important and others are. We don't even stop to think about why we have always read over some commands without feeling that they are meant for us. In fact, our views might seem so obvious that we think others would immediately categorize commands the same way we do.

However, instead of looking back on history to see that God's people have always had a uniquely enlightened sense of morals that the rest of the world would have to discover slowly over the millennia as they became more culturally aware of what caused suffering to other beings, we see that God's people were fine with things like slavery and conquest when the world was fine with them, divided on them when the world was divided, and reliably against them only when the cultural tides of their nations had finally turned against them.

---

springing up at the south, and are now held in slavery, from those originally brought to this country from Africa; and if their increase will do no other good, it will do away the force of the argument, that God cursed Ham, and therefore American slavery is right. If the lineal descendants of Ham are alone to be scripturally enslaved, it is certain that slavery at the south must soon become unscriptural; for thousands are ushered into the world, annually, who, like myself, owe their existence to white fathers, and those fathers most frequently their own masters" (Penguin Classics 1986, pg. 50).

Instead of seeing a permanent code of conduct whose clarity distinguishes it from the muddy morals of the world, we see a confusing history in which God is said to have told people to do things, such as killing a child, that he would later forbid as contrary to his nature, or to give success to people rebelling against government authorities even after he specifically told his people to obey such authorities.

Instead of a law that replaces the need for human beings to figure out what is right, we see a law that still needs to be interpreted according to human thinking and access to background information. We are told that we should follow the commands of scripture whether they fit into our culture or not, but the fact is that in practice we see culture superseding scripture. If an all-knowing being had actually seen a need to give humanity a law-of-all-laws because our ability to determine morals culturally was insufficient, then we would expect that this law would lessen the confusion that surrounds moral choices rather than adding to it.

(2) You're not supposed to actually depend on God to provide for you.

I've heard thousands of sermons in my life, and a good chunk of them were about a topic often titled "managing expectations" or "guarding your heart against bitterness." What these terms actually mean is "preparing yourself for the inevitable fact that God is going to fail you."

While constantly being told that God would always provide for me I was also given a long list of exceptions to what "provide" actually meant in this very special and technical usage. For one, God's provision was said to come in the form of giving you what is best for you, not necessarily what you ask for, and what is best for you might look a lot different from what you expect. For example, you might ask God to protect you or someone else, but it might actually be best for you or that person to get injured or killed; therefore if someone gets injured or killed you cannot say that God didn't provide for them.

Another specification was that God's provision would come at the right time, and not before, and that if now was not the right time, you might or might not be given the privilege of knowing the reasons why. For example, you might pray for a family member to come to know Jesus or for yourself to become more disciplined about budgeting. If nothing happens, it's not because God isn't providing for this need; it's because it isn't time yet (for an unspecified reason) or because there's something else that needs to happen first (often something unspecified) or perhaps because you haven't done something you're supposed to do yet (in which case at least you usually get to know what the holdup is; although it is possible you'll think you know what it is but then still see nothing happen after you've taken care of it).

In addition to God's provision not looking much like provision, it also doesn't look much like it comes from God in many cases. Take the budgeting example. You want to be more responsible with money, so you ask God to help you. If you later go to your pastor and say that you've been praying to be wiser with money and haven't improved, he (or she?!) is going to ask what practical steps you've been taking. If you haven't found a non-supernatural source of instruction on how to budget and taken actions such as developing a plan together with other finite beings, your pastor is going to say of course you can't expect anything to have happened then. When we say God is our father, we don't mean the kind of father who explains things to his children when they ask him directly. When it comes to provision of information too, God's children have to look for some mortal go-between who has what they need. In other words, they have to do the providing themselves and then thank God that they weren't somehow prevented from getting what they needed—or, if they were prevented, they have to choose between concluding that this is God's way of telling them to wait, blaming themselves for not having done something right, or finding something positive that came from the situation and telling themselves that this was the real point all along.

The bottom line is that when you trust God to provide, the word "provide" is basically meaningless. It doesn't mean that God will fulfill the request you made or even that he will clearly give an answer explaining why it wasn't a proper request. You may be left uncertain of whether you are in a waiting period or whether God has said no or whether some seemingly unrelated occurrence is actually God's answer. And while it does make sense that provision would mean ensuring that you have what you need, not necessarily what you want, there is no verifiable way in which people who pray for God's provision can be said to always receive what they need. Parents caring for children might deny them a lot of wants but still keep them safe and prepare them for life, and so they are providing for their children. But when we claim that God always provides his children with what they need, the standard of what qualifies as a need is stretched so far as to go beyond the scope of life itself. If a parent could save their child's life and did not do so, this parent could not be said to have provided appropriate care for their child. But when God allows his people to be murdered or killed in freak accidents we are told that this is not a failure of provision. He guaranteed them eternal life, and that is what's most important, so he can use their death to accomplish a greater good without it being any different from a parent who requires a child to do homework and eat vegetables. Since we can't prove that the promise of life after death is even real, what we are left with is the realization that God's provision is not provision at all but simply a choice to look on the bright side of things, a choice that could be made just the same without belief in God being a factor.

Adding yet another level of frustration is an attitude I would summarize as "Trust God to provide—but don't be stupid about it." Not only are we told that every situation a faithful Christian finds themselves in, including being cheated, neglected, tortured, or killed, counts as God's provision, but at the same time we are told that it's stupid to expect God to do what you ask. People talk as if this is a good attitude to have because it means that you can't go around making bad choices and expecting God to magically fix everything for you—and I'll agree that it is good not to think of things in that way. However, there is a problematic side to this idea as well.

Just think about what is really going on when you have a group of people preaching that there is a divine being who is your father, who loves you like a child, who wants to know you, who wants to interact with you and not remain aloof, whose miraculous power is unleashed by faith, and upon whom you are supposed to depend for all your needs—but then this group criticizes you for not being smart and discerning if you feel that God wants you to do street evangelism in a bad part of town or donate all your money to a missionary. Does God actually communicate with people in a way they can recognize and ask them to take wild leaps of faith and provide for them all the way, or doesn't he? The answer given verbally is yes, while the answer absorbed through experience is no.

It wouldn't be a problem that God's provision differed from what people usually mean by "provision" if true divine communication were a part of the picture. If, when people didn't receive what they prayed for, they instead received an answer stating clearly that they needed to wait or ask for something different or pursue another course of action first, it would all be fine. This would be no different from the parent–child relationship Christianity is supposed to resemble because, while the children don't always get what they want, they do experience communication in regards to their requests. There is a two-sided exchange of information constituting a relationship, and over time the children learn the principles that explain why their parents say no to certain things. However, relationship and exchange of information are exactly what we do not see when it comes to the topic of God's provision, and this is why there is such a demand for sermons preparing people not to become bitter when they experience circumstances that look exactly like what we would expect if there were no one listening to their prayers.

It's easy to see why people would feel tempted to respond in anger when they realize that, no matter what state of lack and need they find themselves in, it will always be called God's provision. It's not hard to see why they feel bitter after pastors tell them that God can do anything and wants to put all the resources of heaven at their disposal but then call them simplistic and irresponsible for naively concluding that this means God might actually do something they ask him to do.

People are simultaneously being told that God will provide and that he won't, and the clear reason why this frustrating act goes on is that for centuries humans have needed a way to keep believing in God in the face of multitudinous failures of provision. It's easier to twist the meaning of a word past recognition than to accept that you have no source of divine help to depend on, but you have to ask if this supposed sense of security is really worth the constant vexation you go through to get it.

(3) You're not supposed to actually expect God to be present in your life.

At a point where I felt I had to keep asking my spiritual leaders why I couldn't find a connection with God, one of them asked me in return if I actually wanted God or if I just wanted an experience. I'll tell you now, it's not a good sign when you're expected to believe you have a relationship with someone without ever having an experience of that person. This is yet another point in regards to which the publicly stated belief and the belief found by inside experience oppose each other.

The importance of God's presence in our lives is preached loud and clear on Sunday mornings. We sing songs about the wonders of being in God's presence, and we're told that we should seek simply to know and enjoy God as a personal being more than we seek to receive good things from him or to hear him telling us what to do.

However, when you start asking around about where you can find God in your life and what it's actually like to experience him or sense his presence, you are quickly made to feel like a naughty chocolate-faced child denying that you've eaten Mom's candy. It's rounds and rounds of, "Aren't you just after an experience? Aren't you failing to exercise faith? Aren't you trying to manipulate God into doing things your way?" As you insist that none of this is the case, you're answered with accusations of, "Then why are you chasing after feelings?"

But people in this situation are not silly children trying to deny some mischief they've gotten into. Not at all—no matter how persistently their frustrated spiritual advisors try to make the questions go away by turning the blame back on the person who wants to find God. These people are, like I was, desperate to meet this loving father they've been told is the most wonderful person in all of existence. When I thought there was a hope of somehow experiencing even a moment of God's presence, I would have done anything to get it. As Chapter 1 describes, I did do anything I had reason to think might work.

I didn't see how this yearning for interaction was any different from the attitude that other Christians praised so highly in the Psalms (Psalm 42:1 NKJV *As the deer pants for the water brooks, so pants my soul for You, O God*). But apparently it was selfish and manipulative. It was me trying to use God to get something I wanted. Now, it still doesn't make sense to me how this could have been a problem since the thing I wanted was *a relationship with God*, but people will think what they have to think to avoid seeing anything that indicates God's absence.

You will be told from just about every source imaginable that seeking God's presence is the best thing you can do, but then when you can't find it and you ask for help, you will be told that God's presence is already with you and if you aren't aware of it you must actually be looking for something else. But, even if I can only speak for myself, I can tell you that at least in my own case I was looking to know God and nothing else would do. If it had been just social interaction I was after, I would have looked to people. I would have actually spent time with friends and family instead of shutting myself in my room for hours on end searching for connection with God.

But human interaction wasn't what I was looking for, and neither was any other experience. I had to have this closeness with God I had heard of, and whatever I thought might facilitate this connection, I did. Eventually I even tried backing off and not pursuing it so hard because a friend told me that that had worked for her. But no matter what I tried, I never became aware of any presence, personal connection, relationship, or anything of the sort. And to cap it all off, when I got to the point where I was really doubting whether anything I had believed was true, I realized that even the people around me who talked about having a very tangible relationship with God didn't really sense or hear him as clearly as I had thought.

As I lost more reasons for faith, I started being more persistent in asking people how they related to God, hoping I would find something that would work for me. Dishearteningly though, as soon as they were pressed for specifics, people were quick to say things like, "I don't really know, maybe it's just my imagination, but I think God speaks to me by..." and they would describe a process that was indeed not marked by anything that necessarily distinguished it from their own thoughts. As this kept happening, I started to feel like everyone believed in God's communication because they thought others were experiencing it, and that it only seemed like others were experiencing it because everyone thought having faith meant believing things that might have been nothing special were actually God's voice and then talking about them as if you were sure you had heard God's voice.

I could have done that too—and I did sometimes for periods of at least months at a time. I could have kept telling myself to be content with saying that finding useful advice in the Bible meant I was hearing from God, even though anyone who meditates on any text can get instruction in the same way. I could have kept telling myself that the fact I was able to learn things from various life circumstances meant God was talking to me, even though anyone who took time to reflect on life could do the same thing. I could have told myself to be satisfied with hearing about the experiences of a few super Christians who sounded sure God was speaking to them miraculously. But the reason why my stamina for telling myself these sorts of things always gave out after a while was that these things just weren't satisfying. They didn't seem anything like the vibrant relationship I had been encouraged to pursue. People talked about God being their joy and their closest friend, but from what I had experienced he seemed like someone very far away sending out generic messages that could have come from anyone. There had to be more. But when I asked about it and then answered people's questions about what I had tried so far and for how long I had been trying it, I was told to either settle for the disappointing, lonely state I was stuck in or admit to being manipulative.

Since that time, as I've thought over other related experiences, I've realized that there were other red flags showing that people didn't really mean what they said about God being present with us when it came down to it. It wasn't just in my own private conversations that this sentiment came out; when I thought about it, there was one thing that people who publicly instructed others on hearing from God had always made clear, and it was that you can't trust what you hear to actually come from God at all. I had heard many sermons and read a couple books on the subject of discerning God's voice, and in the end they all seemed to agree that if the subject you're discussing with God is something that's actually important, you'd better not assume that you know the difference between his voice and your own imagination.

For example, a couple of the churches I attended encouraged people to pray for each other and ask God for "words of knowledge" or "prophetic words" to share with each other.[22] But the church leaders set some very clear boundaries about what could be said during these times. (And thank goodness

---

[22] In my experience, people used "words of knowledge" to refer to pieces of information revealed supernaturally by the Holy Spirit. For example, someone might say that they prayed for a word of knowledge for a person they just met and the Holy Spirit revealed to them that the person was having problems with their family. The name "prophetic words" or "prophecy" was applied to a broader range of things, pretty much any declaration of truth, whether general or specific. I heard it used most often when people gave statements of encouragement or comfort based on scriptural principles.

they did! I've heard disaster stories from churches who did the same thing without rules.) For one, we were not supposed to say anything negative because if we did and it turned out not to have been from God, that could really mess someone up. We also weren't supposed to give people advice about relationships, or any very specific advice at all for that matter. All we were really supposed to do was share encouraging words because we knew for certain that God loves everyone and wants good things for them, so there was no way we could go wrong by sticking to this safe topic.

It would seem that if God's voice was actually something distinguishable from one's own thoughts, those who encourage others to listen for it would focus on explaining the characteristics of this voice[23] rather than on making sure that people only really trust it to be God under circumstances in which it doesn't matter if they're wrong.

To give another example, just as those who want to share God's words with others can only trust what they hear to come from God at times when it doesn't matter if they're right or wrong, those who want to know God's will for their own life are told to take the same precautions. If you actually have a life decision to make, it isn't enough to ask God what to do and get an answer. You need to get confirmation on the answer too. For one thing, if a message you think came from God contradicts anything said in the Bible, it's not

---

[23] When characteristics are explained, they are either things that do nothing to distinguish God's voice from your thoughts (e.g. it is quiet and not pushy, or it is different at different times) or the description is something like, "When God speaks, you just *know* it's him." If this second one were true though, we wouldn't need to establish all these boundaries to protect people from oopsy prophecies.

actually from God. For another, if you think God is telling you to do anything that seems a little unusual or risky you'd better get confirmation from your spiritual leaders and other important people in your life before you go ahead with it. And of course, if you think God told you to do something but circumstances keep making it impossible, perhaps what you heard wasn't really God's voice and God is actually using these roadblocks to lead you in a different direction.

What this all comes down to is that you have a book of instruction and are surrounded by a community of people who try to live by it, and you also have ideas passing through your head, and if these ideas don't contradict the book and don't seem unacceptable to the community, then they are said to come from God. Like I mentioned at the end of Section #3, there are also several ways to explain away any errors that result from this system, such as saying that you only thought you were hearing God tell you something because it was what you wanted to hear or that God did tell you something and if what he said led to a situation that is not good, he was probably trying to teach you patience by putting you in that situation.

My point is that those who listen for God's voice in the hopes of finding connection and relationship are likely to once again be disappointed. There is nothing akin to conversation here. You will never really know this voice, although you'll be told you do know it (at the very same time that you're being told to always double-check what you think it's saying with others). You will only know what it's like to have thoughts and run them through the filter of your community.

God's presence and voice are supposed to be part of your life, but, according to some people, they should be there without your actually experiencing them. At least, if you haven't experienced them and you feel dissatisfied with the fact that your "relationship" with God isn't any different from something made purely of imagination, you'll be told that you are doing something wrong, wanting something you shouldn't want. You should want God to be present in your life. But not really. If "presence" to you includes any aspect of reality, of actually interacting with a personal being, then you are asking too much. Never mind that this sort of loving interaction is held up as the pinnacle of the Christian life; if you have consistently looked for it and not found it, the only honorable thing for you to do is admit that there was something wrong with your wants and not disturb the rest of the community with your leading questions.

(4) You're not supposed to actually think about life in the way the Bible and church traditions suggest you should.

At times, it seemed to me that Christianity was becoming more and more atheistic over the years. Some of this was just because the church I attended growing up was more conservative than the churches I attended as an adult, but some of it is probably due to actual shifts in thinking across the board. My experiences are subjective, but to me it felt like the church was consistently shifting more responsibility off of God and onto man. Regardless of whether that is a churchwide trend though, it's certainly true that I attended churches where the message was preached that God wanted to interact closely, powerfully, and miraculously with people through his Holy Spirit but where it was also common to preach messages along the lines of, "We need to stop waiting for God to do X for us and do it ourselves." For example, "You all need to stop waiting around for God to drop the perfect spouse into your life and go meet people if you don't want to be single forever."

That one's an example we can laugh at a bit and say isn't it silly that some people think romance is this strange and special area of life where they have to let God do everything—but on some levels it's not all that funny. For one thing, some people really do think this because they've been told it all their lives, whether in a direct or in a roundabout way.[24] And for another, it represents a pattern of behavior on the part of the church that shouldn't be overlooked: People are encouraged to depend on God until spiritual leaders realize that dependence on God isn't getting people anywhere, and then these leaders or the next generation of leaders start preaching that we've all been ridiculous and irresponsible to think God would take care of things for us.

In regards to this romance example, at the church I grew up in, I was used to hearing messages and stories with the moral that putting effort into finding romance showed a lack of faith. Good Christians didn't worry about finding the right person for themselves; they just did whatever work God called them to do, trusting that he would bring the right

---

[24] One thing that makes me sad is knowing I have friends who would love to be married and aren't yet either because they think it's mostly up to God to make that happen or because they think that for the time being God is asking them to focus on some pursuit that makes it difficult for them to start a relationship. If they really do want to focus on something other than relationships, more power to them, but if they're struggling to pray their way out of discontentment or sadness over what they think God is asking them to do with their lives, how I wish they could realize they're free to order their own priorities!

person to them at the right time. But at a church I started attending in my early twenties, many of the members had come from backgrounds where they had been told similar things, and almost all of us were single. (Most of them were older than me.) The pastors were very aware that this arrangement didn't line up with the command for humans to "be fruitful and multiply" (which they told us meant quite literally that we should have a lot of kids besides any and all figurative meanings it might have) and so they diligently preached on the importance of human responsibility, of pursuing what was important to you and making things happen, and of trying online dating if you had to.

These messages always included a bit of rhetorical questioning along the lines of, "Why do we think we should just wait for God to act in this part of our lives?" But that's the problem. We think that because we've always been told it, and it makes sense because we've also always been told to pray about major decisions and follow God's will, so when it comes to a decision as big as who to marry, can we risk any possible interference from our own ways? If it wasn't for the fact that waiting on God to lead us in this area just doesn't work in today's world, it would probably sound like great advice. But this pattern repeats over and over again: There is a way of handling a situation that makes sense according to Christian beliefs, and sometimes this course of action is embraced by more traditional churches, but in newer churches and movements that seem to be touching people's hearts and changing their lives more effectively than the older ones, you will be told that this course of action clearly isn't from God because it doesn't work, and you will be offered a more practical and useful course of action that looks a lot like one that non-Christians usually depend on.

This is all somewhat ironically highlighted by talk among various churches about relevance. The churches I attended, from the most conservative to the most progressive one, all wanted Christianity to be relevant, and when the topic was brought up, it was always with wringing of hands over the comparatively low level of influence Christian values and ideas seemed to have on people today when compared to secular ones. All these churches said that because Christians knew the person who had created the world, we should be the most innovative and influential people on the planet. Who else had the privilege of communing with someone who knew everything about every part of life? After spending time with God, we should be overflowing with creative ideas that would revolutionize the world time after time.

And that's just it. That's exactly how things should work if people were actually getting to know a being who created everything, but things don't work that way. Instead, churches keep needing to look to secular trends for new ideas to revitalize them or allow them to deal with real problems in practical ways. I'm not saying that there aren't Christians who come up with good and influential ideas or that Christianity doesn't have characteristics that encourage creativity and exploration, but I am saying that I don't see evidence of a correlation between the amount of time a person spends "with God" and their level of inspiration and enlightenment about life in general.

We've already covered one good example of this: Many people at the church I was raised in, certainly including the leadership, were devoted to studying the Bible and spending regular time in prayer and other activities they felt brought them close to God, but the atmosphere at this church was one in which women were generally encouraged to stick to traditionally feminine roles in life and environmental concerns were viewed with suspicion or flatly dismissed. These attitudes shouldn't be difficult to understand because, while the Bible does mention a few influential women, it nevertheless gives a *general* picture in which men hold roles of power and women support them. And while we can pull out themes of environmental stewardship from many biblical teachings, the Bible also talks about God having the end of the world planned out and maintaining the cycles of nature until then. For hundreds of years, the church harmonized with what we see in the Bible, with the inhabitants of the Christian-influenced Western world mostly following defined gender roles and without any early revelation from God to warn us about modern environmental concerns until they were upon us.

Members of many churches, though, hold ideas that have been updated to fit the times, and so they end up acting out the routine of ascribing all authority to God as long as human beings who they approve of are the ones making the calls on which pieces of doctrine have truly come from God: You're supposed to listen to what the Bible and the church teach you, but then there are times when these teachings conflict with modern morals or just don't work, and so as not to behave in a way you know is immoral or remain stuck in an impractical approach to life, you need to replace those teachings with others, but because God is never wrong and doesn't change, you also can't say that the old teachings your church followed were actually from God—and thus we arrive at a place in which we write off past generations or even our contemporaries as being stubborn and unwilling to listen to God while we ourselves are exceptionally open-eared and soft-hearted to the leading of the Spirit and have finally managed to hear what God was saying after all these years. Yay us! We break ourselves out of predicaments or achieve relevance by doing what works and then identifying scriptural principles that align with it and reinterpreting conflicting passages so that they no longer apply to us (while conflicting principles can always be re-explained as not actually being principles at all but rather collections of individual passages that only seem to contain enough information to outline an underlying principle if you in your human stubbornness insist on grouping them together.)

Just as biblical morals don't change and yet they do, and as God will provide for you but not actually "provide," and as God will be with you but not actually "be" "with" you, in general it's just not right for you to think the Bible means what it says or that the church knows what it's doing. You are stupid, your church family will tell you between the lines, if you thought you could actually trust what you were taught about any of these things and plan your actions accordingly. You are bad if you obeyed the words of your leaders and things didn't work out—Didn't you hear God telling you that that was the right time to rebel? Oh, you thought that was the devil because everything you'd ever been taught said that when a voice prompts you to rebel against what the Bible or the church says, it's the devil? Well, you should have known better. You should have just known.

All of the problems we've discussed here come down to different groups of people telling each other that they should *just know*. If there was a real person keeping the church in line with a real standard of conduct, this confusion shouldn't exist, but it does exist. You will always have other

Christians telling you that the way you think the Bible and the church say to understand life is flawed, and you'll have to choose: Do you believe your conclusion or theirs? I suppose the most important takeaway from these four subsections, besides the venting of the frustrations of so many docile, self-chastising parishioners, is to ask yourself what criteria you use to decide. Is the thing that tips the scale one way or the other the voice of God? Or is it familiarity, fear, compassion, or any other human motivation that could lead different people to different decisions without the need for any of us to single out ourselves or our group as the one special entity who truly hears from God?

3. Truth vs. Manipulation

Romans 1:18–22 NKJV
… the wrath of God is revealed from heaven against all ungodliness and unrighteousness of men, who suppress the truth in unrighteousness, because what may be known of God is manifest in them, for God has shown it to them. For since the creation of the world His invisible attributes are clearly seen, being understood by the things that are made, even His eternal power and Godhead, so that they are without excuse, because, although they knew God, they did not glorify Him as God, nor were thankful, but became futile in their thoughts, and their foolish hearts were darkened. Professing to be wise, they became fools…

The realization that claims of God's love and desire for personal relationship could not be reconciled with my observations of the world, or with the doctrines of salvation and hell, convinced me that Christianity was not a divinely communicated message of truth but a body of brilliant and yet human-made teachings on love collected around a core of ancient Jewish ideas on morality, justice, mercy, atonement, election, and divine judgment of evil. While the claim of perfect judgment and the gospel of love were well-intentioned and powerful, they seemed at their deeper levels to be in contradiction with undeniable facts about how human beings access information. This discrepancy could only be resolved if God as a person interacted with the individual, and I was coming to realize more and more that I was surrounded by people whose reason for believing in this interaction came down to nothing more than the impression that other people were experiencing it.

I would guess that there are many people out there in Evangelical communities, going through the same doubts and frustrations I experienced—asking themselves the same questions about why their "relationship" with God seems so one-sided and what they could possibly be doing wrong—but just like me, they may fight with obvious contradictions for years without ever realizing them for what they are. Why is this? Well, while there may be less incendiary names for the psychological phenomenon I finally recognized as the culprit in my own experiences, I'll call it by the name I think fits it best: gaslighting.

Gaslighting is a form of psychological manipulation in which an abuser, the gaslighter, seeks to control a victim by causing the victim to question their own sanity. By destroying victims' trust in their own ability to understand reality and in the good intentions of the people around them, gaslighters are able to set themselves up as the only source of truth in their victims' lives, creating a state of dependence in which the victims believe they must rely on the gaslighters in order to navigate life successfully. In addition to attacks on victims' sense of sanity, gaslighting also tends to include attacks on victims' sense of worth. Gaslighters try to make victims feel incompetent at life and unworthy of love so that they come to believe their abuser is the only person who will value them and do not turn to outside sources for help or comfort.

In Christianity, there is no intentional campaign of gaslighting and no villain. The perpetrators themselves are ongoing victims who sincerely think they are looking out for the best interests of those they bring into the cycle of abuse. There is no one to blame for the outcome. But that doesn't change the fact that the outcome is nevertheless a state in which people will more readily question their own perceptions of reality than they will seriously consider the possibility that God might not exist, and in which they believe that they are unworthy of love and deserving of hell, that their good works are "like filthy rags" to

God and that they as people only gain worth because God gives it to them, that they don't deserve success in life and that any good thing they receive or accomplish is a gift of God because they couldn't have done it on their own and yet any bad thing that happens to them can't be blamed on God and is just a result of sin in the world, which is ultimately our own fault as humans because we are all guilty of Adam's sin.

To someone who was never taught to believe in God, it might seem obvious that there is a contradiction between the idea that God loves humanity and has always wanted the best for us and the idea that all people were counted guilty because one person sinned. It might seem obvious that the concept of sin coming into the world because of one person's wrong choice was made up in order to answer questions about how God could be good and yet create a world with so much evil and suffering. But to those of us who were taught from infancy that God is good, loving, just, and unchanging, these things are almost impossible to see. The thought that something seems unjust crosses our mind, but because we *know* God is just, we only look for a way to redefine what justice is and never consider that the idea of a just God and the idea of original sin might have been made up by people who didn't see the contradictions.

The same pattern is repeated over and over again: Because it is unthinkable that God might not be kind or fair or even real, we question our ideas of what kindness and fairness truly are or re-set the criteria necessary to accept something as real. We ignore evidence that points toward the conclusion that our beliefs are flawed, and if the evidence itself can't be denied we question the validity of the logic that leads to the conclusion drawn from it instead. Frequently, the corrupting influences of sin on the human mind are cited as an explanation for why seemingly sound logic could fail to lead to a correct conclusion. We are told that sin has corrupted our sense of what is good and fair and that God's ways are beyond our ways. God's plan might not seem just to us now, but that is only because we can't see the entire picture. Our intellect has also been corrupted and so, no matter how logical an argument against God's existence might seem, we have to conclude that it is wrong and that our reasoning skills are leading us astray in this instance.

When I reached the point at which the theological contradictions I had noticed were too obvious to overlook and I was starting to lose hope of being able to believe in God with any satisfying level of certainty, I still felt as if I couldn't stop believing either, like I would always be stuck in limbo. This was because my emotions remained in contradiction to what I could see was true. I could not have made a convincing argument that God was real—all my experience and understanding of the world and scripture contradicted that idea—but I still felt fear of punishment, fear that I was being ungrateful, fear that I was a bad person. My emotions were screaming that I was walking away from my only source of safety, and that emotional pressure was hard to ignore. That's why I've devoted this chapter to explaining the elements of gaslighting that can be part of the Christian experience: Once I started to realize that my emotions were the result of a particular type of psychological manipulation and not an accurate representation of reality, everything changed for me. This is what finally gave me peace of mind and the ability to live my life without daily anxiety, so I want to encourage discussion of this phenomenon as much as possible in case it helps someone else.

Listed below are several short statements and suggestions representing ideas used to keep Christians from changing their beliefs. (Remember, I'm not saying that this is a plot devised by any party to deceive another. People say these things with the best of intentions, but the effect is still to produce a gaslighting situation.) Some of these ideas cause people to doubt their perception of reality. Some have the effect of cutting them off from sources of contradictory information, for example by teaching mistrust of non-Christians. Some target people's sense of worth and competence. Some make them feel that they are ungrateful, selfish, and arrogant if they think God is not good. All are things that I learned in church or from Christian media produced for the purpose of apologetics. I hope that if people can understand the emotional effects these ways of thinking produce they will also be able to find freedom from them.

A: "Everyone has an innate knowledge of God, but some people deny it."

This statement is the very foundation upon which much of the psychological manipulation is based. It is a cure-all to answer almost any challenge to the idea that God is just, and because it makes a claim about a phenomenon that takes place within the minds of others, it is impossible to disprove. It serves the purpose both of making the victim believe that anyone who disagrees with the gaslighter is a liar and of making the victim question their own sanity if they feel that the statement is not true. This is why I have emphasized so insistently that in my search for God I took every precaution I knew of against lying to myself. I can't prove fully to anyone else that that is true, but I can offer the evidence of the sincerity with which I searched for God, always expecting that I would find him in the end, and the fact that I prayed repeatedly over the years that if I was deceiving myself in some way God would bring it to light.

If the claim that everyone actually knows certain Christian ideas are true remains unquestioned, it is a powerful tool for keeping people from changing their beliefs. God is always shown to be just in punishing people because it can always be said that people willfully disobeyed him rather than doing the best they could with the information available to them. Whenever a nonbeliever says that their life experiences contradict Christian claims, their arguments can be dismissed with the assertion that they are lying or deluding themselves. If they know God is real and they've started by denying that fact, everything else they say can be explained away as just part of the logical gymnastics they have to do to keep ignoring the truth.

This assertion of humanity's innate knowledge of God is found, according to some people, clearly stated in scripture. Growing up I learned about the concept from sermons on Romans 1, a passage in which Paul begins to explain the role of God's law and of grace in relation to the concepts of sin and salvation. The relevant passage is as follows, with particularly illustrative phrases in bold:

Romans 1:14–23 NKJV
I am a debtor both to Greeks and to barbarians, both to wise and to unwise. So, as much as is in me, I am ready to preach the gospel to you who are in Rome also. For I am not ashamed of the gospel of Christ, for it is the power of God to salvation for everyone who believes, for the Jew first and also for the Greek. For in it the righteousness of God is revealed from faith to faith; as it is written, "The just shall live by faith." For the wrath of God is revealed from heaven against all ungodliness and unrighteousness of men, who **suppress the truth** *in unrighteousness, because* **what may be known of God is manifest in them, for God has shown it to them**. *For since the creation of the world* **His invisible attributes are clearly seen, being understood by the things that are made, even His eternal power and Godhead**, *so that* **they are without excuse**, *because,* **although they knew God, they did not glorify Him as God, nor were thankful**, *but became futile in their thoughts, and their foolish hearts were darkened.* **Professing to be wise, they became fools**, *and changed the glory of the incorruptible God into an image made like corruptible man—and birds and four-footed animals and creeping things.*

Paul continues in this chapter to refer to unrepentant people as those "who exchanged the truth of God for the lie" (v. 25) and "did not like to retain God in their knowledge" (v. 28) and who "knowing the righteous judgment of God, that those who practice such things [*sins listed earlier in the chapter*] are deserving of death, not only do the same but also approve of those who practice them" (v. 32).

In more recent years I have become aware of people who interpret this passage as meaning that everyone is guilty of wrongdoing even by their own standards because everyone sometimes does things that they think are wrong. But I was brought up hearing that when Romans 1:20 said people were "without excuse," it meant that anyone who was familiar with the Christian gospel and did not accept Jesus as the authority over their life had willfully, knowingly rejected God and chosen a path leading to hell. The possibility that these people could not accept Jesus as the authority of their lives because they were unconvinced that he was God was not acknowledged, and neither was the idea that a person could seek truth and come to the conclusion that God did not exist. Because everyone had an innate knowledge of God, people who had not heard of Christianity must still know that there was some divinity they needed to honor and people who had heard of Christianity must recognize that Christian beliefs provided the correct description of that divinity.

In sermons on the topic, pastors sometimes said that the means by which people knew of God's existence and character was something similar to conscience. Just as people had a natural sense of right and wrong, they also had a natural sense that a certain type of divinity must exist. At other times, pastors speaking on the topic said that the physical world was what made the existence of a certain type of divinity obvious. Because the world was God's creation, people automatically had some idea that there was a creator and that the creator had certain character traits. (This take was particularly popular in the church I grew up in, where ideas of creationism and Intelligent Design were heavily promoted as well.) Either way, the message drawn from the passage was clear: Nonbelievers were guilty of "suppressing the truth."

From my perspective, the claim that, deep down, everyone knows about God seems to constitute an entire worldview. It establishes the rules about which sources of information can be trusted and which can't. (Every source that disagrees with Christian claims about God is suspect.) And if I had never come to question this claim, I think it would have been impossible for me to ever change my beliefs. Thankfully, I found the idea of universal innate knowledge of God difficult to believe in. I did believe in it at one point, by choice, because I believed that everything the Bible said was accurate and hadn't thought to question the interpretation of Romans 1 that was familiar to me, but I found it extremely difficult to picture that people who seemed so sincere in their disbelief or in their failure to realize the importance of spiritual things could actually be lying at the bottom of it all.

It seemed impossible to me that people could know about God's existence with nothing more than an inner sense or their observations of nature to teach them. As I've said, looking back on childhood memories it's hard to tell exactly which ideas formed at what times, but my best recollection of the situation is that at some point when I was very young and before I was familiar with the concept of innate knowledge of God, the thought had crossed my mind that I was glad I had grown up knowing about God because I couldn't see myself ever discovering his existence on my own. If I remember correctly, I arrived at this idea by trying to imagine what it would be like to grow up in the wild without other people around. I was guessing all the things I probably wouldn't know if other people had never told me to think about them: I wouldn't know how to speak any language, I would probably never have thought up the idea of drawing a picture of something, and so on. I didn't see any way I could have known about God in such a situation either because I had never experienced God, and I didn't think that without the benefit of living in a society where I constantly saw people making things and studying the structure of the world that it would ever have occurred to me to wonder if the world had been made by someone.

At some point—I believe it was later and not earlier—I also thought over what my life would probably be like if I had been born into a family that believed in a different religion. Since I couldn't imagine changing my mind about what I had been brought up to believe, I figured that if I had grown up with a different religion I would have believed in it just as strongly as I believed in Christianity. At the time, this view didn't make me wonder if I could trust the religion I had been raised with. I still assumed that Christianity was true and thought God must have known I was one of the people who needed to be born into the right religion in order to believe in it rather than one of the people who convert later in life.

Eventually (again, as far as I remember, this was after I had already thought about the two issues above on my own) I was introduced to the idea that everyone knew God existed because they could see design in nature. Because of the conclusions I had already come to, this made no sense. I already took it for granted that God had created the world just like Genesis 1 described, but it didn't seem possible to me that most individuals could look at the world around them and know about God without anyone introducing the concept of God to them. I realized that some people must be able to come up with a question like "Who made the world?" on their own because otherwise the polytheistic religions of most ancient cultures wouldn't have existed, but to come up with that question all on one's own just by looking at a world of surroundings that from the perspective of a human lifespan seems fairly stable and permanent, seemed like an intellectual leap so great that only the Platos of prehistory could have made it.

I don't know if that impression of mine is accurate, but it seemed almost certain to me because I had never experienced the feeling that the world around me must have been designed by someone. I believed it was designed by God because people had told me it was, but the innate sense that struck me when I looked at and thought about the world was one of apparent purposelessness—not that I didn't see beauty or order; I just didn't see the point. I thought it was odd that so many things were so seemingly independent from and so truly oblivious to each other and that events happened in ways that seemed purely random. Maybe there was a purpose behind everything, but I didn't see how I could have ever arrived at that conclusion if no one had told me about it. The strangeness of how my perceptions differed from what I believed to be true based on what people had taught me would come back to puzzle me consistently over the years, sometimes with a wondering bafflement at how the world could be so different from the appearance it gave and sometimes with pure frustration that I couldn't see things in the way I was supposed to. The most frequently recurring mystery was how I could constantly feel so perfectly alone and unable to reach God when everyone told me God was right there with me.

As you can see, I was being taught to question my perception of reality. I was taught that people knew about God without being told. That didn't seem possible, but I knew my understanding of the situation had to be wrong according to what the Bible said (or at least the interpretation of the Bible I had always heard). For most of my life, the only explanation I could think of was that, since I grew up being told about God, I must have missed the natural signs of his existence that would have stood out to me if I hadn't already been expecting them, kind of like how, when you visit a new place, little details that are different from what you're used to jump out at you while the locals have been seeing them every day for their whole lives without even noticing them.

I wouldn't be able to say to what extent other Christians feel what I felt and to what extent they might actually experience a sense of design pointing to God when they observe nature, or some inner conscience-like certainty that God exists. I can only observe that the claim of innate knowledge of divinity is effective at neatly sweeping away people's questions about how God could be just in punishing limited and imperfect beings who fail to realize who he is. It allows people to say that no one experiences God's judgment except by their own choice to reject him, and I would guess that this is ultimately what led Paul to make the statements found in Romans 1 in the first place. Paul was a logical thinker and gifted theologian, and he wanted things to make sense. He was an expert in the Jewish scriptures, and at his time it wouldn't have been difficult to believe in the accuracy of the picture of world history presented there, which includes all humanity being descended from people who knew God. From his perspective, it would have made sense to say that people were without excuse for doing things (as he understood it) as ridiculous as worshipping pieces of carved wood instead of looking for a creator who was greater than the boundaries of the created world.

The sacrifice one has to make today for continuing to benefit from this neat cleanup is of course to accept that anyone who hears the Christian gospel without being convinced by it is a liar—and this is exactly the position many Christians take and hold to. All my life I have heard Christians sadly remark on the state of "deception" or "self-deception" that unbelievers live in and even try to argue atheists into discovering their buried acknowledgement of God's existence, sometimes on the most nonsensical of notions, such as that a person would not use a phrase or concept with a Christian history behind it unless they actually believed in God somewhere deep down. (For example, I once heard someone claim that people acknowledge God every time they say what year it is because we number years according to a system roughly based on when Jesus lived. But by that logic we must also be acknowledging the existence of the Norse gods when we plan anything on a Tuesday through Friday.)

When I've raised the question of how God could be okay with punishing someone who did their best to find truth and came to the "wrong" conclusion, or why he wouldn't give a person like that a sign to help them, I've been told that people only come to the conclusion that God doesn't exist out of arrogance, that they've already been given everything they need to see that God is real, and that even if God had a face-to-face conversation with them they would still choose not to believe in him. However, this doesn't make sense because in the Bible God does appear and have face-to-face conversations with skeptics, and this does change their minds. Look at Paul himself. As the New Testament tells it, Paul was so devoted to the traditions of Jewish law that he thought Jesus was a false prophet. He actively ran from God's pull on his heart and tried to have Christians silenced. But he completely changed his mind when Jesus supernaturally appeared to him.

Despite this, we are asked to believe that someone like, say, Stephen Hawking, who was so devoted to understanding how the universe works that he spent his life studying it, wouldn't have listened if Jesus had supernaturally revealed himself as the source of it all. Paul was an expert in the scriptures of his day. If his deep knowledge of scripture wasn't enough to make him see that Jesus really was the fulfillment of the law and it took a supernatural experience to open his eyes, then why should a person's deep knowledge of physics be enough to make them see God in the laws of the universe without a supernatural revelation?

The correct Christian answer to this question is that God wouldn't judge someone unfairly, so if Stephen Hawking could have been convinced by a supernatural experience he would have been given one. We can't dispute this possibility since it's all hypothetical, but at the same time there's something unsatisfying about it. There are nonbelievers like Paul and many others who eventually come to believe in God, and there are those who don't. Are the ones who eventually change *not* lying to themselves before they come to believe? Are they honestly mistaken while the ones who never change are the self-deceived ones? If so, why didn't they have an innate knowledge of God all along? Or are the people who change just as self-deceived as anyone else before they become believers? And if they are, why does God undeceive them but abandon the others? If we fall back on the proper Christian answers again, we will have to content ourselves with saying that it's not productive to ask why God does anything, his ways are above our ways after all. But this is simply a branch of the manipulation. Despite the fact that the Bible and Christian tradition place great importance on doing what is right, people are taught that they are arrogant when they want to understand why God's ways sometimes appear to oppose what is right. Because there is no resolution to the contradiction, the only way we can protect our beliefs is by telling ourselves that we are in some way a bad person for questioning them in the first place.

Now, the question might come up, if I'm saying that Christian claims of nonbelievers lying to themselves are not true, and I never experienced this innate sense of God that Christians talk about, do I then think that Christians are lying about having felt this sense? No, at least not the vast majority of them. Part of the strength of the claim that God's existence is obvious could lie in the fact that out of all the people who are raised Christian, the ones who easily accept this idea are probably more likely to remain Christian while the ones who have a hard time accepting this idea are probably more likely to reject other Christian ideas as well. At the same time, people who have a conversion experience later in life may feel as though their eyes have just been opened to something they should have seen all along or as though, looking back, they had witnessed signs of God in their life before and were just hesitant to accept them. In any event, people who have felt a sense that God is real are likely to end up in Christian communities together, swapping similar ideas about similar experiences, and then it can become difficult to believe that someone else could truly never have experienced what they've experienced.

Being surrounded by people who feel that God's existence is obvious and who truly believe it must be obvious to everyone else only adds to the feeling of disconnection from reality that you experience if you don't feel the same way. It makes you wonder what you're not seeing. What sense of yours is defective? What part of your heart is closed to the truth?

I once had a long conversation at a table in a little boba shop with a middle-aged woman who had left the Christian faith years before. It wasn't her first time mentioning this fear to me that day; she was repeating it yet again—What if what God had wanted from her all along was to believe in him *in spite of* logic, *in spite of* conscience? What if somewhere deep down, even though she had devoted her life to God, even though she had searched for him, even though she still wouldn't actually say with finality that she didn't believe in God and remained in a gray area lacking any foundation for faith but still hoping something might someday turn up, *what if,* despite her desire for the God who had never reached out to her, everything that seemed like truth to her was actually self-deception? In other words, what if her reality wasn't real? What if the unpleasant facts of God's absence she had to face weren't facts at all and the truth was that she had willfully walked away from God?

The only difference between this woman who was still fighting her fears after years, and me who had mostly put them behind me after a period of months was that she had grown up in a family that emphasized God's judgment whereas I had grown up in one that emphasized God's love and truth. I couldn't believe that God would trick people. If the only way I could continue to believe in Christianity was to tell myself that my reality was a lie and that God was okay with standing by and ignoring all my petitions from childhood until the present to be undeceived, then I just couldn't believe. Either God was good or he was invented by people who made mistakes. I had no room for the idea of a cruel or neglectful God in my thoughts. My friend hadn't been so lucky when it came to the strain of indoctrination she had been exposed to. The manipulative claims that taught her to question her sanity were more malicious and stronger, more effective at continuing to trigger feelings of fear no matter how much she learned about the inaccuracy of these feelings.

While the intention behind the claim that everyone has an innate knowledge of God is to allow people to keep believing in the faith system they have built their lives on, the results it produces are problematic and even cruel, leading people to question their sanity and live under the fear that things are never as they seem. The teaching is textbook gaslighting and not the sort of idea the church should ever have to rely on to defend itself if its beliefs were based on facts.

B: "Your logic has to be based on faith in something. Put your faith in God's word first and then develop your logic from there. Any logic that contradicts something God has said is faulty."

While Statement A is meant to attack people's direct observations of the world, this statement is meant to attack their reasoning ability, to make them doubt their understanding of reality by suggesting that it might all be built on the wrong foundation. I've heard it presented with different spins, sometimes playing up the apparent craziness of the conclusions some devotees of philosophy have come to, sometimes specifying that logic was damaged by sin just like everything else in creation and so it can't necessarily be trusted to work. Once when I explained to a Christian acquaintance the reasons why I was having trouble believing in God he replied that my logic seemed good but that logic was just a Eurocentric way of looking at the world, invented in Greece, and that people from many cultures around the world wouldn't value it as much as my culture did, so really my conclusions were more of just culturally influenced opinions.[25]

---

[25] This statement tries to appear valid by virtue of its surface-level similarity to other, better-formed ideas. For example, it is important not to simply assume we will be objective while trying to use logic. If we assume our logic is untouched by biases, then our biases will end up ruling us in the name of objectivity just as easily as they rule some people in the name of God's voice. Picture that my acquaintance had said, "Some of the ideas that lead to your conclusion show a Eurocentric bias, and I think if you took into account that not all cultures see those issues the same way, you would end up with a different conclusion." This would have been a valid criticism because it is possible that familiarity with a certain view could have made me give that view too

It's strange that I was offered so many reasons to mistrust the use of logic because the churches I was part of also held logic in high regard. The church I grew up in, for example, devoted large amounts of time and resources to teaching people how to defend their beliefs with logical arguments. It's true that looking back I can see many of their arguments actually contained fallacies and factual errors that all went overlooked, but at the same time I do understand their desire to promote logic. If you think that God created the world and everything in it and that to get closer to truth is to get closer to God, then of course you can't see yourself speaking negatively about processes that allow people to distinguish truth and understand the world.

But somehow while they spoke highly of logic and tried to use it to demonstrate the accuracy of their beliefs, these churches, or individuals within them at least, still came out with statements like the one we're discussing, statements that at bottom mean logic cannot be trusted. These claims grow directly from the need to protect what one believes. There are circumstances in which people are presented with facts whose implications they must deny and yet the facts appear too solid to explain away. The implications still have to be avoided, so it must be the process of drawing implications from facts that is flawed. This is how a community or an individual can end up stating that logic is twisted by sin whenever it points to an idea they dislike even though they claim in general that logic is good and productive.

---

much weight and skewed my conclusions. This criticism is much different from the situation in which both of us agreed that a given line of thought made sense and then one of us tried to invalidate logic itself as something that belongs solely to one culture so that the conclusion could be ignored.

But still, is it really wrong for people to use religious faith as an anchor for their logic? It's true that you have to start with some assumptions about life before you can use logic to learn more. Why shouldn't faith in God be that starting assumption against which a person checks the accuracy of everything else?

The reason why belief in God doesn't work as this sort of foundational assumption is actually very simple. It's the same reason why belief that God does not exist also does not work as a foundation and neither does confidence in democracy or tyranny or the certainty that your neighbor has a cat or almost any other statement or feeling about the world. The reason is that there is a different assumption that must be taken as foundational to everything else if you are to avoid contradicting yourself from the very beginning.

The assumption that forms this necessary foundation to logic is the idea that you can make accurate observations of the world. Of course everyone is mistaken sometimes, but if you are to learn anything about the world, you must begin with faith in the *general* trustworthiness of your perceptions. Why is this? Because if you don't think that you have any ability to distinguish accurate from inaccurate information, then you have no basis on which to claim that a statement such as "God exists" is accurate.

Our perceptions don't have to be perfect, but they have to be good enough to point us in the right direction. For example, think of an optical illusion that makes it seem like a stationary shape on a page is moving. One of our perceptions in this case is completely wrong. We are getting a strong but inaccurate message that the shape is moving. But thanks to the combination of everything we perceive while looking at the illusion, we recognize that single perception of motion as inaccurate. Before we can extend our use of logic, we need to have faith in this general ability of ours to take in information from multiple sources and eventually figure out how to understand it.

If you start with trust in your perception of reality as a foundation, there is always that inescapable chance that you might be wrong. Maybe everything you experience of the world is fake. Maybe your body is actually in a lab somewhere being fed a long and complicated dream. But if you base your logic on trust in your perceptions and this trust is misplaced, it doesn't matter. Whatever that other more real reality might be, you have no access to it. It's more important for you to understand the life that your mind is actually experiencing, and if you were to somehow find out that it was all fake someday, you would still need to rely on your perceptions at that point in order to recognize that the new experience was your real life and to learn the skills you needed to succeed in it.

And if you are wrong in a different way, if you are utterly crazy and your mind is unable to make sense of the input it receives or formulate useful responses to it, this still doesn't matter. In this state, you would have no way of ever telling the difference between a good foundation and a bad one, so if you are actually worried that your mind might be this damaged, you might as well go with whatever makes you happy.

And if you are severely delusional about only one part of life and sane about the rest, and it turns out you need to put your trust in other people when they tell you not to listen to your own thinking about that one subject, then you still need to have faith in the accuracy of the perceptions that led you to recognize there was a problem in that particular area.

There is no evading the need to trust that the way you perceive reality is at least generally correct. Either you have enough understanding of reality to identify and compensate for your weaknesses and eventually find truth, or you don't, and if you don't, it doesn't matter what unfounded claims of truth you randomly grab at.

In contrast to the results that come from trusting your perceptions, picture what happens if you take some more specific assumption as your starting point and turn out to be wrong. Take for example, "Prayer guarantees success in life." This is a statement about a specific part of the reality we live in, not a statement that concerns a hypothetical other world we have no access to. If we are wrong about this idea, we could be making choices based on bad information that have the potential to hurt us right now, and this situation could be avoided. Once again, this is the same reason we cannot use a statement like "Religion is harmful," or "My country can do no wrong," or, "My parents are out to get me," as a foundation for logic. If any of these more specific statements is wrong and we have designated it as the unquestionable standard that shows whether everything else is correct or incorrect, we're trying to navigate to a point on a map with a compass that points east when we think it's pointing north.

In addition to the immediate danger that comes from placing too much faith in these types of statements, there is the risk of self-contradiction as well. If the idea that God exists is our ultimate foundation, then as soon as we observe something that seems to contradict this idea and cannot be explained away, we are in danger of questioning our ability to recognize truth, and if we are not able to recognize truth, then how do we know that the claim of God's existence is true? The same goes for any other statement of this type. They all come with the risk of leading you to doubt your perceptions, at which point you have lost your status as someone who is qualified to evaluate the truth of the original statement.[26]

Trust in one's own perceptions, observations, sanity, has to come before any other step of reasoning is taken. This is not a challenge to religion; it is simply a fact of the way logic works. Starting from this trust you may reach conclusions that support a particular religious system or you may reach conclusions that oppose it, but there is no logically consistent way to bypass this foundation and no reason to try doing so unless you are more committed to a particular predetermined conclusion than to the pursuit of truth.

The claim that belief in God or the Bible should supersede confidence in one's own ability to reason is clear manipulation. As I've said, it's not intended to be manipulative; it's a message preached by people who sincerely believe it. But it is manipulative nonetheless. In order to get people to cave to the assertion that they can't trust their reasoning abilities, the attack

---

[26] Of course, it's possible to use "God exists" as an unfalsifiable statement as well, in which case it can't force you to question your sanity but also can't be used as a foundation to check other ideas against. This is what you would be doing if you believed that there was a God but that we couldn't know anything about who or what it was and if it had any effect whatsoever on the world we observe. That's a separate subject from believing that a specific God who is supposed to influence your life in specific ways exists. In this case, belief in God becomes no different from "what if we're in the matrix" ideas about unknowable other realities. You can have as many unfalsifiable beliefs as you want with no thought to ever having to prove them or keep them consistent with each other, but they won't help you to understand this world we're all living in.

on sanity is once again coupled with an attack on character. People are told that they are arrogant for daring to suggest that human logic could be more trustworthy than God's word. Of course, this attack is all but meaningless since, if God is not real, human logic would certainly be more trustworthy than what he has supposedly said, and if God is real this doesn't change anything I've just said about the reasons why trust in one's own perceptions has to be foundational. Still, the emotional impact of being called arrogant by people you respect might be enough to shock some individuals into starting to believe that they are simply bad and prideful, and detached from reality on top of that.

It is nothing but gaslighting again. People in a position of trust—pastors, motivational speakers, teachers, parents—deliver a message that confuses the victim and back it up with an accusation that undercuts the victim's worth and a threat of how terrible things would be without the gaslighter: *You have to start with faith before you can go on with logic, so don't be tricked into thinking that logic could ever replace your faith in God. It's foolishly arrogant to elevate human reason above God's word, and if you go down that road, you'll be left with no standard of truth, making up reality as you go, and walking farther away from what God wants for your life and closer to his judgment.*

If people are sure that the God they believe in exists, they should never feel that they have to take away someone's tools for identifying truth and error before that person will find God.

C: "Truth is a person."

This is one of those power statements used to drive the point of a sermon home and draw snaps, claps, and amens from the congregation. It sounds downright inspirational—in a world where people's values don't line up and society can fight over what virtue really means perpetually, isn't it nice to know that truth is defined and embodied by Jesus, a real, living person who could be seen and touched and who promises to hear your prayers and give you guidance today? Truth isn't some abstract thing we need to disagree over or wonder about. We can talk to truth himself and experience the certainty in life that everyone longs for.

This idea sounds nice, but the fact is, it's extremely misleading. The appearance it creates and the reality of what it accomplishes are completely different. The message preached is that, without Jesus, people all want their personal views recognized as truth and that we can avoid the confusion by looking to Jesus as an unchanging standard beyond ourselves.

This wouldn't be a problem if Jesus talked to people with a level of clarity that distinguished his voice from their own thoughts.

If you haven't already read Chapter 2, Section #3, go read it. It covers the problems that we actually see coming out of Christian attempts to understand what God is trying to say. Instead of finding coherence and agreement among Christians, we find that different individuals and churches cannot agree even on extremely important questions such as what actually makes a person right with God. You can gather together a bunch of Christians who all believe that they know truth because they know Jesus, and you will find disagreements upon disagreements about what Jesus is saying. Some will come out as arguments about a supposedly universal concept that all sides think the others are misunderstanding, and some will come out as topics about which everyone has agreed that Jesus' instructions will differ from individual to individual. In short, what you get is certainly not a consensus on truth or an unchanging standard.

Then, on top of the fact that this situation is not significantly better than the one it claims to be able to resolve, there is actually an aspect that makes it worse. People in general are prone to clamoring for their opinions to be given the weight of fact, but when they go about their clamoring with the idea that *God is on their side*, things can only become worse than usual. Every time a pastor assures his congregation that they have a direct line to truth and are on more solid ground in this respect than others around them, he is teaching a level of closedmindedness and superiority. He is telling people, "The world has only their feelings to point them to what they think is truth, but you have access to God, the source of ultimate truth." Why should they consider engaging in serious, vulnerable dialogue with others if this is really the case?

The claim that truth is a person is harmful because it fails to produce agreement and gives people the impression that they have the authority of God behind their side of the argument. It is also harmful because it overlooks the importance of educating people about what truth actually is. I agree with everyone who says that we have a problem on our hands if people think they can make up truth for themselves. If we want to address this problem in a way that makes a difference, we have to teach people that truth is correspondence to reality. It's like calculating the trajectory of a moving object to avoid a collision: If this means jumping out of the way of a flying beach ball, you can find the answer yourself with little to no effort, but if it means launching a satellite into an orbit that won't intersect with any other orbit at the wrong time, getting the right answer requires you to depend on tools developed through years of collaboration between many people. And no matter how simple or how complex the problem is, the test of whether your answer to it is correct is whether or not a collision happens when you implement it—it doesn't matter how right the answer felt, how good it sounded, how convenient it was, or anything else.

People need to know that truth often isn't obvious from a snap judgment or an instinctive feeling of certainty. They have to learn how to bring multiple sources of information together so they can find correlations and discrepancies and carefully sort out what is accurate and what is not. In other words, we need to teach critical thinking—a healthy level of skepticism towards our own feelings and opinions and a willingness to listen to others and put everything to the test with the best tools we have available (but not an attitude of perfectionism and hopelessness that leads us to feel as if we know nothing just because we are still learning).

If people are told that God is truth and it's as simple as that, they are vulnerable to overlooking the snap judgments they are actually making. At first glance it seems that the Bible is telling them something or that the Holy Spirit is leading them in a certain way, and if they are overconfident in their privileged connection to God, they might take this as all that is necessary to know what the truth is. This way of thinking does not give appropriate stress to the importance of diligently checking for correspondence to reality by seeing if multiple sources of information on a subject agree, or by thinking of tests that could disprove an idea if it is flawed and carrying out those tests.

It might be worth noting, in fact, that in church I was often told to ignore reality and instead focus on what was called "God's truth" or "spiritual truth." This is not actually as bad as it sounds—it's really just a positive thinking technique—but the ideas behind it are a bit worrying. We would be told things like, "Your physical reality might be that you're struggling financially, but you need to look at things with your spiritual eyes and see that God says you are his favored child and heir to all the riches he has for you." The intention behind this sort of thing is good. It's meant to get people to stop focusing on the daunting nature of whatever problem they are facing and instead visualize themselves overcoming the problem, and many churchgoers take it as just that, just a reason to have a hopeful outlook, so I'm not trying to make it seem like this practice itself is a problem. I just want to point out that there is a lot of power behind this idea that truth can be tied up in God as a person and that the words of this person are the "real" truth and carry more weight than what you are actually experiencing in life. It's a belief with potential to be dangerously misused, although thankfully I haven't personally seen this happen.

What I have seen is a continuation of the habit of making someone feel like a bad person when they raise logical objections to a claim. When someone, usually someone in a position of leadership, feels that God is directing them to work towards a certain goal or telling them that certain things are going to happen in the future, this is taken as a spiritual reality, something that we might not be able to see now but that is as true as anything else because God said it will happen. At this point, anyone who has opposing ideas or who thinks this person didn't really hear from God or who disagrees with the steps being taken to reach that goal or prepare for that future event, is subject to being labeled as all sorts of unsavory things. They may be accused of lacking faith, of being "carnal" rather than spiritual, even of being a false prophet or a divisive person. This goes hand in hand with the idea that truth is a person. Because the idea leads people to overlook the need for critical thinking and misread snap judgments as divine revelation, it creates the false confidence needed to state that one is acting on the words of God and that anyone who disagrees is a liar.

While those who proclaim that truth is a person mean to help people, the tactic is counterproductive and ends up being manipulative. The intention is to point to an authority who will provide greater consistency and clarity, but as Chapter 2, Section #3 explains, this authority doesn't appear to actually communicate with anyone, so people still end up disagreeing widely about what they think is being said and may feel that they have divine authority backing up their views. They are told in addition to this that there is a more important truth than the reality they actually observe around them and that it is controlled by this authority they supposedly have access to. The result of all this is that, instead of taking responsibility on themselves to see whether various claims match up with their best and most careful understanding of reality, people have handed responsibility over to someone else. They think that person is God, but since we have no evidence that God has actually taken on this responsibility, it seems that their trust is unknowingly resting on human beings. Sometimes it might end up resting on their own feelings, which they mistake for divine communication, and other times it might end up resting on people around them, especially church leaders. This all makes it easy to overlook bias and unquestioned instinct because people don't recognize these feelings for what they are, and even to be lied to because when someone like a pastor makes claims about "spiritual reality" people are open to the idea that these claims could contradict everything they are able to observe about life and still be true.

You could hardly find a better example of gaslighting than the claim that truth is a person because the goal of a gaslighter is to be the only source of information a victim trusts. Saying that Jesus is truth is meant to make truth easier to find, but what it actually does is establish that each individual does not have the ability to find out what is true on their own and must listen to the supposed words of Jesus above their own conclusions. These words of Jesus are actually the consensus of a community or the declarations of an influential person mistaking their own thoughts and feelings for the divine communication they expect to hear, but because outside sources of information, like an individual's own logic, are seen as untrustworthy, dissenters can be ignored or pressured into changing by being labeled false prophets.

D: "Everything in the world has been damaged by sin, including your conscience."

Like Statement B, which seeks to discredit logic, this claim is another desperate attempt to defend beliefs against challenges that can't be dismissed under the normal rules of engagement. It usually turns up as a response to the question of how God could do something that seems unjust, such as considering all humanity guilty of something that Adam and Eve did wrong or allowing someone to spend eternity in hell as punishment for choices made with very limited time and understanding. Since everyone knows these things are not just, we are told that our sense of justice can't be trusted and if we were perfect, we would see why the way God is said to do things is best.

This claim also turns up as a way of explaining why some people don't feel bad about doing things that certain groups say are against God's law. For example, at a conservative church where people think that God doesn't want them to listen to certain music or watch certain movies, newcomers who can't see what the big deal is might be told that, because the human conscience has been damaged by sin, there are some things that are wrong and yet don't cause them to feel any negative reaction. Therefore, instead of trusting their own sense of right and wrong, these newcomers need to be retaught by their church community what is right and wrong.

Before I go on explaining the problem with the claim that conscience is broken by sin, let me note that I'm not trying to replace this claim with a rosy view of a world in which everyone always agrees on what is right and what is wrong. Unfortunately, there are disagreements. I completely understand why religious claims of absolute morality are so appealing and why, if they were true, it would be thoroughly irresponsible for humanity to try to decide their own moral laws rather than following divine law. The only problem is that no matter how great of an improvement an absolute divine law would be, we have no reason to think it exists if we have no reason to think God exists. Since I've already stated my reasons for coming to the latter conclusion repeatedly, I'll leave things at that.

The important thing to understand is that for most if not all people who find themselves in the position to question Christianity, the moral alternative to divine law is not depravity but a commitment to do what helps others and avoid what harms them. This is partly because people naturally feel empathy for each other and partly because it's far more enjoyable to work together trying to maintain peace and safety than it is to have everyone fighting.

So, I'm not claiming that moral questions are easy or that everyone's feelings will line up perfectly, but I am claiming that we have good guidelines with which to answer moral questions: things like empathy and the agreement to work together so that everyone gets more of what they want. I am also claiming that when someone tells you to ignore your understanding of these guidelines and instead follow commands that have no comprehensible explanation behind them, this is *dangerous*.

This is psychological manipulation at its worst. Just as with everything in this chapter, even this attack is unintentional and meant to be helpful, and it stems from the fact that people have already placed all their hope and confidence in certain religious claims and will, knowingly or unknowingly, give up almost anything else before they will give up what they think is guaranteeing them eternal life. But the effects don't improve just because the intention is not malicious.

As with many of these claims, what we have here is again a combined attack on sanity and character. When a person suggests that it isn't right for God to punish people for things they didn't do or send them to hell eternally for small, temporary mistakes, this person is coming from a place where they have some amount of trust in their perception of right and wrong and also in their simple desire that right would be done instead of wrong. In order to quash this sentiment, which would reveal an inconsistency in Christian beliefs if it were acknowledged as correct, the person is told that something about their understanding of the world is broken. They do not really understand right and wrong because this is perfect knowledge that only God has. And if they still protest, they are, as usual, slapped with the charge of arrogance. How dare they claim that a finite individual could understand what is right better than God can? The goal is to get this person to accept a set of rules given by God as superior to what seems in their eyes to do the greatest good for the greatest number of people. The problem, of course, is that the many groups who claim to be God's followers do not even agree on what this set of rules is.

The requirement to place religious morals over morals determined by conscience and empathy sets up a situation in which people can end up blindly doing what others tell them without allowing themselves the veto power to say, "I won't go along with this because I know it's wrong."

I had some experience with this myself, although thankfully it was mild—I'd say it had more to do with tact vs. jerkiness than with right vs. wrong. For example, when I was in junior high and high school, I thought that God wanted me to tell anyone I could about him, including by joining "street evangelism" groups to tell strangers about why they needed Jesus. I absolutely hated everything about doing this because it obviously required throwing out things like tact, consideration, and general good-neighbor-li-ness and embracing the fact that you would have to be a bit of a jerk, bother people, and even mislead them. (That's no exaggeration; the people who did a lot of street evangelism sometimes recommended that we start conversations with people under the pretense of being interested in some other subject. Their reasoning was that people needed to hear this message but didn't want to, so if we could by any means get them into a conversation where they ended up hearing it, we would be doing them a favor.)

Under any other circumstances I would have said that this sort of behavior was clearly undesirable and refused to participate. But I was convinced that my desire not to be a nuisance to people was actually just a selfish and sinful fear that stood in the way of the greater good. Thankfully I don't think this ever led to anything more harmful than making a few people at Huntington Beach Pier feel ticked off, but the manner of thinking behind it isn't far from what leads people in cults to do things they wouldn't have considered otherwise, like distancing themselves from family and friends—Even if it doesn't seem right, an authority who has made some very big and attractive promises tells them it's for the greater good.

Looking back, I'm so glad certain circumstances never came up in my life because they could have led to worse consequences than simply annoying someone. The most likely problem that could have arisen would have been if any of my Christian friends had done something that would have been considered "living in unrepentant sin," meaning doing anything the church said was wrong and not making an effort to change. At least two of the churches I attended were very clear that if someone claimed to be Christian but habitually made the same bad choices and didn't try to change, the best thing to do for the community and for this person would be to avoid them. To maintain an intact relationship with them would be like commending someone who was sick and refused to see a doctor. At the church I grew up in, I don't remember people getting very specific about what this withdrawal included, but at one of the churches I attended later, they were very specific, to the point of actually calling the process "excommunication" and saying you had to block the person on social media sites among other things.

Now, this situation is most likely to arise if the person is doing something that only the church considers wrong—since otherwise another party would probably be dealing with the problem already—so it is most likely to involve a "sin" that doesn't cause any apparent harm to anyone, such as if an unmarried couple is living together or if someone participates in the practices of a religion other than Christianity. If I had known someone who was involved in a "sin" like this, even if I couldn't explain why their actions were wrong or harmful to anyone, I would have gone along with the instruction to distance myself from them. I would have believed what I was told: that my feelings of sadness and fear of hurting the person were simply incorrect and stemmed from the flaws in my modern, slightly broken sense of morality.

If individuals within a church or any other group believe that they can trust their sense of right and wrong and should not listen to influences that tell them to violate it, they all serve as failsafes against the group doing anything too harmful. In contrast to this, telling people that their knowledge of what is right has been ruined by sin makes them dependent on a central source of morals and ethics and means that there is no failsafe to intervene when this source is wrong. But even though the churches I was part of warned against giving up this authority of conscience in other circumstances, they insisted upon it when it came to holding God blameless in all cases.

When church congregations doubt their conscience and get used to accepting moral positions they do not understand, they are considerably more than just an annoyance. They may use these moral positions to guide decisions such as how to vote, which means they are taking actions that directly affect the lives of others according to a standard that doesn't need to prove its worth to them. Things are wrong or right because God said so, God is not required to reveal to people why some things that don't hurt anyone are wrong or why his plan of judgment is right, and people are willing to keep believing that the teachings of their church are the words of God despite the fact that other churches have heard contradictory words from God on the same subjects.

The claim that your conscience is damaged by sin and should be superseded by the guidance of a spiritual authority needs to be recognized as a ploy for control. Even if the people perpetuating it don't realize how dangerous it is, even if they think they're bringing their followers to God, they are guilty of turning congregations into private armies that can be sent to the polls or rallied to shun undesirables on command. They are guilty of tearing down people's confidence in what is right and replacing it with blind dependence so that they remain submissive, without the strength of moral convictions that could encourage them to run from their abusers.

E: "God is paradoxical."

This statement is a wonderful, terrible example of how well-meaning and intelligent Christian thinkers gaslight themselves on God's behalf. I believe I first began to hear the declaration that God is paradoxical when I was in college. It was said with such interest and fascination by pondering, inquisitive types, the types of people who also spoke of reflecting deeply on the difficulty of reconciling human suffering with God's goodness or the seemingly predictable and explicable natural workings of the world with the inexplicable spiritual reality said to lie behind them. But when they talked about God's paradoxical nature, they spoke as if they were happy that God was so difficult to understand, so contradictory at first glance. Things were so much more interesting that way, they said.

In the years after college I continued to hear the idea raised with frequency. Everyone seemed taken with the wonder of divine paradoxes and the challenge of "holding beliefs in tension" (a wording that has a distinctly more pleasant ring to it than "accepting that your cognitive dissonance isn't going anywhere"). While acknowledging that contradictions (at least seem to) exist is a step in the right direction, there are two aspects of this popular claim that God is paradoxical that ought to be concerning.

First, this claim can be used to silence criticisms of Christianity without addressing them. When someone points out an inconsistency, it is possible to say that there is no need to find a resolution, that we shouldn't even expect there to be a resolution in this life, because God is paradoxical. He doesn't have to make sense because that's just not who he is. His ways look contradictory to us, but that's only because the grander way in which they harmonize is beyond us. Thus, no criticism matters because we can't understand what is being criticized anyway.

The idea isn't always used this way. Some people use it to make much more responsible points by actually explaining surprising ways in which supposed contradictions end up being resolved. When this is the goal, I don't have a problem with a person's interest in paradoxes. Manipulation only starts to happen when the concept of paradox is used to belittle people who want to feel confident that God's behavior lives up to godly standards. If God is just, people want his behavior to be just, and they will speak up when it doesn't look that way. If the idea of paradox is accepted, it's easy to call them overly simplistic or narrow-minded and end the discussion there, and in accordance with the common theme here, this teaches people to stay quiet by communicating that they are bad for having a problem with the way things are in the first place. It teaches them that the very willingness to state that something doesn't seem right and search for a resolution isn't reasonable; it's a defiant attempt to limit God.

Second, it's somewhat disturbing that people have reframed an old pain as something to be happy about. Not that this is completely new—positive references to God's mysterious ways are an ancient phenomenon. But as our values have diverged from those of the ancient world and we've come to see more problems with Christian teachings (for example, seeing the conquest of the Promised Land as God ordering genocide), the response to the increasing difficulty of believing that God is good has been to say that God is paradoxical and to speak as if this is part of what makes him wonderful.

Clearly I don't believe that God is a real person capable of treating anyone in an abusive manner, but when you tell people who believe God is real that he acts in certain ways and they believe you, those claims have the impact of real actions on them. It's sad that people feel such a need for a perfect higher power to save them from their problems and such a burden to make that higher power the object of their hopes and desires, that they will reinterpret his apparent mistreatment of humanity in a positive light. This is little different from a victim insisting that their abuser's attempts to control and manipulate their life are actually signs of concern and even love. The Christians who sincerely feel troubled by difficult parts of the Bible and want to know how God could behave or instruct people to behave in ways that seem reprehensible deserve better than to be told that we just can't understand how God's apparently cruel actions fit into his loving nature and that in fact we should be happy and awed at how impossible it is to understand him.

F: "You know that God is speaking to you when you have a thought you definitely wouldn't have come up with on your own."

This is just one specific embodiment of the feeling that teaches people to attribute whatever good they do to God and to blame themselves for whatever bad they do. Another statement in the same vein I have heard dozens of times runs along the lines of, "Aren't you glad God calls his people sheep? Sheep aren't very smart or strong or impressive, so we know we can all make the cut." I would bore you by trying to compile a comprehensive list of all the types of statements preachers pepper their sermons with that imply everyone listening is a loser, so I'll restrain myself; those two illustrate the concept well enough.

The point is that human shortcomings are a beloved topic at church, and the problem with this is not that it's inaccurate to say human beings have all kinds of failures and shortcomings—we clearly do according to our own ideals—but that the topic is presented in a way that makes each individual see their own nature as worse than it actually is. It's one thing for me to think that I've done wrong things but can improve; that's a beneficial way of thinking. It's another for me to think that I am a bad person through and through, that anything good I've done should actually be attributed to someone else, and that I need to turn to that person for help if I'm ever going to do anything good again. This disempowering sentiment comes through in a multitude of comments you can't help hearing when you grow up in a conservative Christian environment, comments that say we humans are childish, wayward, unintelligent, stubborn, unreasonable, hopeless cases, but God in all his grace and goodness just keeps forgiving us.

In an environment like this, people who already know they have good ideas and don't experience the feeling that any of their thoughts have been dropped into their head from outside are in effect pressured to give up the confidence they possess in their own imaginative or problem-solving skills. Those who are blunt enough to say that their best ideas aren't beyond the bounds of natural human inventiveness may be told, as per usual, that they are being arrogant. You see, the claim that God gives you thoughts you wouldn't have come up with is a self-fulfilling prophecy as long as anyone who doesn't agree it's being fulfilled can be discredited as having too much pride to admit the truth.

Telling people that they're wrong about where their own thoughts come from discourages a realistic view of life. When people are able to acknowledge what they're good at, they are exercising honesty and objectivity, but when a church shames people for being able to say positive things about themselves, it teaches them useless criteria to bend their perceptions around: You can generally attribute certain outcomes to certain causes *except* when trying to understand yourself; then you need to worry about things not really being as they seem.

It also creates the distressing feeling that your efforts to do right are all backfiring and you can't understand why. You know that there's nothing different about these thoughts people are telling you should be counted as messages from God. You want to hear from God and you know it can't be right to just settle for something you know isn't God. You don't want your church family to think you're arrogant and resistant to God, but they're telling you that they know some of your own ideas aren't really yours—and how could they know that? How do they know what God is saying to you and how he's saying it? You aren't willing to settle for these slapdash assumptions. You want the real thing. You're like Jacob, tenaciously holding on to whatever revelation of God you have, saying "I won't let go until you bless me," or like the unclean woman who clawed her way through the crowd to touch the hem of Jesus' garment; you have to have the real thing, that real contact, and that's all you'll settle for. But your devotion isn't getting you anywhere. It never has. And as you watch the model good Christians blossom into their ministry lives, you sink into the dismal realization that either God doesn't talk to you or you're dumber than you thought and his voice is less grand and less personal than you hoped.

Another undesirable outcome that can go along with this way of thinking is that people may be directed away from realistic methods of developing their talents. Because insight is seen as being given by God from outside of oneself, people may be encouraged to focus on things like prayer and scripture reading above all else, the assumption being that God will supernaturally give them more wisdom as they commune with him than they could cultivate through any other means. Some church communities even suffer from a level of anti-education sentiment because they teach that studying and learning only develop the mind and are inferior to devotional pursuits that develop the spirit. If individuals in these environments undertake to become the people their church tells them they should be, they may end up as something lesser than what they could have made themselves by focusing on natural ways to improve their skills.

I remember hearing a pastor refer to a question he had been asked, *People sometimes ask me why non-Christians are often more accomplished at what they do than Christians are...* and he went on to explain that people who didn't spend time developing their spiritual life did have more time to excel at creative pursuits than devoted Christians did but that we needed to keep the cost in perspective: Having a spiritual life was more valuable than any human achievement. Something about this—about the idea that nonbelievers were doing more tangible good, touching people's lives in deeper and more lasting ways, than Christians were and that that was fine—didn't sit right at the time, and now I have to wonder if this phenomenon isn't only due to the Christian lifestyle coming with a set of demanding time commitments but also to the fact that people are directed away from natural sources of self-development and pressured to see themselves as no good.

Many people, sadly, don't even need to be pressured to see themselves this way. The abuse begins when they're too young to have an idea of who they are yet or when they come into the church fresh out of situations that have already stripped them of confidence. When they're told that they are lesser beings with lesser thoughts, not capable of achieving higher levels of understanding on their own, lucky that God doesn't expect them to be any more impressive than a sheep, they believe it.

Abusive behavior seeks to compensate for a shortcoming of the abuser, or in this case, the church ends up perpetrating abusive behavior because it hides the shortcomings of God. A human gaslighter might believe they are incapable of attracting the love, loyalty, and respect of others, and so they resort to trying to make others feel worthless and helpless because that is the only way the gaslighter appears competent enough in comparison for another person to need them. In the same way, the church resorts to preaching that people are worse than they actually are so that they continue to have a need for God, and one specific outworking of this is telling them that they aren't capable of deep insights and aren't honest or modest enough to give credit to God, because in this way God gets to end up looking like a real source of information instead of like a made-up idea. Abusive human beings don't consciously say to themselves, "I really don't think anyone likes me. How can I manipulate people into cooperating with me anyway?" If they were that aware of their motivations, they might find a better solution than manipulation. And neither are the people who together make up the church consciously plotting to say that humans are evil and stupid so that God appears good and wise in comparison. The manipulative claims arise naturally as answers to defend the belief that God is perfect when someone points out imperfections or the belief that he is communicative when someone points out that he doesn't communicate with them.

In the community I came from, people talked about the sorts of denigrating statements you encounter in church in a very positive light. Saying that God gave you ideas that were too good to be your own, or saying that God called his people sheep, was an encouragement and a point of bonding over relatable experiences—friends would agree that yes, they knew that feeling of recognizing a Holy Spirit thought! or yes, they too were glad God set a low bar. But, normalized as they have become, these claims need to be exposed as the manipulative tools that they are. If an all-powerful and deeply loving and personal God communicates with his people, then acknowledging what he's saying shouldn't be any more confusing than acknowledging what anyone else says, and people shouldn't have to be shamed into recognizing his voice.

G: "Can't you see God working through all the good things that have come together in your life?"

When I expressed my own difficulty in finding God in my life, I was told that his presence was apparent in every good thing that happened to me. I was blessed, and that should be clear—to say God wasn't telling me he loved me through that would be ungrateful. Following the pattern of this chapter, this claim blatantly tells you that your perception is wrong—things that seem like nothing more than natural turns of events are actually messages from God—and that you are a bad person for not perceiving things differently—in this case you are ungrateful.

Like all the other manipulative responses to people's search for God we have here, this one proves twisted and harmful upon examination. The twisted thing about it is, if I am supposed to interpret the general happiness and prosperity of my life as signs of God's love, then how am I supposed to interpret the suffering of so many others? Most Christians are indeed aware that this is a problem, and I've heard plenty of sermons stating that when bad things happen to people it doesn't mean God is judging them. Truly, how could we conclude anything else when it's clear that terrible things sometimes happen to very good, even very godly people? It should also be extremely simple to observe that good things happen to people who live bad lives (and to people from all religions and those who don't believe in God). It's nice if you enjoy the idea that positive events in your life are gifts from God, but it's not kind or reasonable to call others ungrateful for not seeing the good in their lives as proof that God is interacting with them.

Even before I had trouble believing in God, I simply felt dissatisfied and lonely if this was truly the way he communicated because it didn't feel like communication—it felt random. Good and bad could happen to anyone, anytime, with no discernible pattern except that of how your own efforts could influence the likelihood of an outcome, and I was being called ungrateful for not saying that this impersonal probability game was actually a sign of the intervention of a divine person on my behalf. Like other claims we've seen here, this one tries to swap out the topic under discussion without being caught doing so: While the person trying to find God is asking for reasonable evidence that God is real or present, the person defending God responds as if the question being asked was actually, "I know God is real, but is he good?" or "I know God is real, but do I actually have to do what he says?" The answers suggest, "Shame on you; of course you already know how you should respond to God," and never addresses the real question of how we know God is even there to be responded to. When the concept of gratitude is twisted in this way, it deserves to be called out as manipulative. You cannot be ungrateful if you are honestly not sure that there is anyone to be grateful to, so the accusation serves only to hide the real issue.

The good and bad events of life don't deserve to be called communication from God any more than they deserve to be called communication from Morgan Freeman. Good things happen to people who don't know Morgan Freeman as much as to people who do. They even happen to people who haven't heard of Morgan Freeman. (It's rumored they might even happen to people who hate Morgan Freeman, but researchers haven't been able to find anyone who hates Morgan Freeman to confirm this hypothesis.) If the way this world functions has been shaped by the outworking of natural laws of physics over long periods of time, rather than by the direct intervention of Morgan Freeman, there's no reason to think that we should see fewer good things happening in people's lives than we do. In short, if there's a correlation between the ups and downs of a person's life and their standing with God or with Morgan Freeman, we really have no idea what it is. Calling skeptics ungrateful for the good in their life is nothing more than an attempt to use emotion to distract from the fact that there's no particular link between positive events and one's relationship or lack of relationship with God.

H: "You need to manage your expectations and guard your heart against bitterness."

As Chapter 2, Section #4, discusses, pastors are very aware on some level of the need to condition people not to see God's absence as absence. Their sermons on navigating the vexations of the Christian life, no matter how well-meaning, lean extra hard into gaslighting when they touch on the topic of bitterness against God.

I recall my slight surprise a handful of years ago upon hearing a pastor state that sometimes we need to forgive God. Yes, that is actually what was said. *We* need to forgive *God*. Not that there is really anything to forgive God for, it was explained, because of course God hadn't done anything wrong, but there were sure to be times when we felt mad at God, when we felt completely justified in being mad at God, and at those times it was best not to try to understand why God wasn't actually in the wrong but simply to forgive him so that we could free ourselves of bitterness. Perhaps I shouldn't have been surprised, but at the time it hadn't occurred to me yet how problematic all the other advice I'd heard on bitterness was. Today it all sounds just as backwards as the idea that limited beings should ever have to be the ones forgiving an infinite and perfect being.

All the bitterness prevention advice given at church boils down to the same strategy of getting people to agree that there is no standard of conduct we can hold God to and that we are bad if we think there is. Under the pretense of warding off entitlement, church leaders get congregations to make a mental commitment to accept every instance of abandonment joyfully. With stirring calls to loyalty they ask, will you still love God *even if*? Will you still follow him even if he doesn't do what you want? Will you still obey him even if it feels like everything is going wrong? In the moment, agreeing to remain loyal no matter what feels like committing to be mature about things, agreeing not to demand your own way all the time. You think you're reminding yourself to be wise and count on someone who won't let you down even when you don't understand his methods. But when God never shows up, never reaches out to you, never makes himself known, never intervenes, none of this is ever enough to justify a re-evaluation of whether you're really exercising maturity or just taking abuse.

A person who is mature and not selfishly entitled will put up with some inconvenience for the greater good and go out on a limb to some degree for those who have proven themselves in the past, but there has to be a limit. Crying bitterness when someone expresses dissatisfaction in a "relationship" to which God has never contributed, is abuse: Instead of holding the source of the problem accountable, this sort of response tries to make the victim blame themself for being too demanding. As I've stressed many times already, no one intends for this abuse to happen. It is the natural result of already having fully accepted that God can do no wrong and therefore having to find fault in some other party when explaining the neglect God's people experience. But it is still harmful to tell someone who has been let down by God that the problem is not God's careful withholding of affection and that in fact the problem lies with them for feeling hurt after having experienced what anyone can see is abandonment.

What I'm advocating here isn't that people hold on to their feelings of hurt—even given the assumption that I'm completely right and God was never there for you at all, and even if God was always there but was a huge jerk who let you down on purpose, it wouldn't help you at all to keep stewing over your anger. The thing I want to see change is the disempowering and accusatory nature of these talks on bitterness—because the subject as I personally encountered it always showed up to disempower or to accuse. It would come in a sermon preemptively to entice us to forfeit our claims to proper treatment—the kind of treatment that any party should afford their child, their beloved, their friend, yes, even their servant—and declare that we would accept any suffering God put us through no matter how apparently meaningless it was or how firmly he denied us any communication in the midst of it. Or it would come in answer to the complaints of the neglected, telling them that they were the only one in the wrong and that their feelings were wicked.

Instead of these abusive approaches, advice that seeks to free people from bitterness should start by acknowledging that there is a real problem underlying the anger-inducing experiences shared by so many Christians. God should be held accountable for his absence, or rather, the concept of God should be evaluated and weighed against these experiences before being blindly accepted as true and accurate. It's just not fair to expect healing from bitterness to take place simply because you've instructed the victim to tell themself nothing bad actually happened, suck it up, and keep proclaiming the one who abandoned them as a wonderful friend. In order to heal from their bitter feelings, they should be instructed to acknowledge the full extent of how wrong the other party was and then let their negativity go for the sake of their own benefit.

I: "Don't be so legalistic."

In one of my last ditch conversations with a pastor, trying to see if there was any hope of saving my faith, I mentioned that the Bible's condemnation of some actions that are not ethically wrong troubled me. The pastor's response was that I wouldn't have such a hard time believing if I didn't take such a legalistic view of the Bible. After a lifetime of begging God to please let me have a relationship with him and guide me in how to live, that accusation was like a slap in the face. I felt like asking how it could be legalistic to reach out for contact with someone over and over again and then, in the absence of any communication, do your best to objectively interpret their last written instructions and live by them. How could it be legalistic to have believed the Bible when it said that God was holy and would not tolerate sin or allow his people to get away with misrepresenting him? How was it legalistic to believe that the many, many warnings about being on the wrong track when you think you're on the right one were actually serious and worth listening to?

While I agree now that the world would be better off if Christians didn't actually listen to the Bible and simply threw out any of its teachings that caused ethical problems, I still have to point out that this free and easy interpretation of the Bible is employed by churches selectively in ways that contribute to the atmosphere of gaslighting that exists in Christianity. When the church is in offense mode, when its leaders are talking to audiences they expect no challenges from (for example, young people who live mostly within a Christian community, like the groups of kids who are usually found at Christian schools or camps) they will tell you that their ideas of right and wrong are taken from the Bible and are correct, and they will say that while the highest commandment is to love everyone, we can't know what the most loving way to behave towards others is without having God tell us. We might feel that it's loving not to interfere in others' lives if they aren't hurting anyone, but God tells us in the Bible that some actions are bad for us even though they don't seem to be bad, so the most loving thing to do is to preach against those actions. If we were left to our own devices, we would all have different ideas about what it means to love each other and would live in chaos instead of truly showing love to the world.

But when the church is in defense mode, when the leaders are facing the disquieting questions of someone who has looked in all the right places and never found a sign of God, then they fall back on accusations of legalism and tell you that you should have known what it really meant to love people all along. You can point to passages of the Bible that are inaccurate in some way or that contain ethically reprehensible commands, but in that moment, those will always be the passages that weren't supposed to be taken literally or that don't apply to us today, and it will always be your fault for not seeing that.

Like I said, I'm fine with Christians deciding not to listen to the Bible about what is right and what is wrong. I'm fine with them saying that the specifics don't matter, that the instructions aren't for today, that we should actually just follow our conscience, our gut, what have you. I think it's great if they decide that the principle of love is the most important thing and that we can figure everything else out from there. All I'm asking for is a little bit of thought about *why* this is okay. *What caused* the writers of the Bible to record figurative explanations in a way many people can't distinguish from literal explanations or to write down inaccuracies or to flow from timeless commands for all people into instructions meant only for one group at one time without any distinction as to which is which? Whatever your explanation is for why some people are being legalistic when they take the words of the Bible at face value, how did it occur? Were biblical writers recording normal human ideas instead of words from God? Did God intend the Bible simply to capture the way people understood him at various moments in history and not to instruct people about how to live later on? Figure out what the explanation is and then ask how it affects your understanding of the entire Bible. That's all I'm asking.

If when it comes to determining right and wrong we should trust our gut over our most careful objective interpretations of what the Bible says, then shouldn't we trust our gut over what the Bible says in every area? If not, by what principle can we identify which parts of the Bible are okay to ignore in favor of our gut feeling and which are not okay to ignore? I was called legalistic for saying that the Bible condemns actions that are not unethical and therefore the Bible seems more like a fallible human document shaped by cultural prejudices than a perfect divine document. The idea behind rejecting my analysis as legalism is clearly that the Bible cannot be wrong so I should have assumed any part of it that contradicted an ethical principle was not literal or not meant for us today. In other words, instead of looking at the Bible as a guide to right and wrong, I should have determined right and wrong separately and then used my conclusions as a guide to which parts of the Bible actually mattered. My sin was thinking that it was possible to come to some sort of understanding of what biblical authors likely intended their words to mean and then evaluate whether this meaning seemed ethical or not.

Forgive my legalism in saying that we can't have it both ways. Either the teachings of the Bible supersede our gut feelings whether we like it or not and we need to bring our ideas into alignment with these teachings, or our gut feelings supersede the teachings of the Bible and we can dismiss any biblical claim that we feel to be unfair or incorrect. When church leaders accuse doubting Christians of being legalistic, this is just as lazy as if they were to say that the government had covered up all the evidence for their favorite conspiracy theory: Just as any and every lack of evidence for something can be explained away with "because the government deleted it," every intolerant command recorded in the Bible can be explained away with "you're legalistic for taking that one seriously." As long as the church can keep bending the standards for interpreting the meaning of the Bible to dodge accusations as needed, they can never be wrong.

All I ask of those who are devoted to never being wrong though is that they admit this isn't really the same thing as being right. They've created something unfalsifiable, an impenetrable defense for whatever treasured beliefs they keep wrapped within it, but I wish that those who feel the need to live in the realm of the unfalsifiable wouldn't reach out of it to contribute to the gaslighting of people searching for truth. I wish they wouldn't try to shock and shame people away from examining reality objectively just because they're afraid of what these people might find.

4. Brave Old World

Ecclesiastes 1:2 NIV
"Meaningless! Meaningless!" says the Teacher. "Utterly meaningless! Everything is meaningless."

This is the last chapter, and there are two reasons why it exists. The first is that when I decided to turn all these notes I had been writing into a book, I felt that they focused too exclusively on the positives that go along with the decision to give up religion. Since no decision of this magnitude is ever 100 percent positive in its outcomes, I thought it would be unrealistic not to discuss the points among my new views I found difficult to accept.

The second is that as I organized and expanded on my material, I realized that I had a particular audience at the back of my mind: I was writing for people in situations similar to mine, those who know the good side of Christianity well and are used to thinking about every part of life in a way that is infused with biblical teaching but who at the same time feel that something doesn't add up, that their faith brings them more stress than joy, that God never seems to be there, or that he requires them to become someone they are not without ever empowering them to do so. I wanted people like me to know they can be free from the burden of finding excuses for beliefs that don't make sense, but I also realized that they would probably face the same difficulties I had faced, and for many the transition might be harder, scarier, and not as quick. In addition, I don't only want to validate the suspicions of those who feel that something is deeply wrong with what they've been told to believe: By talking about the things I was afraid to lose and how I dealt with the loss, I hope I can offer some modicum of encouragement to anyone who has come to question Christianity for any reason at all, even those who happen to be reading this after having arrived at a place of doubt through no willingness of their own.

Thankfully, there are also other resources available on this same subject. I don't know how many people will find my particular problems and solutions relatable, but chances are *someone* has already been through whatever it is you're going through and their story is out there—from people sharing what it's like to be nonreligious in a demographic where that just isn't expected to people running support groups for those in ministry-based careers who have come to question their beliefs; it's all out there. My point is that, while you may have grown up like me in a Christian bubble, feeling that a Christian worldview was the only thing that made sense or provided purpose, and while you may have been told again and again that there is no true happiness apart from Jesus, that unbelievers are always searching for something to make them whole, or that nonreligious people won't treat you with love and respect, the truth is that the world is full of people living fulfilled and exciting lives without God and some of them understand exactly what you're going through and want to help you find whatever you need in order to grieve, adjust, and then thrive from this point on. (See "Additional Resources" after this chapter for a few places to start making these connections.)

Anyway, to finish my own story for now, I'll return to the point at which I finally admitted that I had exhausted my options for finding God and had no reason left with which to convince myself he was real. This was a shocking, strange new reality that had suddenly opened up in front of me.

Losing my belief in God felt similar to the sensation children have when they are happily peddling their first bike, totally secure, and then look back and realize that no one is holding them up. Even though nothing has changed from a moment before and they've been handling things fine on their own, the sudden realization that they are on their own makes them feel out of control and incapable, terrified that they're going to crash at any second.

For perhaps a couple months after I realized I could no longer believe in God, it felt to me like the world had lost every security measure and failsafe. For one, I had always believed that God meant for people to live at certain times and that if there was anything you were meant to do in your life, you didn't have to worry about dying before you had done it. I had rough ideas of things I wanted to accomplish, and I thought that, whichever of those things were really important, I would be sure to accomplish them as long as I lived for God. I didn't have to worry over whether my life would count for something. But suddenly that idea evaporated. For a short time, maybe a handful of weeks, I lived in constant fear that I was going to die in some random accident or attack of a disease without having ever accomplished anything that was important to me—because there was no one looking out for me and no plan, so what was to stop it?

I eventually calmed down from the shock and got used to the fact that life still went on day to day without requiring a higher power to run it from behind the scenes. If I, along with almost everyone I knew for that matter, had made it this long without God looking out for me, then the odds of life going on as usual for a good while must have been in my favor. But there were other concerns that didn't just go away as time passed. These were things that had to be wrestled with, and the parts of them that I couldn't explain away I had to accept.

There are three things that are lost along with religion that I think we absolutely need to talk about, for many reasons: Because the fear of losing them held me back from searching for truth with the thoroughness my questions deserved. Because many religious people far oversimplify what their loss means and use it to scare others away from searching thoroughly for truth as well. Because some non-religious people are uneasy about these topics too and keep them swept under the rug in their minds rather than working through them. Because even though I had to give up these things, I'm still far happier today than I ever was when I was Christian. And because the good that these three things offer is also often oversimplified and, beneath the surface, is not as wonderful as it's made to seem.

These three very misunderstood things that are lost along with a belief in God are eternity, ultimate meaning or purpose, and an objective moral standard.

I know, pretty heavy. If you've only ever heard the conservative Christian perspective on the topic, this sounds like an insurmountable loss. Thankfully not many people today are that insulated from other perspectives, but even if you happen to be the exception, don't worry; there is more to this subject than the harsh intro.

Below, I discuss why each of these ideas is not as it may seem and why its loss is tangible but not the disaster it is claimed to be.

Eternity

To some people, the idea that a grown adult could really believe they were going to live forever must sound preposterous, but that's what I and most of the people I knew thought and based our decisions on. For many people coming from that background, admitting that there is no life after death is hard, frightening, and sad. I imagine it must be harder the more a person looked forward to the idea of heaven or the more they've given up in their life thinking they'll be rewarded in an afterlife. In fact, I'm afraid of how hard the loss of eternity might be on certain people I know; I haven't talked to those people about my reasons for leaving religion for fear that they might find them convincing and that their quality of life might be lessened by that. Maybe I'm underestimating these individuals by thinking that they wouldn't be able to handle the change, and perhaps I'm even doing them a disservice by not challenging them to accept the truth when truth is something they value—but when I see how they've devoted their life to serving God over the decades and hear how fondly they talk about spending eternity with him, I feel that trying to convince them to change their beliefs would be like trying to destroy their life's work and take away their goals and hopes. When it comes to younger people, I don't worry. I want them to change their minds now, if it's at all possible to convince them, *before* they become someone who has spent the majority of their life working towards a goal that won't pay off.

While I'm aware that there are Christians who don't think much about eternity or an afterlife, the community I came from viewed eternal life as the most important consideration a person could have, and for good reason since Christianity is built on the idea that Jesus conquered death and incorporates many afterlife-focused claims (such as that repayment for good and evil actions happens in the afterlife). My community was not at all unique in this way, as a vast variety of churches use talk of heaven to comfort people and assure them that wrongs will be righted someday.

The idea of eternity in the form of heaven or a restored earth appeals to people for different reasons. Some truly view God as a beloved person they have communicated with throughout their lives and look forward to being able to interact with him face to face. Others see eternity as a promise of reunion that helps them to cope with the death of loved ones. Many just want the security of believing that justice will be served—that no secret evil really goes unpunished and no hidden victim was ever really abandoned. And most probably have some amount of simple relief that they don't really, truly have to deal with the idea of their own existence coming to an end.

The hopes for all these future benefits and more lie behind the claims you may have heard in church that people who don't believe in eternity lead a lessened existence. In the way of thinking I grew up with, the ideas of joy and peace were tightly linked to the idea of eternal life, and a general picture was painted that nonbelievers lived in a state of angst and fear of death, never truly fulfilled or happy because God created everyone to desire more than a temporary existence.

If God (or something equally as supernatural) does not exist, there is certainly no chance that I'm going to live forever, so by the logic I was raised with I should be constantly miserable and dissatisfied. I've discovered, though, that this is not the case. I *was* worried at first—when I started to run out of reasons to believe in God, I was afraid that the increasingly undeniable dismal facts were going to condemn me to unhappiness. If I and everyone else were simply going to vanish someday with no memory of anything that had ever happened and the world wasn't destined to be restored to a state where everyone got to live a truly good life, how was I supposed to accept this reality after having grown used to a much more attractive one?

One thing that does need to be said on the subject is that it sucks. Finding out that you will only exist for a very limited amount of time, that you will never see your dead loved ones again, and that there is no cosmic justice for all the victims of greed and cruelty over the millennia, is painful and not an experience to be downplayed. I have to admit that the last point is particularly bitter, and I really don't think there's anything that softens it. It's horrible that every wrongful death really means the end of everything for the victim, and I completely understand if the repulsiveness of that thought alone is enough to cause some people to maintain religious beliefs rather than face it. But I can't pretend that their belief in ultimate justice makes things any better for the oppressed—the possibility exists for it to make things worse by causing people to perceive the stakes as lower than they actually are. And I can't pretend that it's reasonable to say a belief system must be true because it's nicer than the alterative.

Should the extremely unfortunate reality of injustice make you miserable though? I think not. Only you can control whether it does, but I can tell you that it shouldn't, because your misery is another sentiment that won't in itself do a damn thing for people who are suffering. You should feel sadness, but it should drive you to actions taken in the hope of making whatever improvement, large or small, that it's currently realistic for you to make. The sadness shouldn't be allowed to turn into a paralyzing misery—because if it does, the world is left with just one more suffering person and one less person efficiently using their skills and resources to help others.

Losing a belief in God forces you to grow up in this respect. You're made to see that an already ugly facet of life is even uglier than it seemed before and that it's up to us to do the imperfect things we can in order to help. It would be dishonest to portray a transition away from religion as easy and free from deeply saddening awakenings like this one.

The more personal implications of the loss of eternity are also difficult to deal with; there's no denying that either. It can be wonderful to feel that everything will work out in the end and that you will always, always have tomorrow, and so it can be distressing to find out otherwise. Not that the thought of eternal life seems wonderful to everyone, I should mention—and this other side of the coin will help to explain why the good things that are preached about eternity are oversimplified.

Some Christians find the idea of eternity frightening. It feels suffocating and imprisoning. They wonder what they could possibly do for all eternity that would seem worthwhile. If I cite only personal encounters that I remember, a conversation comes to mind in which a devoutly religious friend remarked that she found the idea of heaven "scary." Then there is another in which I asked a Christian acquaintance what he thought of eternal life and he responded with no pause at all, "It terrifies me!" I remember hearing a pastor in a sermon describe how as a child the thought of eternity made him feel panicky and claustrophobic, and I remember hearing similar childhood memories recounted by someone who left Christianity as a young adult about running to his mother's room for comfort one night after getting himself all worked up over the trapped feeling that thinking about eternity gave him. I myself struggled with the question of whether a person could go for long without becoming listless if there was no need for them to fend off any kind of pain or suffering, either on their own behalf or someone else's: Should we wish that, even after all the improvements we could accomplish with no time constraints, there would always be some pain and suffering left in eternity to provide us with motivation?

Another downside of eternal life as presented by most conservative churches is that it includes eternal punishment for some people. I would guess that most people who think they are going to heaven worry about at least one friend or family member of theirs going to hell. Growing up in church, you certainly hear questions raised about how those in heaven can be happy when some people they loved on earth are eternally separated from them and suffering. The answer I heard given was that in heaven you will have no memory of the people you would miss and feel sorry for, an answer that always felt a little lacking somehow.

For me, the relief of knowing that no one is going to hell did a lot to make up for the disappointment of knowing that I'm not going to heaven. I suppose this change in beliefs would be rougher on someone who started off thinking that everyone (or at least everyone good) goes to heaven—I have to say I don't relish the idea of having written anything that would rob people of an all-positive belief like that, and I'm banking on the likelihood that people who practice a feel-good version of Christianity that gives them nothing to be dissatisfied with won't be looking around for books that ask them to examine how well their beliefs correlate with reality.

Whether a person's idea of eternity includes hell or not though, it is bound to have certain problems that reveal the shortsightedness of the claim that hope and joy only truly come from knowing you will live forever. The eternity that seems able to deliver what people really want hasn't actually been promised anywhere—in one sense. What I mean is that people want an eternity with a guarantee of happiness or fulfillment or whatever name you choose to give the state you would need to be in in order to keep wanting to live forever. If we look at what the Bible says, we see that it does promise an eternity in which people are happy, but at the same time the details it mentions about eternity don't account for *how* everyone could be happy indefinitely, and generations of Christian thinkers haven't been able to come up with an explanation. So we do have a promise of eternal happiness, but it's a promise that comes with no substantiation or even a hint of how it could be possible when it seems to contradict everything we know about ourselves.

The Bible describes the afterlife as a place with no tears, suffering, or pain, and this naturally leads people to wonder how long it would take to get bored under such conditions. In answer to this, theologians have proposed all sorts of wonderful possibilities for what people might do for eternity. Some focus on the idea of heaven as a place where all our desires will be fulfilled: Everyone will get along, and we'll all be able to learn what we always wanted to learn and accomplish what we always wanted to accomplish. We'll be able to spend as much time as we want pursuing the smallest interest. We'll have deep, fascinating conversations with anyone and everyone, and most importantly we'll have perfect communion with God. Other views of the afterlife focus more on the idea of a restored earth and of how much satisfying work there will be to do: People will continue to devote themselves to things like art and science, and we will have forever to explore this vast universe that we can currently only dream of seeing a tiny fraction of. Life will go on as usual in many ways, but without the fear of losing anyone or of having your pursuits cut short. And there are many other ideas of what eternity will be like with varying degrees of desirability and of basis in biblical teachings.

The problem that none of them address satisfactorily though is, what will motivate people and keep them from being bored into stupor after millions or billions of years of life with no real problems to face? Even if we had heart-breaking problems like those we are constantly trying to fix today, would the need to see them solved be enough to provide motivation over *that long* of a time? If you eventually managed to fix all the problems, boredom would start to set in. If you hadn't solved them after a few billion years of trying, would you lose motivation? Additionally, would the fact that no one dies itself be enough to take away motivation because even if someone had a bad life at a given point they would always have an eternity left to live a good life? How many people's existence would be defined by the fact that there was no real need even to provide food for themselves to stay alive?

The Bible says little about heaven at all and nothing about human fears that eternity couldn't really be good. Personally, I find that strange because the New Testament talks about eternal life as the reason for living a Christian life now. For instance, Paul writes in I Corinthians 15:19, "If in this life only we have hope in Christ, we are of all men the most pitiable" (NKJV). If eternity is supposed to be motivating enough to make you choose a lifestyle that would be "pitiable" without it, then it seems reasonable that the Bible would explain how eternity can be good when everything we know about the idea suggests it is not good. The only answer to this concern is to say that heaven or eternity is about being with God more than anything else and that our ability to experience God now is so limited that we can't see all the aspects of his nature that will keep us amazed forever.

For people like me who can't say they've ever experienced God, this comes down to saying that you should live in a way that is often unpleasant because someone whose existence you have no good reason to believe in said so, and if you do, you will end up in a situation that the person who might not exist said is good, although you can't see how it's good and no one has ever been able to explain how it could be good, but it should actually be fine because the person whose existence you have never seen a sign of also supposedly has characteristics that resolve this impossible situation, although no one can explain what those characteristics might be either. And also if you don't go along with the whole thing the only other option is eternal torment.

Even for people who talk about experiencing God to some degree, the situation is bleak. I know because I've heard friends and acquaintances, from those who struggled with constant doubt to those who felt secure enough in their faith to go into fulltime ministry, express their worries about what eternity could possibly be. The only difference between them and me was that they thought they had experienced God, and they just didn't see how the being they had experienced could be enough to make eternity work. Even for someone who has a sense that God is a wonderful person and an important part of their life, if they ever start to ask themself the questions about motivation I've mentioned here, it's difficult to ever go back to an unperturbed happiness on the topic, and of course some of them never experienced such a happiness in the first place because they weren't able to experience it while knowing that many people were headed for hell. If these pensive devotees persist in voicing their worries to leaders who are supposed to advise them, they are told not to worry because we just can't understand any of it—or possibly reprimanded for their presumptuousness in accusing God of not being enough for them.

By talking through all the uncertainties and negative feelings that can exist around the topic of heaven, I want to show that when religious people say nonreligious people are missing the hope and joy of eternal life, it's really not that simple.

At the same time though, suddenly having the concept of mortality become real to you for the first time can be difficult whether for the reasons I mentioned earlier or for others, and it might be helpful to know how others have worked through this change, so I'll end this section by talking about things that helped me to have joy in my life even while accepting that everything has to end. As I already stated, the realization that no one is going to hell is a big positive. No one is going to suffer forever. No one is going to have regrets. Even though I won't be in heaven, I won't experience anything negative either, and that doesn't seem like such a bad trade for the certainty that no kind but non-Christian person is condemned to unending punishment—especially when I couldn't really convince myself that heaven was a good idea anyway. The thoughts that I'll list out here all offer the same sobering, adult type of comfort. There isn't anything in existence to match the fairytale bliss of someone who believes in eternal life without ever having stopped to think about how it works. But there are a lot of things better than living with the grudging acceptance of hell and the indomitable fear that there's no way heaven could be what people hope it's going to be.

- Your eternity is now. -

In some ways, a limited lifetime is not all that different from an eternity because, while you don't live forever, the only experience of the world you have is one in which you are alive. Your life will keep going, keep moving, keep changing, until the point at which you are unable to know that this is no longer happening; there will never be a time when you are not alive but wishing that you were.

This realization hit me like never before after I was put under anesthesia for a few hours for a minor surgery. I had never experienced such a perfect nothingness before that, not even while sleeping. From sleep, I always woke up with some sense of time having passed, probably due to the sounds and other sensations that manage to drift into a slumbering consciousness. Waking up from anesthesia felt utterly different, as if a segment of time had simply been snipped out of existence and deleted. It was strange the degree to which, in that state, I didn't realize that I had left anything, that I was missing out on anything, or that there was anything to go back to.

It is, certainly, difficult to picture what it really means to be dead and how completely devoid of any negative it is, but to me it seems like a mental exercise worth trying in order to develop an understanding of how little reason we have to be afraid. I've found myself thinking about the concept often over the last couple years: It takes quite a while to grow accustomed to, but thankfully I can spare a couple minutes a week to think about such imponderables.

One facet of the topic that stands out to me, perhaps just because of its irony, perhaps because it is a nice thing to take note of, is how much the primary description of heaven I always heard in church does *not* differ from what a nonreligious person is left with. This brief, much-referenced description says, "'And God will wipe away every tear from their eyes; there shall be no more death, nor sorrow, nor crying. There shall be no more pain, for the former things have passed away'" (Revelation 21:4, NKJV). The chapter this verse is found in and the next chapter contain other details about what the "new heaven" and "new earth" (Revelation 21:1) will be like, but none of those details took on quite the life of its own that this one did. I believe this is because the details given about what *will* be part of the afterlife are odd, somewhat hard to make sense of, and not as universally appealing as this one list of what *won't* be part of it. The few affirmative details the Bible gives about eternity just don't speak to people as powerfully as seems fitting for something so all-important, and although Christian thinkers have made suggestions to fill in the gaps, we're still left with a lot of vague maybes and uncertain hopes. But when people hear the promise of no more sorrow, they *want* that, and they know they want it. No longer believing in eternity, I'm a little sad to not have the option of imagining a nondescript future in which all good things come together in an impossibly perfect way forever, but it's also not terrible to remind myself, "I know that doesn't work anyway, and at least dead people still get the one part of heaven most of the world was able to agree on."

Even the first point of the verse, "there shall be no more death," seems meaningful to me in this context. The only time you can fear death is while you're alive. Once you're dead, you won't actually experience whatever it was you were afraid of, nor will you experience the pain of being separated from others who have died. Not that I imagine this point enables anyone to simply toss aside a fear that is quite deeply ingrained and natural. Like the fear of hell, this isn't a feeling to be logicked out of. You can tell yourself that worrying about an unavoidable future that doesn't actually involve any suffering anyway is a waste of time, but it doesn't necessarily remove all worry. You have to give yourself time. Leaving a belief in eternity is like finding yourself on another planet, surrounded by an alien society. If you are to thrive in this new world where reality confounds your expectations, you must allow yourself time to grow gradually through the discomfort of adjusting to the unfamiliar. As you choose to face the fact over and over again that your life is right now, that it's not found in some other world and it's not forever, you will get used to that idea, and the fear that might seem inseparable from it right now will slowly wear off.

- Your desires for freedom now matter. -

Because this life is all you have, your desires to get and to give freedom in this life are deeply important. There is no "greater good" of an afterlife to overshadow them with its supposed grandeur. If meeting a friend for coffee on Sunday mornings brings more pleasure or inspiration to your life than attending church, you should do it. Your enjoyment right now is actually worth something, while commands and traditions stating that church attendance helps keep you on the road to heaven have no substance to back them up and do nothing to benefit you. Within the wide realm of all the things that don't harm anyone, you are free to order these little details of your life in the way that suits you best: to read what you want, to live where you want, to prioritize as you want, to associate with whom you want, to say yes or no when *you* want to. If your choice makes life on earth better, that's all there is to it; it doesn't need to be weighed against the sometimes unintuitive rules of achieving an afterlife.[27]

It is valid and important for you to take steps, both the big ones and the small daily ones, towards defending and improving your own mental and physical health, your wellbeing, and your satisfaction with the structure of your life. There will be times when it is right to sacrifice for the good of others, but you won't be trapped in a lifestyle where you constantly have to sacrifice what benefits you now for some far-off, uncertain goal or threat.

All the same principles go for questions of justice and equality and improvement of life for others as well. When you see a problem in this country or on this planet—when you know someone is being taken advantage of, when you know your own community is being taken advantage of, when you know the way we do things now needs to be improved—you don't even need to consider listening to anyone who says that it's up to God to work it all out in the end or that challenging authority is spiritual rebellion. Your concern to see others respected and valued in this life is right, and it matters infinitely more than all the hollow threats about where those who make waves spend eternity.

- You are always young. -

The most frightening aspect of immortality, I think, is the idea of all you might outgrow as your numbers of experiences stretched towards the infinite. Would you become bored with things it would be unthinkable to tire of in this life? Would you perhaps

---

[27] If someone even *tries* to make it sound like I'm saying you should do whatever sounds good in the moment without thinking about the long term effects... Don't be that person. Don't be the person who didn't even read the footnote highlighting the already glaringly obvious point.

even become bored of the people who mean everything to you now? Of course it's impossible to know, but what we do know is that in this life we will never be more than children in our knowledge. With all the vastness of experience and information that exists, and all the great depth you could delve into on any one interest, you can't outgrow wonder and humility in this lifetime except by your own choice, and it would be a bad choice. There will always be so much that you don't know and haven't experienced. Let that be a positive! You haven't reached the end of all you have to explore yet, and you aren't going to.

- Life is light. -

Whatever anxiousness you might have about your own mistakes and bad decisions, at least none of them have eternal effects. I don't know how many people share the weight of worry that the thought of eternal consequences used to give me, but I know in my case that one of the positives I experienced after changing my beliefs was a sense of lightness about life. A weight that I hadn't realized was so heavy had disappeared: It was the weight of apprehension over all the unknown, forever inescapable ramifications that any of my actions might have.

While there are still plenty of things in life to be taken seriously, you don't have to take yourself too seriously. When deciding how to spend your time and how to interact with people, the factors that come into play are things you are able to make sense of: people's needs and feelings, your balance of work and enjoyment—it is familiar things like these you have to take into account. You'll do your best, and the results won't be perfect, but none of the imperfections can exist on the scale of the eternal, and there is also no need to wonder if perhaps the choices that seem best for everyone in the here and now could perhaps be damaging eternally.

- A grieving process isn't a failing. -

All the good and bad advice about how to cope with the loss of something as monumental as eternity can only take you so far—most likely not very far at all in terms of how you feel day to day. I think it's important to keep concepts like the ones I've listed above in mind, in order to eventually develop a new framework for thinking about life, but the most effective remedy to any shock and grief that comes along with a major worldview shift is simply giving yourself time to adjust. While all the logic of why the change isn't so bad might be clear to you from the beginning, your emotions might be slow to catch up, and there's nothing wrong with that.

In the transition, don't run from your new realizations. Don't try to distract yourself from thinking about the less-than-ideal nature of reality. Face the problems and ponder them; otherwise, you become a fugitive, never quite at peace or at rest, afraid of quiet and stillness and anything that might allow your thoughts to drift to places you can't accept.

It's unfortunate that so many of us gained our first grounding in reality in an unrealistic world in which immortality existed and consequentially we find it hard to leave this concept behind, but the same thing could have happened with any idea. We could have been brought up believing in magic or telepathy. Think of anything in life that you wish were different, any impossible thing that would make the world more ideal, and it could have been the too-good-to-be-true object you were raised to long for. Alternative fantasies, any fantasies you weren't raised to see as reality, probably sound silly to you, and you can say that of course all those things would be nice but you aren't going to waste time feeling upset that they aren't real. Unlikely as it might sound now, you can put the idea of eternity in its place as well;

against all the practice you had in valuing this thing above all else, you can start to build up a counterweight of practice in letting go of it, but, depending on exactly what your history is with the idea of eternity, this process might not be easy or quick in any way.

Leaving a faith tradition is a loss. It is accompanied by a grieving process. The process takes time, and it is vital that you not rush yourself. I encourage anyone who is in the midst of giving up old beliefs and even anyone who gave them up long ago but is left with any lingering negativity: Talk to a grief counselor, a religious trauma counselor, or any type of counselor or therapist you feel comfortable with. The need for this type of counseling is well known and shouldn't be surprising to any professional who does not specifically confine themself to working only with clients of one faith. There are even organizations and networks of people who can help you find this sort of counseling for free. (See "Additional Resources" on the page after this chapter.) You might have to try things out with a few counselors before you find someone whose style works for you, but the investment is worth it. And if you aren't going to talk to a professional, for Pete's sake at least talk to someone who's got your back and who doesn't put you through any of the things I talked about in Chapter 3 or anything that resembles them in any way when you bring up the issue.

Meaning or Purpose

Without an intelligent, deliberate creator, you can't have a meaning to life of the sort Christianity promises, and without eternity, you can't have purpose on the scale it promises. The community that raised me looked upon people living without this sort of cosmic, ultimate meaning and purpose as the most pitiable bankrupts. They spoke of the aimlessness, the hopelessness, the unfulfilled longings, and the dread of death that darkened their fretful existence and reminded us that we had living within us the light and joy that the whole world hungered for. Just as with eternal life though, God-given meaning and purpose don't remain as wonderful as they seem when you think them over, and having to do without them is not exactly the agony it's made out to be.

Speaking as a former Christian, I can tell you that purpose is always a problem, even if you do have God and eternity. In fact, the more time you have to work with, the worse the problem becomes. With eternity, it's utterly insufferable.

I was always the sort of person who had to ask why I was doing something, what the point was. And I often felt dissatisfied because, no matter what point I came up with, I could always think one step ahead, on to another level at which the purpose I had pictured no longer mattered. In my childhood, there was one phrase in particular that tended to start me off down these dissatisfying trails of thought. It was a phrase that sometimes turned up in nature documentaries: "for the preservation of the species." Some serene-voiced narrator talking about rattlesnakes or penguins or ants would comment on what feats these creatures achieved for the preservation of the species. Anything to ensure another generation would go on. When I heard that, I always pictured to myself how terrible it would be if that was the only thing people lived for. If your life didn't mean anything in itself but you lived so that someone else could live an equally pointless life so that someone else could live an equally pointless life and so on, there really was no point, and the whole idea felt too dreary to dwell on. Thank goodness we get to do things to enjoy ourselves, I would think, instead of having to fight for survival just long enough to reproduce. Somehow in my mind the whole problem was always completely resolved by virtue of my having access to all the construction paper and markers I could want. I couldn't imagine living without arts and crafts, but thankfully I didn't have to.

As a young adult, I found these sorts of concerns returning in a new context: Sure, the thrill of creation and discovery was enough to make life feel worthwhile if you only thought about the here and now, but I knew that what really mattered was eternity. For the hope of eternal life, I frequently took time away from the activities I felt drawn to in order to spend it on others that were much less enjoyable but felt deeply meaningful because they were said to have eternal value. Having the hope of eternity had to be inherently more meaningful than living for the present, I thought, because there was an obvious purpose for everything: Everything would last in some way. The concept of putting in work and preparation now for something you would get to enjoy in the future made sense. Why pursue God now? For an eternal closeness with him. Why do earthly activities with excellence? Because those activities and the effects they had on others would in some way contribute to our experience of eternity. I never had to deal with a question along the lines of, "Why do anything now if the effects aren't going to last anyway?"

But eventually I realized that there was another question that was just as troubling: "What's the point of eternity?" As the previous section details, when thinking about eternal life there's an uncomfortable tug-of-war between selfish and altruistic motivations. Is pleasure the point of the whole thing? I'm living this Christian life now for the enjoyment of eternity later, but is it really enough to just live for pleasure forever? Wouldn't it feel more meaningful, wouldn't I have more of a sense of purpose, if there were problems that needed to be solved in eternity? And the thought process goes on from there with the ideas I've already addressed. It was disturbing to me that Christianity didn't offer any escape from the cycle of always asking, "What's the point of this?" being given an answer, and then asking, "But what's the point of *that*?" The supernatural provided no clear barrier beyond which things were suddenly endowed with unquestionable purposefulness. Finding nothing useful by going in circles, I had to content myself with simply not thinking about it. I could tell myself that this life mattered because it affected eternity, and after that I had to stop: Build a wall. Cut the edges off the map. Beyond this point there's nothing worth seeing.

What I only started to realize after losing the beliefs that had at least been supplying me with purpose for the present was that the be-all-end-all sort of purpose I wanted religion to provide didn't even exist. Perpetually-satisfying purpose is an imagined concept, just as impossible as a square triangle. If you can't be satisfied in doing anything until you've asked why you're doing it and received an unassailable answer, then you just aren't going to be satisfied in doing anything. No matter what next level of scope and impact each answer takes you to, you will always be able to ask why again. You aren't going to arrive someday at a mystical ultimate answer about which it's impossible to ask yet again what the point is.

Contentment doesn't require a grand or eternal purpose at all though. Some things you do because you want to. Some things you don't want to do but you do anyway because they lead to something you want. If you think you need many more layers than that, certainly if you think you need more layers than fit in the observable universe, then the only way to achieve contentment is to change your thinking.

There are people who are happy because they spend their days helping their children to thrive. They don't need to ask why they want their children to thrive. It's a motivation that needs no greater purpose. There are people who are happy because they work to combat famine or disease. They don't need to ask why they don't want others to be in danger of these things. They just want it. There are people who are happy because they live to experience the beauty of nature or to produce art. There are many people who find happiness in combinations of several different motivations. But there are also people who are never happy because they find a way to devalue every form of enjoyment and accomplishment by comparing it with something they imagine to be greater. Neither religion nor anything else one imagines to be a source of ultimate purpose can bring happiness within that attitude. The attitude itself has to be changed.

And that is why I see no problem in simply lacking a source of ultimate purpose. Without God and eternity, you still have numerous sources of intrinsic and nearly intrinsic satisfaction and purposefulness, and if these sources aren't enough for you, religion probably wouldn't have been enough either, just as it wasn't for me. Like me, you will probably take a while to adjust if religion was a source of some level of purpose for you, but adjusting your attitude is a slow process that really gets you somewhere in the end, unlike the supposedly instant solution of labeling eternal life as all the purpose you will ever need.

I believe it's also important to clearly acknowledge that there is not one perfect purpose out there towards which everyone should be striving. This is important because purpose enslaves. Great purposes are demanding masters and difficult to leave behind, whereas smaller, simpler purposes can be disobeyed or abandoned more easily if a conflict of interests arises. An ostensibly ultimate purpose will hold you to it even against your better judgment. Purpose is not necessarily the same thing as happiness either and may require the sacrifice of happiness. When I had little doubt in my original beliefs, I was mostly unhappy but very full of purpose as far as the idea of getting to heaven took me (even though there was still dissatisfaction if I let myself wonder why that goal itself mattered). I had a reason to live a certain way, and I believed it would lead to happiness eventually, but the sacrifices it demanded made the present unhappy. For me the primary sacrifices were that I was constrained to follow "God's" commands even if I didn't see how they could be ethical and that I had to devote large amounts of time to Christian activities. If I had thought that Christianity was a system to serve me and that I could disregard the parts of it that didn't work for me, it would not have felt real enough to provide a strong sense of purpose.

Pursuing anything that feels important enough to bestow a sense of purpose will involve sacrifice on some level, so you should think about what kinds of sacrifices you're willing to make. It's important to realize that there isn't one best, greatest, only worthwhile purpose that everyone must take the good and bad of, but that instead, you are free to choose purposes that don't make demands you're unwilling to comply with.

Similar principles to all these apply when it comes to meaning as well. If human beings had been created deliberately by a higher power, then you might be like a knife or a lightbulb: a thing made by a designer for a specific purpose or range of purposes. And then life might have a specific meaning too. Like a test or a game, it would have a predetermined goal that you were supposed to arrive at if you did it right. I don't think that's a bad thing to be without at all. It might sound convenient to simply be told there was an ultimate, cosmic meaning for your existence and to therefore know exactly what you were supposed to do with your life, but it's more freeing to have a choice. Like I've already covered, as illustrated by my own experience, it's possible to believe that you do have a predetermined cosmic meaning and to be unhappy with it, to wonder whether it's actually good and valuable in the end, and even to wish yourself annihilated in order to be rid of its complications.

Instead of being handed a meaning you have no say in, without God you are free to spend your time on what is meaningful to you. I'm allowed now to search for the truth, to discuss my search, and to act according to what I find out without fearing that this pursuit is outside of or in contradiction to my intended purpose for existence. This search for truth and the ability to share and discuss it with others is deeply meaningful to me. It is something I naturally want to engage in and feel satisfied engaging in without needing a reason. It is something I want to do regardless of how fleeting my life or even the world itself might be. You too have no need for meaning to be handed to you from a supernatural realm. Cosmic meaning is as imaginary as eternal purpose, but everyday, earthly, human meaning is all around you. You don't need to ask a deity or enlightened being to reveal something that matters beyond the edge of your ability to question; you already know, or can discover with some effort, what matters to you and those around you.

To sum this all up, there was a time when I was afraid of the possibility of losing my beliefs because I thought my life would have no meaning or purpose without them, but losing those beliefs only brought me to realize that the exalted level of meaning and purpose I was afraid to lose had never been achievable in the first place and that all the sources of simple, intrinsic meaning and purpose all around me were still just as accessible as before, in my specific case, even more accessible than before. From the perspective I have now, the threat of meaninglessness I was raised with almost appears to have been made in bad faith, like a mechanic telling you that, sure, you can go to the guys down the street for a better deal, but *they* won't throw in a free flux capacitor tune-up. I don't think it actually was a deliberate lie—I'm aware that I was raised in a community of mechanics who believed cars were sacred and were consequently a little afraid to study their inner workings too closely and had simply accepted the age-old tradition that a car does have a flux capacitor inside somewhere. I know our spiritual leaders thought they were protecting people with what they preached to us, but what they actually accomplished was to encourage the cultivation of a desire for something fake. I simply hope that by taking this critical look at things I can point at least one person towards a method of redirecting that insatiable desire for cosmic purpose towards things that are real and satisfying.

An Objective Moral Standard

Church and Christian media introduced me to plenty of Sunday school characters as a child, both specific individuals and stock types. There was Elijah, brimming with miracles; Jonah, complaining and selfish; the New Testament believer, bold and full of life in the face of danger; the establishment lackey, driven by greed and hateful of believers for challenging the existing world order. Among all these characters, the morally depraved nonbeliever fit right in. The person who thought there was no God was depicted as anything from a psychopathic villain to a suffering lost soul spitting out bitter adages on the worthlessness of human life to cope with their own despair. The image lived on far beyond Sunday school as well, continuing to arise with varying levels of depth in discussions meant for teenagers and adults. When I began to talk over my religious doubt with people in my late twenties, fear of the chaos society would undergo without Christian moral standards was still brought up as a primary reason why Christianity had to be true, and as far as I know it continues to be used as a technique of fearmongering for people of all ages in the types of communities I came out of.

The Christian message here is that we have a moral law that works: We follow the rules that God has recorded in the Bible, and we are able to have peace and justice. Take that clear, understandable, dependable set of laws away, and you get a world in which people will do whatever they feel like doing with no concern for the effect they have on others. Instead of being concrete, right and wrong will shift with cultural tides, be left open to interpretation, and generate perpetual disagreements as everyone fights to bring their own opinion to prominence.

If God is not real, then, just as my Sunday school teachers feared, the moral requirements found in the Bible are not the words of divinity and therefore do not necessarily represent a standard we must live by and therefore should have their rightness and usefulness evaluated by human beings and be thrown out if they prove less than worthy. Just as we've seen with the Christian ideas of eternity and of purpose though, what Christianity promises on this topic is really not as great as it's made out to be and the alternative is really not that bad. In fact, despite the claims that a religious standard of morality is more objective and concrete than any other, in real life the Christian moral code has all the same shortcomings as do sets of rules that admit to having been agreed upon by human consensus.

As we've already covered in Chapter 2, Section #3, it's a misconception even to say that there is one Christian moral code. When a Christian says that the Bible provides us with an objective moral standard, I can't be sure what they picture that standard to be unless I already know many details about their specific set of beliefs. If an editor were to tell me that they planned to mark up a text according to *The Chicago Manual of Style*, I would know what decisions they were going to make almost down to the comma, but when a Christian says that we need to bring society into alignment with the moral standard of the Bible, I haven't a clue what that means in practice for any moral question. Lawyers can cite specific passages of legal codes and decisions made by courts that give fairly clear guidance on the legality of most things—yes, there are always legal battles still to be fought, and situations constantly arise that defy quick and easy answers, but at least decisions are reached and details are recorded, and at least the vast complexity of it all is acknowledged. When it comes to Christian morality, people state that it's all just as *simple* as doing what God says and yet various churches cannot agree on whether many actions are right or wrong even though they are all trying to do what God says.

Christian moral codes are lacking in objectivity at every level, beginning with the level at which one decides which rules are included in the code and which are not. As I explain in Chapter 2, Section #3, and Chapter 2, Section #4, Point (1), you can identify many passages in the Bible that clearly give commands about right and wrong, but some churches say these commands are for all people while some say they were only meant for a specific group at a specific time. From the beginning, human decisions about which rules really count have been introduced, and the deviation from objectivity continues as each church interprets what the rules they do decide to keep actually mean. As a microcosm for all this, let's take the Ten Commandments, found in Exodus 20:1–17. If this revered passage of scripture were part of an objective moral standard, a standard so concrete and so above human wisdom that our mere respect for its words would singlehandedly guide our moral decisions more effectively than would all human legal and ethical deliberation, then, honestly, I don't think we would find the confusion and the throwing out of rules we actually see surrounding it.

I'd like to draw your attention to three commands that have inspired particularly high levels of confusion: the command not to "misuse" or "take in vain" God's name (verse 7), the command to observe the Sabbath (verses 8–11), and the command not to commit adultery (verse 14). (And while some of the other commandments on the list might be easier to agree on, keep in mind that they're not perfectly objective either: Churches can't even agree on which specific actions violate the command not to murder and which don't.[28]) If morality decided by human beings is too messy because it requires going through processes of disagreeing and reaching a consensus, then morality taken from the Bible is no better because it requires the same processes, as illustrated by the following.

First, the command not to misuse God's name is left wide open to interpretation, much, much wider than should be the case if it is intended to perfectly, clearly let people know which actions are wrong so they can avoid them. In some communities, people feel it is obvious that this commandment strictly prohibits using phrases like "Oh my God" to express surprise, while in other communities people can't understand what could be problematic about habitually calling out to the most important person in your life at moments of strong emotion. I've heard people point out that it would make more sense to interpret this commandment as condemning careless claims of divine support and favor—throwing around the notion that God told you to do something just so others will go along with it for instance—and I agree that it would make more sense to interpret it this way. But the fact that some existing interpretations of this commandment are better than others doesn't take away the problem that the Bible says not to misuse God's name, gives no specifics on what "misuse" means, and therefore creates a situation in which we don't really know whether something as seemingly unimportant as involuntarily repeating words of surprise is morally wrong. If there is a defined, objective

---

[28] For example, some sects think pacifism is necessary while others don't consider killing in war to be murder. For another example, some believers in the God of the Bible at some times have not considered the killing of a "servant" or slave to be a crime equal to the killing of a free man, while your average Christian today would consider it all murder. See Exodus 21:20–21, 28–32.

meaning behind the command, then some people who want to follow God's laws must still be doing the wrong thing, even though they have this set of rules to help them, because different people who all want to obey God come to different conclusions about what obedience to this command really means.

But perhaps there isn't one specific meaning behind the command you'll say. Perhaps true obedience really does look different for different people. That's a possibility worth considering, and the first detail about it we need to consider is that it is referring to a subjective moral standard, not an objective one. Perhaps God gave humanity vague laws on purpose so that each individual could act according to what they felt in their heart was the true meaning of each law. Sure. But if so, that means human convictions are the authority on which behaviors are moral, and different people are free to follow different moral standards. As I mentioned in Chapter 2, Section #3, and Chapter 2, Section #4, Point (1), the range of convictions that honest, serious, God-fearing churches hold on the commands of scripture easily includes the conviction that a command doesn't need to be followed at all because it was meant for somebody else.

To some degree, that is the case with the Exodus 20 commandment to observe the Sabbath. We know that this originally meant refraining from work on the last day of the week. However, in Christian times the practice shifted to apply to the first day of the week instead, and besides that, many people don't think there's actually anything morally wrong about working on any old day of the week and claim that this commandment is simply stressing the importance of building restful times into your life. So, is it objective? Is the original understanding that one should rest on Saturday a moral requirement? Is the command concrete, or did it change to mean Sunday and/or something more general? On a related note, if God's law is objective and superior to the laws of conduct we could make for ourselves, then what are we supposed to make of the fact that scripture also commanded God's people to kill anyone who did not observe the Sabbath?

Exodus 31:12–15 NIV
Then the Lord said to Moses, "Say to the Israelites, 'You must observe my Sabbaths. This will be a sign between me and you for the generations to come, so you may know that I am the Lord, who makes you holy. Observe the Sabbath, because it is holy to you. Anyone who desecrates it is to be put to death; those who do any work on that day must be cut off from their people. For six days work is to be done, but the seventh day is a day of sabbath rest, holy to the Lord. Whoever does any work on the Sabbath day is to be put to death.'"

This added information does make the commandment seem more concrete and objective, but it is very difficult to understand how objective morality could have somehow changed from requiring a death penalty for working on Saturday to saying it doesn't really matter. Was it truly right for God to have demanded punishment at first? Is it truly right for no punishment to be demanded now? Did right change, and if so, why? Is depending on a standard as fluid as this really better than living by our own careful deliberation on which actions are helpful and which are harmful?

Finally, consider the commandment not to commit adultery. This one is particularly interesting because in the New Testament Jesus provides some details on what "adultery" includes, which should help to avoid the type of confusion seen over the command about taking God's name in vain. Speaking to a crowd, Jesus says the following.

Matthew 5:31–32 NIV
"It has been said, 'Anyone who divorces his wife must give her a certificate of divorce.' But I tell you that anyone who divorces his wife, except for sexual immorality, makes her the victim of adultery, and anyone who marries a divorced woman commits adultery."

There are two interesting things to note about Jesus' words. One, the original commandment against adultery apparently wasn't enough to make it clear that divorce counted as adultery, and so Jesus needs to explain that. Two, although we have here an Old Testament commandment backed up by a specific teaching of Jesus himself in the New Testament, we are still left with the moral problem of "That just doesn't sound right," and with disagreement between churches. Some churches hold to this teaching exactly as stated here, but many don't feel moral peace about the statement unless they add in a few more caveats they think Jesus must have intended. For example, of course the last part, that anyone who marries a divorced woman commits adultery, can't really mean exactly what it says. A woman in an abusive relationship shouldn't have to choose between staying married to a violent man or being single forever, and one whose husband left her shouldn't be prohibited from finding someone more faithful. And even though the first part says a man can only divorce his wife for reasons of sexual immorality, surely that doesn't mean he'll be considered an "adulterer" for leaving a woman who is abusive either.

These three commands, like the ones discussed in Chapter 2, show that the communication of morals in the Bible isn't a simple solution for the discomfort or imperfection of identifying right and wrong. Despite the existence of these commands, either we do not really know what the specific standard we will be held to is and can only hope we're getting it right, or the standard is different for everyone. Either way, those who believe they have a moral standard given by God have to exercise their own reasoning ability to determine what is right just as those who don't believe in God do. The idea that religion provides objective morals simply does not hold up, but the good news is that this means we've been doing at least tolerably without a perfect standard so far, so our efforts to evaluate whether various moral laws are just and worthy will likely bring improvement rather than a collapse of order.

That last point is worth spending a little more time on: By admitting that there is no divine being who has given us a perfect moral code, we aren't necessarily throwing out Christian morality at all. If there is no God, then Christianity is a set of ideas reached by human consensus just like any other ideology, and whatever advice on morals it contains *might* be excellent. The point of all this isn't to get rid of all morals with religious roots but to be aware that each moral recommendation should be evaluated for the worth of the results it produces and not simply accepted because it appears in a holy book. Because there are so many different interpretations of what any moral rule in the Bible means, each interpretation needs to be evaluated separately.

None of this necessarily discounts the idea that Christianity has historically had a positive moral influence on people. That is a completely separate question, one for historians to answer. Since I'm no history expert, I can only offer my own rather uninformed opinion: I could be persuaded to change my mind if the evidence to the contrary is convincing, but currently I would say that, with its glorification of charity and humility, Christianity has exerted a positive moral influence over the centuries. By detailing the reasons why I don't think Christian morality is supernatural or more objective than other sources of morality, I am not trying to deny its importance in the development of the cultures it forms a part of; I am denying that it needed to have a supernatural origin in order to produce its positive influence.

As I've covered throughout this book, Christianity seems human in origin to me. It can be a helpful philosophy when humans acknowledge that it is imperfect and selectively choose its beneficial ideas to live by, but when we assume that it came from beyond ourselves, we end up being bound to it in whatever form our church community happens to embrace, which could include ideas that are inaccurate and harmful. When we admit that the helpful morals we've gained from Christian thinking over the centuries are still human ideas and that interpretation and deliberation have always been necessary, we can then allow ourselves to separate out what is harmful more effectively.

It would be nice if we possessed a moral standard that was free of flaws and required no guesswork to make sense of. But such a thing simply does not exist. The fact that Christians claim they have a moral code that is both perfect and objective does not make it so. This doesn't mean Christian morality is bad necessarily, just that it isn't inherently superior to moral codes derived from other sources: Any source is most likely going to contain some helpful rules and some harmful or useless ones.

Here is where a defender of Christian morality might feel the need to interject that I'm missing the point entirely. It's not actually objectivity that matters, they might say. The threat of atheism leading to societal collapse doesn't arise because human beings need to be told in detail what is right and what is wrong. Human beings may even know right and wrong on their own in fact. The real problem is that, regardless of what right actually *is*, people won't *do* right if they don't have the threat of divine judgment scaring them into it. In this case, it's not so much the specifics of the rules found in the Bible that matter as the idea that there is a rule-giver who can punish you in an afterlife.

The idea of a cosmic judge is another proposition that would, or could under the right conditions, be great if it were true: I think we'd all prefer to believe that right and wrong were never truly overlooked. But just as the supposedly objective biblical standard takes a lot of subjective interpreting, the threat of divine judgment seems to require a lot of help from human agents of enforcement. Again, Christians can say that the biblical system of morality is superior to other systems all they want, but I just don't see it with this point any more than with the previous one. The claim seems inaccurate.

It's not that I think a belief in divine judgment is completely ineffectual: I'd wager there have been more than zero people in the history of the world who have thought twice about doing something wrong because they believed God was watching them. But belief in divine judgment has never existed in an isolated system where it was charged to keep order without help from human self-interest, human empathy, human discipline, and human punishment.[29] You can say that finding the most

---

[29] I am curious to know who would volunteer to live in a society where the only means of keeping order was people's belief in divine punishment. We've always had a mix of religious and secular influences on behavior, but if I had to pick between living in a society where we

effective way to prevent wrongdoing is as simple as telling people that a cosmic judge knows all their actions, but such a simplistic statement glosses over several things: For one, people who believe in God do wrong things, knowing they are wrong, all the time—either in a moment of weakness or in a pattern of uncontrolled weakness. For another, some people who believe in God do wrong things thinking that God has authorized or even commanded them. And for another, just because the people of a society no longer believe in God doesn't mean that they no longer feel concern for the wellbeing of those around them or that they somehow become shortsighted enough to think that acting in disorderly, dishonest ways will make them happier than cooperation will.

Even in times and places where the vast majority of people shared some sort of Christian belief, we've never had a perfect world without a need to rely on human peacekeeping—from parents disciplining their children to governments penalizing crimes. If you've been made to feel any guilt or fear over your unbelief and the moral effects it might have on the world around you, please see these threats of moral decay for what they are: nothing more than fearmongering. At the end of the day, most people just want to know they can live a life free of danger and harassment. Most of us are never even going to consider trading that security for some risky shot at selfish gain, not only because it's a stupid gamble but also because most of us can't stand the thought of causing suffering to others. And when it comes to

---

only kept a belief in divine judgment and threw out all our secular forms of behavior management, or of living in a society where we kept secular education, secular law enforcement, secular rehabilitation programs, and so on with no belief in divine judgment, I'd pick the latter. I think removing the secular elements would bring a greater risk of some sort of moral decline than removing the religious ones would.

the exceptions who don't play by the rules the rest of society would prefer, it's not as if our arsenal of crime prevention strategies is depleted by the loss of the option to verbally threaten people with eternal damnation.

Part of the problem with expecting divine judgment to be an effective deterrent to bad behavior is the very fact we've been discussing here: that scriptural moral rules aren't as objective as they claim to be. We can see this played out in the Bible itself, for instance, with Jesus' accusations against the Pharisees in the Gospels. Jesus rails against the members of this very rule-conscious sect for bordering on ridiculous with their attempts to keep every tiny detail of God's law while at the same time overlooking the more important big concepts of being merciful, just, and charitable to those in need around them. The Pharisees thought they were doing what was necessary to avoid God's judgment, but Jesus tells them they are failing miserably. Looking at these stories with modern eyes, most of us probably agree that the Pharisees' behavior towards the less fortunate members of their community (as described in the Gospels) is wrong. Although they believed in God, paid close attention to scripture, and bent their daily behavior around a fear of divine judgment, they still didn't do what was right.

The idea that God is watching you is no silver bullet for making the world more just and kind. There are as many factors influencing the possible ways people will respond to the idea as there are with any other means of promoting right behavior. Like the Pharisees, some people may be certain that they know the right way to live to avoid divine judgment, while other groups of people who fear divine judgment just as strongly look upon their beliefs as ridiculous and misguided. For some people, divine judgment might be an added reason to obey human laws and standards. For others, it could be a motivation in the opposite direction, reminding them that if their understanding of divine law contradicts human law, they had better stick to divine law since it comes with worse punishments.

It would be easy to reverse the tales of godless immorality I was told in church and paint a picture of theocratic horrors to counter them: Scare stories of inquisitions, crusades, purity killings, and criminals convinced that God's voice had commanded their actions. I could fight fire with fire and claim that the real threat of moral decay in our world comes from religion. But what good would that do? The fact is there are both nonreligious and religious people who put love and truth first in their lives, and those people tend to both care about the wellbeing of those around them and find effective ways to secure it. And then there are both nonreligious and religious people who will sacrifice everything, including love and truth, for some sort of agenda, whether it's personal gain, a political cause, or what have you. And there are both nonreligious and religious ideas and institutions that will threaten people with suffering, death, and damnation for showing disloyalty. People who prioritize their agenda over love and truth, or are forced to act as if they did, either place little value on the wellbeing of others or fail to work towards it effectively even if they place great value on it because they won't question the flaws in their methods.

Neither lack of religion nor adherence to any particular religion leads on its own to social chaos. And neither is a guarantee on its own of order or happiness. There are too many factors more in the realm of psychology and sociology than of theology that have a larger influence on such things—factors that you can find many people of all sorts of religious and nonreligious backgrounds agreeing upon in fact because there doesn't have to be a one to one correlation between your theological position and your ideas about things like education and motivation. The one particular criticism of Christianity I'm trying to make here is that the version of Christianity an individual practices *can* itself be an agenda that the individual places above a search for truth, and this *can* result in that individual making harmful choices and never questioning them because they think their choices are built on flawless divine revelation. (For example, instead of studying the actual effects of various approaches to positively influencing behavior, some people may think that their understanding of what the Bible says about morals and discipline is all they need to know and therefore never attempt to find out if there are any ways in which it backfires.) The same thing could happen with an overblown commitment to a nonreligious position too: Any time that reaching a predetermined conclusion becomes more important than figuring out what actually works best, you're going to end up with a less happy social structure than you could have otherwise had.

The important thing is that, unlike the Sunday school spiel says, you don't need to be Christian in order to figure out what works, and you are certainly better off mistrusting anything that claims to be a perfect answer to all moral needs.

* * *

This world we live in is full of problems that have no perfect solutions and can only be chipped away at slowly with vast efforts of cooperation. The claims made in Christianity are enticing, with their promises of guaranteed, ultimate, all-satisfying remedies, but the habit of oversimplifying life's difficulties can be harmful, especially when those who choose to face unpleasant complexities are looked down upon and villainized.

If you, like me, were told all your life that you could never be happy—and the world could never function—without eternity, cosmic purpose, and a divine moral law, then you've been done a disservice, and unfortunately you may be in for a lot of growing pains in the coming months or, more likely, years. But you have not lost the ability to be happy, and neither has the world lost its ability to function, after all. You still have the same desire to thrive that you always have, the same conscience, the same love for your family and friends, and the same curiosity to know what's true and what's not. And so do the people around you.

The loss of God can feel like the most monumental, world-shaking event that could happen, but the truth is the world hasn't actually changed just because you've changed your mind. Your belief system was always a man-made thing, and in some respects it served you well for a time. It hasn't gone anywhere even though you see it differently now, and in some ways you can still draw upon positive parts of it. Take faith for starters. If your community achieved things because you believed God would make them possible, you still have that ability. God was never there and yet somehow you still knew what goals were worthy of your faith. In a community of people coming to consensus on what to place faith in, which out-of-reach goals to pour attention and effort into, you can still be part of turning the seemingly impossible into reality.

Because Christian concepts originated ultimately from human minds, you will find that the characteristics of God you loved are still with you as you interact with other people. Love and inspiration and strength in all their various manifestations are, unfortunately, more than just a prayer away, but are still a part of this world. You do need to work: to find your community, to choose your friends, to invest in your relationships rather than letting others carry them all. But while seeking out and fostering healthy relationships with people is not as easy as just declaring that God is there for you, it ensures that the support you build into your life is tangible and able to be understood. Making an effort to know others well and to see the world and its problems from their perspective is also vital if we want to make the present as good as it can be. Coming to understand others' needs, communing with them, and meditating on their words and experiences allows us to discover drive and motivation and to build knowledge and empathy that inform our moral choices.

I think it says something about humanity that we came up with a story in which a God who has everything decides to become a human and experience human suffering, all out of love. Maybe what it says is that we're awfully self-centered, but I think it reveals the importance we place on sharing experiences as well. If you've gone through a deconversion, then you know what it's like to leave one world for another, to be divested of something glorious and find yourself limited in strange new ways. Now you know what it is like to be fully mortal. In our case, this wasn't by choice and we are certainly not better than anyone else. Nevertheless, we find ourselves forced to pay attention for the first time to the depths of this human experience we are all sharing. We are from earth now, not visitors with a dad who can pull strings to get us out of the rough parts of the stay, but true locals with nowhere else to go.

Instead of pining for the reality we were once able to believe in, we have the opportunity to be more present than ever with our neighbors. Now we know that the marks of their griefs can't be erased, and the importance of their joys can't be diminished, by comparison to anything in a world beyond. Now we know that nothing is simple or perfect, but together we are all working through what is real. I maintain that through all this we really haven't lost much and only need to realign our emotions and expectations with our new understanding of the world. For the goal of knowing the truth and loving each other in ways that are practical, the discomfort of this realignment is a price worth paying.

Additional Resources

recoveringfromreligion.org
Recovering from Religion is an organization formed to help people who are in the process of leaving a religion or who have suffered trauma from religion. Their website provides access to both professional counseling and peer counseling as well as other resources, including for those who are just looking for a community to connect with.

Moral Combat by Sikivu Hutchinson
An informed position on theology is *not* all you need in order to do good rather than just hoping you aren't doing harm. Sikivu Hutchinson discusses the high social cost of unbelief among minorities and why the largely racially-homogenous public face of atheism makes it even harder for those who don't fit the demographic to pursue their religious skepticism. In doing so, she highlights the intellectual contributions of black American skeptics over the last two centuries and calls for unity over social justice issues.

Genetically Modified Skeptic YouTube Channel
Drew McCoy, a young man who left his conservative church after encountering intellectual obstacles to belief, makes videos on why communication between theists and atheists breaks down and how to improve it, among a variety of related topics.

clergyproject.org
The Clergy Project is an organization focused on supporting people in ministry careers who no longer believe in the supernatural, including those who have never told anyone about their change in beliefs and want to remain anonymous. They offer an online forum and assistance for those who need help transitioning to a different career field.

More from the author at
nihilistshavemorefun.com

www.ingramcontent.com/pod-product-compliance
Lightning Source LLC
LaVergne TN
LVHW041247080426
835510LV00009B/631